C0-ATZ-050

Dear Prof. Boettke:
As you said inspiring
to inquiry + inspiring to activism
& Thanks for inspiring re!
Joseph -

FREEDOM
CHAMPIONS

STORIES FROM THE FRONT LINES IN THE WAR OF IDEAS

30 Case Studies by Intellectual Entrepreneurs
Who Champion the Cause of Freedom

Edited by
Colleen Dyble and Jean Baugh

with an Introduction and Epilogue
by Brad Lips

30TH ANNIVERSARY

ATLAS
NETWORK

Published in the United States of America by
Atlas Economic Research Foundation
1201 L Street NW
Washington D.C. 20005
AtlasNetwork.org

Twelve chapters in this volume were first published by the
Institute of Economic Affairs, London, July 2008

The Atlas Economic Research Foundation is a nonprofit
organization connecting a global network of free market
organizations and individuals to the ideas and resources
needed to advance the cause of liberty.

The mission of Atlas is to discover, develop
and support Intellectual Entrepreneurs worldwide
who advance the Atlas vision of a society of
free and responsible individuals.

ISBN 978-0-615-42726-3

Many Atlas publications are translated into languages other than
English or are reprinted. Permission to translate or to reprint should
be sought from the Chief Executive Officer at the address above.

Cover design by Berman and Company.

Printed and bound in the United States of America.

Dedicated to the Intellectual Entrepreneurs
of yesterday, today, and tomorrow.

FREEDOM CHAMPIONS

STORIES FROM THE FRONT LINES IN THE WAR OF IDEAS

CONTENTS

THINK TANK LESSONS

A WORLDWIDE BATTLE

* The twelve chapters marked with asterisks originally appeared in
Taming Leviathon: Waging the War of Ideas, published by the
Institute of Economic Affairs.

PREFACE

by Colleen Dyble

During my eight years working for the Atlas Economic Research Foundation, I was constantly amazed by the Freedom Champions with whom we had the privilege of working. I was inspired by their passion for making their countries more prosperous and by the personal and professional sacrifices they endured to start and run free-market think tanks. I was impressed by their thoughtfulness in developing public policy solutions based on classical liberal principles. I was deeply moved by the struggles faced by those working within countries hostile to liberty.

Each individual had a story of outrage that compelled them to take positive action to confront corruption, abuse of individual rights, unrestrained government, and other threats to freedom. These stories made an impact on me. They ultimately prompted my move from DC to Lima, Peru, where I could engage more intimately in the challenges of promoting free-market solutions to poverty via microfinance.

Of course, these stories have inspired others as well. During Atlas's first year of operation, there were about a dozen free-market think tanks in operation. There are now more than 400 such organizations spread all over the globe.

Atlas has facilitated the growth of the think tank network by connecting those who aspire to become Freedom Champions with their more experienced peers, who can show them successful models to replicate, and teach fundamental principles of effective intellectual entrepreneurship as it's called at Atlas.

On the occasion of Atlas's 30th anniversary, we have collected 30 short essays from 30 individuals who have been on the front lines of the war of ideas. *Freedom Champions: Stories from the Front Lines in the War of Ideas* is organized into three parts.

The first third of the book showcases Intellectual Entrepreneurs' stories of how their institutes grew to have an impact. In their stories, you'll feel the "passion for liberty" – to borrow Gerardo Bongiovanni's phrase – and you'll understand how essential this is for a think tank's success.

The second section concentrates on best practices for think tanks. These essays – beginning with John Goodman's not-to-be-missed "What Is a Think Tank?" (Chapter 11) – get to the heart of how think tanks must operate like well-run businesses to have a lasting impact.

The final section includes some of the many different countries and cultures that are now touched by the Atlas network, including Belarus, Kyrgyzstan and the Republic of Georgia.

Of the 30 think tanks featured in this book, seven predate the founding of Atlas in 1981, five were founded in the 1980s, ten were founded in the 1990s and eight were founded in the 2000s. We selected five from Latin America, five from Eastern Europe, four from Western Europe, four from the United States and Canada, three from the Middle East (including the Caucauses), two from Australia and New Zealand, and two from Africa.

Twelve of these stories were originally published by the Institute of Economic Affairs in a book I edited called *Taming Leviathan: Waging the War of Ideas Around the World*, which itself was inspired by John Blundell's *Waging the War of Ideas*.

I hope these stories inspire, motivate and provide useful strategies for those of you already running think tanks.

If you are not already part of the Atlas think tank network, *Freedom Champions: Stories from the Front Lines in the War of Ideas* is sure to make you pause and reflect on the threats to freedom that concern you deeply. I hope you will consider how you can best contribute to this worldwide freedom movement that has grown from efforts like those described by the contributors to this book.

INTRODUCTION

ADVANCING LIBERTY DEPENDS UPON SUCCESSFUL INTELLECTUAL ENTREPRENEURSHIP

by Brad Lips, CEO
Atlas Economic Research Foundation

Entrepreneurship is a hot topic. The last three decades have seen the number of U.S. universities offering courses or programs in entrepreneurship grow more than sixfold. Gates and Jobs and Bezos and Whitman became household names as the world visibly changed as a result of their entrepreneurial successes.

In economic literature, too, the role of the entrepreneur is no longer neglected as it once was. The development of nations most clearly depends not just on the macro-economic variables of your old Samuelson text book, but on the creativity and courage of entrepreneurs who perceive new opportunities to earn profits by providing valued goods and services.

Ayn Rand's most famous novel *Atlas Shrugged* – enjoying a surge in popularity now, five decades after its release – put this lesson at its heart. Rand asked us to envision a world in which entrepreneurs and other innovators went on strike. Persuasively, she depicts a society stagnating, and then disintegrating, in the absence of entrepreneurs who know how to create value in a free market.

The villains in Rand's novel are people that you might classify as "political entrepreneurs." They accrue prestige and influence by using the power of government to interfere in economic affairs to create politically desirable outcomes. They fail to anticipate the consequences of public policies that take resources out of the private economy, displace voluntary problem-solving activities, and reward dependency rather than creativity and resilience.

Sound familiar? All over the world, we see headlines that echo the dystopian vision of *Atlas Shrugged*.

What can be done to restrain the growth of government, so that it doesn't infringe upon the creativity of entrepreneurs in the voluntary sectors?

This book presents the stories of Freedom Champions who are answering this question. As you read about their efforts to move the climate of opinion in the direction of greater individual liberty, you will learn about a different kind of entrepreneurship. At Atlas, we believe that "intellectual entrepreneurship" is the most important factor for protecting and advancing freedom.

DEFINING "INTELLECTUAL ENTREPRENEURSHIP"

To be successful, any new organization needs a leader, or leadership team, with entrepreneurial talent. We call it "intellectual entrepreneurship" when such skills are applied to the war of ideas – that is, the ideological contest over whether public policies will protect individuals' freedoms or limit them.

Atlas president Alex Chafuen has given a concise definition of an Intellectual Entrepreneur. That is, someone with talent to (1) discover opportunities (an unsatisfied need) in the field of ideas, (2) attract and deploy material and human resources to capitalize on those opportunities, and (3) turn ideas into action.[1]

Of course, truly effective Intellectual Entrepreneurs need more than talent; they need wisdom. I won't attempt to reprise the many lessons that the Atlas team has learned through its years of providing service to aspiring Intellectual Entrepreneurs. I'll just mention one.

It's the one that John Blundell, who preceded Alex Chafuen as president of Atlas, emphasized as "absolutely key" at the very top of a list of management lessons he prepared for think tank leaders: independence.

Intellectual Entrepreneurs will have the most influence on the long-term climate of ideas when they refuse to hitch their wagons to any particular political party. Staying above the fray of partisan politics allows an organization to engage with opinion leaders of all ideological persuasions. Think tanks gain credibility when they shun funding from government agencies, and when they remain skeptical of taking corporate funding that might come with strings attached. They must cultivate a donor base that expects, first and foremost, the think tank to remain independent and committed to core principles over the long term.

This essential lesson was born from a conversation had by Atlas's eventual founder, Antony Fisher, and the great economist and social theorist F.A. Hayek in 1945. A bit of background may help to clarify how.

---

1   "From Intellectual Entrepreneur to Institute Leader," Alex Chafuen, *Atlas Year in Review 2004*, pp. 18-19.

THE FISHER STORY

Antony Fisher was a Royal Air Force pilot in World War II. His brother fought alongside him, and was killed in the Battle of Britain. Having sacrificed so much to win the War and preserve individual freedom in the UK, Fisher was alarmed by the election of a Labor Party government that was set on nationalizing all the major industries and using central planning to run the economy.

In the April 1945 edition of *The Reader's Digest*, Fisher came across a condensed version of F.A. Hayek's *The Road to Serfdom*, which explains how central planning inevitably erodes individual liberty and enables tyranny. He sought out the book's author, who was then teaching at the London School of Economics. Fisher told Hayek that he agreed with every word in the book, and was going to go into politics to save Britain from socialism. Hayek advised Fisher that this would be a waste of time. In a democracy, politicians follow public opinion. Fisher should not be strategizing about how to get elected to Parliament; rather, he needed to develop a strategy for *changing public opinion*. Only after the public was persuaded against socialism, Hayek said, would there be any chance for political reform.

Hayek made a similar point just four years later in his essay, *The Intellectuals and Socialism*:

> "We need intellectual leaders who are prepared to resist the blandishments of power and influence and who are willing to work for an ideal... They must be men who are willing to stick to principles and to fight for their full realization, however remote. The practical compromises they must leave to the politicians."[2]

Thanks to his conversation with Hayek, Antony Fisher did not go into politics. He instead established a chicken farming business, and as he achieved commercial success and put a chicken-in-every-pot in the UK, Fisher kept Hayek's challenge in mind. By 1955, he used his business profits to launch the Institute of Economic Affairs (IEA), the first free-market think tank in Britain and one of the very few to exist at that time anywhere in the world.

Over time, the IEA had an enormous impact by producing scholarly studies that were written in clear English to be accessible to educated lay-

---

2   Friedrich A. Hayek, *The Intellectuals and Socialism* (London: The Institute of Economic Affairs, 1998 reprint), p. 26.

people. Its scholars engaged in public debate with journalists and academics, and the IEA remained completely independent of party politics. As the consequences of socialist policies revealed themselves, the institute became a trusted independent source of alternative proposals. In 1979, Margaret Thatcher was elected Prime Minister and credited the IEA with providing the intellectual foundation for her political victory. The next year, she wrote in support of Fisher's ambition to replicate the IEA model wherever it could take root. This was the impetus for creating the Atlas Economic Research Foundation.

Thatcher wrote, "I applaud your aim to build on the success of the IEA in Europe, America, and further afield. I believe it deserves the most urgent and generous support of all concerned with the restoration of the market economy as the foundation of a free society."[3]

Hayek too testified to the urgent need: "The future of civilization may really depend on whether we catch the ear of a large enough part of the upcoming generation of intellectuals all over the world fast enough. And I am more convinced than ever that the method practiced by the IEA is the only one which promises any real results.... In building up that institute and trying the technique elsewhere, you have developed a technique by which more has been achieved in the right direction than in any other manner. This ought to be used to create similar institutes all over the world..."[4]

With this encouragement, Antony Fisher and his wife Dorian (pictured above) established the Atlas Economic Research Foundation in 1981 to create new fronts in the war of ideas.

3   Margaret Thatcher, letter to Antony Fisher, February 20, 1980.
4   Friedrich A. Hayek, letter to Antony Fisher, December 30, 1980.

WINNING THE WAR OF THE IDEAS

At the time of Atlas's founding, Antony and Dorian resided in San Francisco, California, in the same apartment building as their friends Milton and Rose Friedman. After receiving the 1976 Nobel Prize in Economics and emerging as a surprising TV star (thanks to the 1980 series, *Free To Choose*, produced by Bob Chitester), Milton Friedman authored a preface to the new edition of his landmark book, *Capitalism and Freedom*. It contained this noteworthy passage, which gets to the heart of how policy change occurs:

> "Only a crisis – actual or perceived – produces real change. When that crisis occurs, the actions that are taken depend on the ideas that are lying around. That, I believe, is our basic function: to develop alternatives to existing policies, to keep them alive and available until the politically impossible becomes politically inevitable."[5]

The above quote has been misused by Naomi Klein to advance a theory that Friedman wanted to cause crises to create an ideological opportunity. Actually, Friedman is providing simple common sense: the war of ideas is fought over the long-term. It requires patience. There are periods when reforms are politically impossible. Nonetheless, we need to be ready in advance, because you don't know when opportunities for change will arise.

But ready how? Friedman doesn't say what to do to ensure our ideas are the ones that are "lying around."

Simply, you need *people* to advance the ideas – talented, principled people with sound ideas and the credibility to spread them. It's best when these people have the entrepreneurial talent to develop institutions that run like effective businesses, so they are constantly winning new adherents and strengthening the understanding of free-market economics. These are the ingredients for a sustained, long-term effort at shifting the climate of ideas.

We're all better off for those Intellectual Entrepreneurs who have devoted their lives to the challenge of moving public opinion toward greater liberty. We're in debt to the pioneers of this sector: Fisher and his colleagues at the IEA, Leonard Read (Foundation for Economic Education) and F.A. "Baldy" Harper (Institute for Humane Studies) to name just a few. Their names are less known than the Information Age entrepreneurs that I cited

---

5   Milton Friedman, *Capitalism and Freedom* (Chicago: University of Chicago Press, 1982 reissue), p. ix.

at the outset of this chapter, but they and their heirs in this field – Ed Crane (Cato Institute), Ed Feulner (Heritage Foundation) and those contributing to this volume, among others – are having an impact on the world that is even more important to mankind's future well-being.

I urge you to read, and learn from, their stories.

- Giancarlo Ibárgüen explains how the late Manual Ayau and other Guatemalan businessmen grew their small think tank into a major university.

- Michel Kelly-Gagnon shows that for young think tanks to grow to have success like the Montreal Economic Institute, they must spend as much or more time on the "tank" part of the equation, as they do on the "think" part.

- Parth Shah explains the different models of think tanks he has observed in the marketplace, and how he selected the most appropriate strategy for the Centre for Civil Society in New Delhi, India.

And that's only the beginning. This book contains 30 such stories, each selected to celebrate the 30th anniversary of the Atlas Economic Research Foundation, a network of people and resources which exists to advise, train, and support Intellectual Entrepreneurs who are working to transform our world for the better.

At the conclusion of the book, I've added a short epilogue with some observations about new opportunities (and new challenges) for Intellectual Entrepreneurs in the early decades of the 21st century.

For the moment, I invite you to enjoy 30 case studies presented by Freedom Champions who are connected by the Atlas Network. Each of them provides insight on how intellectual entrepreneurship, paired with a commitment to the principles of a free society, can improve the prospects for liberty.

CASE STUDIES
IN ENTREPRENEURSHIP

A Short Story of the Free Market Triumphing

Elena Leontjeva
Lithuanian Free Market Institute
(Lithuania)

CHAPTER

When I was a child, I never saw bubblegum, only a wrapper, which somebody brought to school for our amusement. Yet I learned from an empty wrapper that the bubblegum must exist. In the same way I discovered there must be the market, even though there was no market in my environment. 'Market', the word itself, sounded sinful. No wonder! This was a time when socialism was being 'developed' and embraced as never before. Naturally, we did not know about such things as free choice, supply and demand, bubblegum and bananas. The content of a sweet-smelling bubblegum wrapper was beyond my wildest imagination when I was eleven, but when I was sixteen that all changed. My dream came true and I started working at a newly launched bubblegum production facility, the second one in the USSR. It looked as if the socialist state could catch up with the market.

While working at the conveyor belt, however, I witnessed striking social injustice and economic inconsistency, which led me to the question: what changes must be made to make the system work and prevent people from being pushed to one single solution – stealing from their workplaces? For a while I studied mathematical programming, economics and industrial planning, hoping that this would be the way to improve the system. Unfortunately, my work as a programmer did not make the country any better and made me feel disillusioned. I remember the day back in 1986 when I realized that socialism must be improved by way of market forces and I started to contemplate how exactly the market would alter the system. I was still expecting to reconcile the market with socialism, however, and it took me several years of personal perestroika to comprehend that the market implies private property and that the system will not be saved by increasing the 'independence' and 'self-finance' of state enterprises.

In 1990, Lithuania declared independence and thus broke the Soviet empire. Freedom of speech and movement allowed people like me to bring ideas into action. For five young economists led by Professor Glaveckas, this meant establishing a think tank which we called without compromise the Lithuanian Free Market Institute (LFMI). There was no doubt in our minds that it was time to contribute to building a new order; one based on individual liberty and limited government. Many scholars and professionals joined us, excited by the idea of building a new Lithuania. I dropped out of postgraduate studies without regret and ventured into the newly established institute. We were privileged with only a month or two of academic serenity to sketch out the free market principles before life provided a chance for us to jump into the reform-making process.

A new law on commercial banking came under consideration in parliament, and since we knew that a well-functioning market starts with capital allocation, we outlined a proposal on banking principles in Lithuania. Even though we were young and inexperienced, our proposal competed on an equal footing with the official draft of the central bank and even won the sympathies of the members of the economic committee of the parliament. This was the start of our success, but also of continuous hardship. The central bank became our long-term opponent and made our lives truly difficult. At one point, our one-room office was taken away, but we persevered and continued to contemplate the future of banking while sitting in entrance halls and other unsuitable places. One of these places was a conference hall in the central bank, which we dared to use since it was always empty and had a table and chairs on the stage. Looking back, the situation seems rather ironic: the system attempted to push us out of the arena and, in response, we climbed on to the stage.

The allergic reaction of some statesmen towards us was understandable; we were a new 'beast' in public life: a non-profit private institution which instructed authorities how to run the country. We did not wish to be arrogant, but our mission required us to visualize where and how to move forward, to enlighten people and to steer those in power in the right direction. In addition, we vowed that we would not accept government funds, a principle that we followed strictly. This made the authorities worry: we had a state-level agenda, but no state affiliation. Yet, at that time, private funds were seldom available. As a result, our finances were uncomplicated and recorded in a thin notebook. This notebook did not reflect the most crucial donation: our efforts, which were donated for free to the free market cause. This was the key investment which formed the foundation of the Institute.

Despite all the difficulties that we faced during the early years of our think tank, it was a very precious time. There was no alternative to freedom in people's souls and minds. Free trade and private property had no bona fide alternative. To be able to provide people with bread, not to mention sausages and bananas, former socialist states had no other solution but the free market. Some countries realized this right away and others not until much later. Lithuania was the first in the former USSR to liberalize prices and started mass privatization, around the same time as the Czechs.

Lithuanians enjoyed the most freedom when the reforms were being commenced. Old socialist rules and regulations did not have moral support among the rulers or the general public. Almost instantaneously people could trade without restrictions, do business without regulations, cross borders without customs and create wealth without paying excessive tax. This was the time when most of the initial capital in Lithuania was being created and, more importantly, when people were learning principles that they were never taught in their socialist schools. Responding to the needs of the day, we developed the legal framework for, and contributed to the founding of, the first Lithuanian commodities market. This gave people a platform on which to exchange goods at a time when there was a shortage of almost all goods and, more importantly, buyers and sellers did not have a mechanism for interacting with one another.

The next issue that needed addressing emerged from mass privatization: almost all people became shareholders of former state companies, but they had no rights in the companies and no mechanism for trading their shares. Our response to this problem was to develop a set of legal principles for the capital market and the stock exchange. This not only allowed the trading of shares and bonds on the market, but also made it possible to raise capital and define shareholders' rights. As a result of these efforts, the first stock exchange in the former USSR was opened in Lithuania in 1993. The development of the Securities and Exchange Commission followed.

In our work to develop a system of institutions, our aim was to provide the impetus for the adoption of a minimum set of rules to protect private property, rather than giving way to interventionist regulations. Beginning in 1993, Western countries and donor institutions began to transfer their 'know-how' to our soil, and while they were often our allies in promoting a reform agenda, at other times we had to fight against their efforts to bring about more intervention and rent-seeking behavior. It is well known that our region suffered from bank bankruptcies in the mid-1990s. The primary reason was that while donors worked hard to introduce capital adequacy and other sophisticated ratios into the banking system, nobody noticed that there was no proper mortgage system, so the same property could be used as collateral multiple times. I recall many more cases where shallow interventionist regulations preceded indispensable rules.

Reflecting back on those times, I regret that we were not able to address all of the pressing issues of the day, yet I know that we always chose the most important ones that would result in a chain reaction. The most vivid example of this is the introduction of the currency board in Lithuania. When Lithuania was getting ready to replace the Soviet ruble with its national currency, litas, we were promoting the idea that money should be separated from the state, although at that time it didn't sound very attractive. But when the new currency was introduced and the central bank launched harsh interventions that led to a remarkable appreciation of the young (or new) national currency, the economy was brought to a standstill. We felt the need to explain to people that it was not the market which made the national currency rise, but the central bank, which is a typical central planning authority. We told people there could be no genuine market if currency remained in the hands of central planners. Since many academic economists and public officials were great enthusiasts of the traditional (interventionist) central bank, it was crucial to show people that there might be an alternative. Only 50 years ago Lithuania enjoyed the gold standard and people still had memories of sound litas, so we appealed to people's hearts and minds, explaining the benefits of gold and other sound money. The currency board model was a kind of a modern version of sound and relatively independent money. Explaining to people its essence, which is very simple, and which was called by opponents the 'lavatory principle', was only the first step. Let me give you the basics as well: the central bank can issue currency only in exchange for foreign reserves and gold, which must be kept in its vaults, and must exchange any amount of national currency at the fixed exchange rate and vice versa. This operating principle means that the hands of the central bank are tied – no credit expansion, no interventions, no relevance.

Sure, very few people shared the vision that turning the central bank into a 'lavatory' could save our freedom. Fortunately, among those few was the prime minister. We kept sending numerous policy papers to statesmen, appealing to people through the media and speaking to the business elite and politicians. Despite widespread skepticism and the hardcore opposition of the central bank, the currency board model was introduced on 1 April 1994 through the Litas Credibility Law. This law tied the national currency, the litas, to the US dollar at a fixed exchange rate and required that all money in circulation be fully backed by gold and foreign reserves. Despite critics' prophesies that the currency board would not survive and that it was on the brink of crashing, thirteen years have passed and the system is still alive. It has survived many crises as well as official political plans to dismantle it. Thanks to the currency board, people's money was never devalued or used to cover bank losses, treasury shortfalls or to finance the grand plans of statesmen. For thirteen years people were protected from central bank interventions and currency fluctuations caused by the central planning authority. Needless to say, the currency board broke down artificial barriers that separated Lithuania from global money and capital markets, and interest rates decreased at a rapid rate that even we found surprising.

After the implementation of the Litas Credibility Law, there was no shortage of local and foreign critics who claimed that a developing economy would not survive without some currency devaluations and that such devaluations would help to promote exports. As the US dollar appreciated, many began panicking and worrying that the devaluation of the litas was imminent. The interest groups lobbying for devaluation were so powerful that it is a miracle that the devaluation never actually happened. These groups were happy to support the euro as the new peg instead of the US dollar, since the euro at that time was steadily weakening. In 2002, this was done as part of national efforts to join the European Union. Unbelievably, from that time onwards the euro started to appreciate! It would be difficult for graph-lovers to counter my guess that the currency which Lithuania chooses as an anchor is always strengthening and that this fact alone is responsible for developments on the Forex market. On a more serious note, our history is proof to devaluation devotees that it is still possible to prosper economically and to have fast-growing exports without this economic 'remedy'.

Since the monetary system was now in order, we turned to other areas of importance. At this time, there was a lot of concern about the country's competitiveness, so we provided comprehensive policy proposals and suggested that officials should focus on addressing the burden of the state: taxation, expenditure and regulation. Our fight on this front has been quite productive: personal income tax was set at a flat rate and remains flat despite many attempts to implement progressive rates. The property tax for individuals that has been on the government agenda for about a decade has never been introduced (except recently for commercial property). The discussions on the corporate profit tax have been varied. At one point, the idea of abolishing the corporate tax became so popular that it was included in the electoral programs of two competing parties. Reinvested profits have not been taxed, which has helped to boost private sector development. Unfortunately, owing to harmonization pressure from the European Union, the Lithuanian government did not dare abolish the corporate profit tax and even returned to the old practice of taxing all profits by a universal tariff, which is currently at 15 per cent.

Our efforts to retreat from the pay-as-you-go social insurance system have been partially successful – the transition is set in motion and private pension funds have already become common. Needless to say, more radical steps need to be taken. Working at a think tank requires a lot of patience; there were times back in the 1990s when proposing the introduction of private pension insurance provoked harsh criticism and disbelief that it could ever be implemented. My highly esteemed Chilean friend, José Piñera, said that some people believe that a private pension system succeeded in Chile only because it is a very long and narrow country. If, in less than a decade, private pensions were successfully introduced in petite and heart-shaped Lithuania, tell me, what else is impossible?

What is noteworthy about LFMI is that life gradually required us to engage in an exceedingly wide variety of topics. How can one work on budget issues and not touch upon agriculture? How do you address agriculture and not tackle the most interventionist case: white sugar? These questions led us to get involved in almost every topic associated with economic and social policy. These topics included pensions, social redistribution and welfare, the functions of government and strategic planning, as well as a nationwide initiative on reducing the size of the state, which came to be known as 'sunset'. We launched an assault on business over-regulation, known as 'sunrise', and engaged in the topics of competition policy, market entry and licensing. We introduced the concepts of education reform and vouchers and put forward the idea of the private sector becoming involved in health insurance and provision. The Institute developed solutions for fighting corruption and engaged in issues related to public administration, transportation, the energy sector and the knowledge economy. This is in addition to our own field: NGO regulations, philanthropy and the principles and procedures of law-making.

Although such wide-ranging engagement is common sense and frequently leads to good luck, it is tiring and consuming. People expect us to act on any issue that becomes hot on the public agenda. Journalists call us on matters that go far beyond our expertise.

LFMI is an interesting case since it is a truly genuine domestic initiative which, in the early years, had no helping hand from abroad and almost no access to foreign know-how. It was not until after 1993 that we developed relationships with foreign partners. In addition, being one of the first think tanks in Lithuania also meant that there was no history of nongovernmental organizations in the country or a tradition of private funding to support such initiatives, so we were leaders in defining what it meant to be a think tank. We were also pioneers in conducting independent research and advocacy, educating the public, engaging in nonpartisan policy efforts and actively fundraising for our activities. Every skill beyond our initial mission has been developed in response to daily demands, and we have learned to be inventive and very efficient. Our scope and our output always looked suspiciously big vis-à-vis our budget, and I have heard people say that we must employ at least 100 people. We have become an incubator for countless statesmen and stateswomen, and LFMI staff have been highly desired, and from time to time recruited, as ministers, deputy ministers, state councilors, central bank board members, and advisers to the president and prime minister. Early members of the Institute currently hold top positions within private industry as well as finance and public administration. LFMI fellows teach at universities and publish widely in the press. Many of them become 'celebrities', since they frequently appear on television and radio.

It is not yet the right time to rest on laurels, however. Our homeland today is the European Union, and the many similarities between the EU and the Soviet Union make me worry. Lithuania's accession to the EU and the transfer of the ideas of the welfare state from the West pushed us off the free market road on to what must be a 'road to serfdom'. The ideological climate in Lithuania is deteriorating. After years of confidence in spontaneous order, many people started to presume that changes in the market could be foreseen and that instead of waiting until the market brought desired results, authorities could intervene and 'take care' of the changes. The massive transfer of EU subsidies makes our people believe that the 'center', whatever that is, knows better about where to invest and whom to favor. The economy is being damaged by enormous central support and harmonization, and it is increasingly difficult to find a genuine market around. All of this is a great misfortune, but we know from our socialist past that bad times are never forever.

I will admit that it is not easy to address the infinite policy matters and countless institutions of the EU. We feel obliged to speak to people, however, about the vicious omnipotence of the Union and the principles that would make the EU downsize to a sound level. Dealing with this matter from just a utilitarian point of view is fruitless. We need to begin talking to people about faith and the moral foundations of liberty. If people are not ready to accept the spontaneous way of life, then the prospects of freedom are dim. Without a deep acceptance of spontaneity, people will always seek to set up institutions that attempt to provide certainty, which will most likely be institutions of serfdom.

Reclaiming a Free Market Tradition in Quebec

Michel Kelly-Gagnon
Montreal Economic Institute
(Canada)

Quebec is in a particular situation in North America. Everybody knows of course that the majority of its citizens speak French and that its culture is, up to a point, different from that of the rest of the continent. In political and intellectual matters too, Quebec society follows its own path. For a long time in the 19th and early 20th century, Quebec had a lively classical liberal tradition. This was reinforced by the influence of a strong Catholic Church, which controlled health and education services and did not favor government intervention in society and the economy.

This is a little known fact, but until the 1960s, Canada as a whole had a government that was as small, and in some respects smaller, than that of the United States. Interventionist fads (such as the creation of a central bank, income tax, unemployment insurance and other welfare programs) were usually implemented first in the United States and then in Canada several years later. Quebec itself had, until the 1950s, one of the least interventionist governments on the continent. During the Great Depression, a Quebec premier criticized Roosevelt's New Deal as 'a Socialistic venture bordering on Communism'!

It was only in the 1960s that we caught up and eventually surpassed the Americans in terms of growing the size of the state. As is often the case, Quebec politicians went further and built one of the most extensive welfare states on the continent, drawing inspiration from Europe's social democracies. Not only that, but the old classical liberal tradition was literally wiped out. The growing nationalist and separatist movement became aligned with left-wing sentiment. Quebecois identity was increasingly defined as one based on a more 'caring' and collectivist approach, shielding its inhabitants from what another Quebec premier described in the 1990s as the 'cold winds' of conservatism prevailing in English-speaking North America. By 1980, almost nobody in Quebec, among the intellectual and political class, openly defended a free market approach, even though these ideas were likely still shared by a not insignificant portion of the population at large.

FINDING LIKE-MINDED SOULS

This is the environment in which I grew up. As a young man (I'm now 38) I had always been attracted to an individualist's view of life. But apart from some readings – in particular, Ayn Rand's novels and pamphlets by Frederick Bastiat – I had no access to a body of literature that defended this point of view. It was totally absent in Quebec's media. And remember, these were pre-Internet times, when finding something that was not part of the mainstream was quite difficult.

I actually discovered free market economics while doing my university degree in law. I took a course on law and economics given by one of the few academics in the province who had a classical liberal perspective, Professor Ejan Mackaay at the University of Montreal. I was immediately attracted to this discipline, seeing that it expressed in an organized way the intuitions that I had about how the world works. After that, my interest was piqued and I actively searched for books and magazines with a libertarian perspective, mostly coming from the United States. The Cato Institute and *Reason* magazine, in particular, were especially important for me during those formative years.

I can pinpoint with precision the moment when Quebec's free market tradition was being taken out of limbo and relaunched in its current form. It happened on a winter evening, in January 1995, at the house of a friend of mine in suburban Montreal. Five people who shared the same libertarian principles met as a group for the first time. Four of us were young men in our twenties. The other one was Pierre Lemieux, probably the best-known Quebec defender of freedom abroad, who had written several books and had tried to keep the flame alive in a rather isolated fashion for the previous twenty years.

All would not only become my friends, but in some cases, close colleagues in years that followed. We discussed various ways we could spread free market ideas. The meeting was also very special because Mr Lemieux had brought his laptop and showed us what exactly this thing we had only heard about, the Internet, actually looked like and explained how it worked.

BUILDING INSTITUTIONS

The first outcome from the meeting was the founding of a discussion group called the Friends of Liberty, which went on to meet every month for the next couple of years. This was a way not only to share ideas, but to enlarge our circle of like-minded souls, by encouraging members of the group to bring a friend, family member or work colleague. We realized that there were more of us than we first thought, and after some time, our network went from four to a few dozen people.

That was the old, slow way to build a movement, however, and we set out to develop more efficient ways. In early 1998, one of the original participants at our first meeting, Martin Masse, launched Quebecoislibre.org, which, to this day, is still the main French-speaking libertarian magazine on the Web. Although Internet access was still modest at the time, especially outside of the cities, isolated Quebecers who shared these ideas could see, for the first time, that they were not alone.

However, despite the dynamism of its volunteer contributors, this was not a professional organization and it could never have caught the attention of the mainstream media and reached a wide audience. It also appeared very much like an activist group when what we needed was a more objective approach based on sound research to convince business people, journalists and the political class that we had serious solutions to offer to public policy problems.

This is why in 1998, I accepted the challenge of trying to relaunch the Montreal Economic Institute (MEI), a think tank that had been set up in July 1987 by Mr Lemieux and some of his business people, but had never managed to raise any funds nor publish much. In essence, MEI was an empty shell, with only a few thousand dollars in the bank, not enough to pay for a telephone, a fax line or official letterhead. I started its initial operations in the mezzanine of my condominium.

By the end of the year 2000, however, our budget had already surpassed C$600,000. We had a secretary, an in-house economist, Martin Masse (my friend from *Le Québécois Libre*) had joined us as director of publications, and I had also hired someone to take care of communications and events. During that year, we also managed to issue twelve publications. Soon after, Pierre Desrochers, another member of our 'Fab Four' group in 1995 who had recently finished his PhD, became our director of research. By the middle of the decade, we had a dozen employees, an annual budget close to C$1.5M, and had become one of the main players in Quebec's public policy debates. We were later dubbed by Quebec's association of journalists as 'the most overexposed source of information in Quebec' with over 1,500 media hits per year (all of which are listed on our website). While they certainly didn't mean it as a compliment, we took it as such.

LESSONS FOR YOUNG THINK TANKS

To what can we attribute this rapid progress? It is not my innovative research on public policies! As I mentioned previously, I was trained as a lawyer, not as an economist. More generally, I would describe myself as a man of action who likes ideas, rather than as an intellectual. Indeed, I am first and foremost an entrepreneur and a popularizer of ideas, not a thinker. And I believe that is one major factor that made a difference.

One crucial mistake that many people launching think tanks tend to make is to focus too much on the 'think' and not enough on building the 'tank'. With all due respect to my academic friends, they have a tendency to believe that the main challenge in terms of influencing intellectual debates is to publish weighty papers that are well-researched and contain well-argued ideas. They rarely care about making sure those ideas reach the general public. They are almost never interested in generating the flow of funds that will finance the activities of the organization.

That is why putting academics in charge of a think tank often leads to failure. Like any other type of enterprise, a think tank has to be run by entrepreneurs who see the big picture and focus on finding opportunities for development, not on one aspect of production only, in this case, the content of publications.

Right from the start, I understood my job as being the fundraiser and organizer-in-chief, and not the researcher-in-chief. We received seed money from foundations helping new think tanks, including the Atlas Economic Research Foundation. But a few important contacts in Montreal's business world were also instrumental in opening doors and getting support from corporate donors across Canada.

My approach to research was also not one that most academics would find appropriate. I thought that there was no point in trying to reinvent the wheel and devoting huge resources to studies that organizations in other countries had already done in similar contexts. Especially for a young organization with a limited research capacity, adapting what was done elsewhere to a Quebec or Canadian context made a lot more sense, even if we get no points for originality. My main preoccupation was to make sure that we had the biggest bang possible for our buck. Consequently, we put a lot of thinking and effort into the systematic marketing of our studies instead.

We tried to determine what kind of topic would be in the news several months ahead, based on expected government consultations and decisions, conferences or other events that were planned in advance. This insured that any contribution we might have would be topical and of interest to journalists.

We also put a lot of emphasis on clarity, brevity and visual attractiveness. Whether you like it or not, most people, including journalists, don't have time to read a 50-page study and are likely to get bored with dry and complicated prose. The publication format that became our trademark was a four-page, easy-to-read and concise 'Economic Note', containing some graphs and illustrations. After devoting fifteen minutes to reading this, you understood the most important points of any public policy issue. We also published larger research papers and even books, but it's the Economic Notes that gave us our widest media coverage.

Finally, one of my most cherished goals was to provide economic education to business people, parents, students, and the 'average Joe,' as opposed to debating policies with interest groups and university professors, as someone with a strong academic slant would be more likely to do.

One of our first breakthroughs in the media was a regular column that I was invited to contribute to in *Les Affaires*, Quebec's main business publication. I used it to try to demystify economic theory and debunk fallacies in a very simple and accessible way, as I believe Frédéric Bastiat would do if he were alive today. A few years later, one of our senior economists, Nathalie Elgrably, also got a weekly column in *Le Journal de Montréal*, a tabloid newspaper which has the largest circulation in the province. In this publication, sex, sports and crime are issues that are always well covered. Some of my more educated friends sometimes look down on this publication but I actually made it a point of honour to be published by it. These days, we also publish weekly 'economic tidbits' in Montreal's free dailies and in about 30 regional weeklies. I believe we are one of the few think tanks in North America to benefit from such regular exposure in mass publications that are read by ordinary people. This is one of the achievements that I am the most proud of.

OUR IMPACT ON THE CLIMATE OF OPINION

The issue where we have had the largest impact is undoubtedly in the evaluation of school performance. In 2000, we teamed up with the Fraser Institute, one of the best known and oldest free market think tanks in the world, to produce a Secondary School Report Card that compared student results in Quebec's 475 public and private schools, adjusting for social background and other variables. This study got a huge amount of coverage in every region of the province and became as widely popular among parents as it was vociferously denounced by the education establishment. It made the cover page of *L'Actualité* (which is the Quebec equivalent of *Time* magazine). It introduced a novel idea in this society, which is that the performance of schools and other government institutions can and should be evaluated to see if taxpayers are getting their money's worth, and that competition is good not just in the private but also in the public sector.

Health care is another area where the existence of sacred cows did not permit any meaningful debate to take place a decade ago. At the beginning, our approach was to show that even in such social-democratic countries as Sweden there was more competition and private provision of services than in Canada. Over the years, we published studies on various aspects of healthcare reform and broke many of the current taboos. Today, we can debate these things openly without being accused of wanting to destroy Canadian identity.

On several other topics as well, our contribution sometimes sparked debates and controversies that lasted for months. One of the best examples of these was the privatization of the provincial government monopoly over the distribution of alcohol, an anachronism dating back to the 1930s.

It is important to have these debates, even though they don't lead to immediate changes in public policy. They show that there are better alternatives than the usual solution of throwing more government money at the problem, and they force people to consider them. They acquaint the population with concepts and ideas that they were not familiar with. They provide a wealth of data and arguments that will be ready to use whenever the debate flares up again. They set the stage for reform whenever a government finds it politically advantageous to go forward with it.

CLASSICAL LIBERALISM REBORN

During the first years of our existence, some activist groups who did not like what we stood for were questioning not only our public policy prescriptions but the very legitimacy of our participation in these debates. Today, this is no longer the case. The MEI is a well-established institution and some of its board members are part of the 'who's who' of Quebec's business community. In that sense, we have managed to achieve something that would have seen quite ambitious fifteen years ago: the rebirth of Quebec's classical, liberal tradition after its almost complete disappearance from the scene in the previous decades. There is now an official political party with seats at our provincial legislature that defends these ideas (albeit very imperfectly).

In my own career I also experienced a detour before returning to my previous situation. In March 2006, I accepted the position of president of the Conseil du Patronat du Québec, the province's main business association. The fact that the head of the MEI could be sought after to preside over such an important Quebec institution is testimony to how prominent our views had become.

This was, of course, an influential place from which to try to impact public policy, especially on economic issues. However, I realized that lobbying on behalf of business people is not quite the same thing as lobbying for freer markets. At times, I felt very constrained in this new environment and accepted an offer to come back to MEI in February 2009.

So this is a bit like a new beginning for me. Yet our institute is still going strong as a key player in Quebec's public policy debates, and we have the accumulated capital of a decade of work to help us carry on our mission.

03

A Model for Winning Liberty

Giancarlo Ibárgüen S.
Universidad Francisco Marroquín
(Guatemala)

'REBELLIOUS IMPROVISERS'

In 1958, on the eve of Castro's takeover of Cuba, that one of Latin America's first classical liberal think tanks was born. It evolved out of discussions involving a Guatemalan businessman, Manuel 'Muso' Ayau, and a cluster of friends who were concerned about the poverty of their country and what to do about it. At their modest think tank, the Center for Economic and Social Studies (CEES), they set about studying, writing pamphlets and translating the texts of great classical liberal thinkers into Spanish and mailing them to anyone in Latin America who might or should be interested. The words in these pamphlets echoed throughout Latin America. Peruvian Enrique Ghersi tells us that it was a pamphlet by Ayau in the 1970s, *Ten Lessons for Underdevelopment*, that 'awakened in me the vocation and commitment to defend liberty'. Enrique went on to co-author, with Hernando de Soto, the landmark book *The Other Path*.

CEES was also active in bringing renowned economists to Guatemala to defend the philosophy of freedom and make a case for economic liberty. These visitors included: Henry Hazlitt (1964), Ludwig von Mises (1964), Friedrich Hayek (1965), Leonard Read (1965) and Ludwig Erhard (1968).

CEES pamphlets consistently challenged socialist and Keynesian economic theory and explained the relationship between capital, wages and employment. They questioned the policy of full employment and its impact on salary levels. These pamphlets made the causes and effects of inflation clear and they opposed currency manipulation, import substitution, price controls, minimum wages and agrarian reform. They championed the relationship between free trade and economic growth and the role of the entrepreneur and property rights. Aged thirteen, already an avid reader of the CEES publications that my father received, I sought out Ayau as a mentor. As with Ghersi, he awakened in me a desire to defend liberty.

The decision to found the Universidad Francisco Marroquín (UFM) in 1971 was in direct response to the increasing influence of socialism in academia. The success of the Fabian Society convinced members of CEES that the education of the influential elite was the most important determining factor in the destiny of a country. When they undertook this courageous enterprise, they did so in an environment that was intellectually hostile, politically dangerous and which called for personal risk and sacrifice. Guatemala was the foremost territory for Marxism in Latin America and the first communist experiment – long before Cuba. In the international communist movement, Guatemala was the place to be (Che Guevara was active in Guatemala before going to Cuba). The movement took root in the national university and from there it spread to the private universities. When UFM was founded, guerrilla activity was at its most aggressive.

When Ayau and his supporters – 'rebellious improvisers', as they called themselves – established UFM, they did what few persons have ever accomplished or even dared to attempt. They developed a new model for promoting classical liberal ideas in the world. Ayau applied his great entrepreneurial spirit and creativity to designing an institution that has evolved into something far more significant than an imprint of the man, and with a projection far beyond his country or lifetime.

ENTREPRENEURSHIP IN IDEAS

Rigoberto Juárez-Paz developed a foundational document for UFM, Philosophy/Ideario, which is based on classical liberal philosophy and encompasses all aspects of the institutional structure – its organization, administration, teaching activities and relationship to society. Although we are a non-profit institution, we run the university as a for-profit entrepreneurial venture in that we subject our own decisions and activities, and those of our staff, to the law of supply and demand.

Flying in the face of traditional academia, UFM does not offer tenure, our board members are business people and entrepreneurs, and our department chairs are required to balance their budgets. In order for us to fulfill our social role as educators, the university does not engage in the political and social issues of the day; rather it focuses on essential themes that transcend contemporary issues. We believe UFM to be globally unique for another reason: we teach all students, regardless of academic discipline (we offer degrees in architecture, business administration, dentistry, economics, education, law, medicine, political and social sciences, psychology and public accounting), the causes and origins of the wealth of nations.

Four core semester-long courses form part of the curriculum for all of the undergraduate degree programs and these four courses are compressed into two for the graduate-level programs. Two of the courses, which take a look at economic processes, begin with an analysis of comparative advantage as a fundamental component of the development of human society. The curriculum also covers competition and entrepreneurship, price formation, the role of private property, money and banking, inflation, credit and interest rates, the role of government and the costs of government intervention. The other two courses look at liberty as a philosophical concept. One is based on Friedrich Hayek's *The Constitution of Liberty* and its analyses of the evolution of the concepts of liberty, the rule of law, the use of knowledge in society and the creative power of the free society. The other course contains readings from Ludwig von Mises' Human Action and Liberalism, focuses on Austrian economics and the influence of philosophy in the history of economic thought, and provides a critical analysis of socialism. Undergraduate students are required to take a fifth course which educates them through a process of analyzing real day-to-day issues using the knowledge and tools they have gained in the core courses.

UFM HIGHLIGHTS

As civilized human beings, we are inheritors, neither of an inquiry about ourselves and the world, nor of an accumulating body of information, but of a conversation begun in the primeval forest and extended and made more articulate in the course of centuries ... Education, properly speaking, is an initiation ... in which we acquire the intellectual and moral habits appropriate to conversation.

—Michael Oakeshott

REACHING THE BEST AND THE BRIGHTEST

When we recruit students, we look for the most brilliant minds from all walks of life and those most likely to become future leaders. Unfortunately, despite our deferred tuition program, many cannot afford to study at UFM. The majority of Guatemalans are very poor, so staying in school and out of the workforce long enough to graduate from high school is already a sacrifice most families cannot afford. In 1996 we established the program known as ITA (Impulso al Talento Académico/Promoting Academic Talent) to identify the most qualified, passionate, motivated and poorest students. As well as full tuition, the program covers room and board, public transportation, books and basic personal expenses.

ITA students have fire in their bellies – they establish goals and fight to achieve them. Despite the huge gap in education level, ITA students quickly rise to the top of the class and actively drive discussions with their questions. Most of them go on to participate in graduate programs abroad and all of them are committed to changing their country and making sure others do not have to endure the poverty they have experienced.

CREATING A CULTURE OF INDEPENDENT THOUGHT

In 2003, we began an in-house revolution. We began shifting the focus of what happens in the classroom from teaching to learning through the intensive use of Socratic practice. We are moving from a culture of command and control, where the teacher is the center of the student's experience, to a more dynamic model whereby the students are actively engaged in facilitating their own learning. This model allows students, under the leadership of their teacher, to learn to take responsibility for their learning process and ownership of their curriculum.

Student-centered classrooms facilitate an environment of complex social interactions and behavioral rules which create a culture of intellectual independence, innovation, discovery and genuine learning. We believe that the Socratic method is the best way for students to explore the meaning of liberty. The Hayekian and market process analogies to learning and school culture are numerous and will not be lost on our students.

CHALLENGING THE MYTHS

David Hume points out in his essay 'Of the First Principles of Government' that when all is said and done, it is public opinion that establishes the limits to liberty. The greatest threats to liberty have been historical myths. Even those that may seem far fetched frequently contribute to the formation of present-day public opinion. For example, the socialist myth is responsible for the death of over a hundred million of our fellow human beings and for the poverty and low living standards of hundreds of millions more. With this in mind, in 2006 UFM established the program Explorations on History, to promote the continuing re-examination of history. We consider this program vital to the future of liberty, in the most literal sense of the word.

FOCUS ON LIBERTY IN LATIN AMERICA

In 2004, the Liberty Fund in Indianapolis selected UFM as a co-sponsor of the program Exploraciones sobre la Libertad (Explorations on Liberty), a Spanish-language version of the Liberty Fund colloquia which is directed towards native Spanish speakers. Held in Guatemala, this program is targeted primarily, though not exclusively, at a Latin American audience. The program falls on fertile soil; much has been accomplished in the past four decades to cultivate classical liberal thought in Latin America. UFM's long-standing network of scholars and opinion-makers throughout Latin America is reaching new and stimulating intellectual communities, providing a rich source of networking for participants.

MULTIPLIER EFFECTS

The importance of UFM's programs is palpable in Guatemala. Members of the UFM 'family' have gone on to found a policy think tank, three public policy pressure groups and the first public choice center in Latin

America. Their newspaper columns appear daily in the Guatemalan press and they dominate the influential sphere of talk radio. UFM graduates have mastered the art of taking an abstract idea and putting it into simple language that is culturally relevant and understood by all. Any public debate must take into account a well-documented classical liberal point of view.

Unfortunately, in countries like Guatemala opportunities to change the entrenched and twisted institutional base are fleeting. Luckily, windows of political opportunity do open up and offer us the chance to extend individual liberty by ratcheting down the role of the state as it relates to a particular policy measure or even constitutional reform. UFM has fostered a critical mass of classical liberal thinkers who span several generations and professions. Each has the intellectual ability to recognize opportunities and the courage to honor their convictions and seize them.

MISSION POSSIBLE

The mission of Universidad Francisco Marroquín is to teach and disseminate the ethical, legal and economic principles of a society of free and responsible persons.

Members of the classical liberal community formed by UFM have been directly responsible for the reforms that have had a huge and tangible impact on individual liberty in Guatemala. Sometimes they have participated in reforms as outsiders, sometimes from key positions on the inside. To spotlight the most successful: in 1989 Guatemala's central bank abandoned fixed exchange rates; in 1993 a constitutional reform prohibited the central bank from lending to the government; in 1996 Guatemala's Congress passed the most liberal telecommunications law in the world; and in 2001 legislation was changed to allow competing currencies – an idea advocated by Hayek! As a result of these reforms we have monetary stability, the ability to make contracts in any currency, and phones widely available for everyone. The impact of each of these systemic changes has been so positive that no politicians dare talk of removing them.

The case of telecoms reform in Guatemala is a perfect illustration of the importance of UFM graduates being ready to engage in policy battles. The government nationalized telecommunications in 1971 and by the 1980s setting up a phone line took years and cost thousands of dollars. Just getting a dial tone could take up to fifteen minutes. In response to this, messages and invitations were shuttled on motorbikes around town. The poor and rural areas were cut off from all phone communication. Manuel Ayau fought the state monopoly from its inception. The factor that made the most difference in fighting this battle was the team of UFM graduates who were operating from the inside. In 1995, with a UFM graduate sitting on the congressional committee on telecommunications, a legislative plan to introduce competition into the telecoms market was hatched. The door opened further when the new president appointed him head of the state telephone monopoly. This resulted in very liberal telecommunications laws which successfully privatized phone companies. In 2007, Guatemala boasted 9 million cellular lines for a population of 13 million and some of the cheapest rates in the world.

As I write, it is election season in Guatemala. An international political adviser recently commented to one of the candidates that he was trying to figure out why there was no talk from any of the candidates or in the media about raising taxes, agrarian reform or other populist formulas. What, he asked, had happened in Guatemala to make it so different from the rest of Latin America?

JUST THE BEGINNING

The telephone liberalization coincided with the arrival of the Internet. UFM was the first campus to be fully wireless and we continue to aggressively use technology to enhance the learning process. Our new media department provides audio and video streaming of lectures to clients around the world. Both in-house and visiting speakers have been featured, the latter including Israel Kirzner, Vernon Smith and José Maria Aznar. In addition, the department hosts the Spanish version of Milton and Rose Friedman's *Free to Choose* series and is currently working on a project to fully digitize the entire collection of our Ludwig von Mises Library. The possibilities for the dissemination of ideas of liberty are unlimited!

The founding of UFM was inspired by the example of others who were already engaged in promoting classical liberal ideas. It was the encouragement of scholars, promoters of ideas and friends at organizations such as the Foundation for Economic Education, the Mont Pelerin Society and Liberty Fund that convinced the founders of UFM to take up the daunting challenge of founding a classical liberal university in a poor country where the battle of ideas had moved beyond rhetoric and into the realm of violence.

Today, UFM is a unique and durable venture in the world of ideas; one that transcends Guatemala's borders. UFM has evolved into a model that can be emulated. We believe that UFM can inspire others around the world to undertake and succeed at great enterprises that will continue to expand human liberty everywhere.

We take with us the challenge of leading a revolution that will change the course of history in our country. But not with arms, threats or violence; not from ideological trenches that lead us to see enemies in our own brothers and sisters. Rather through open and frank dialogue, through respectful questioning and through the triumph of ideas.

—Edwin Xol, magna cum laude, ITA scholarship recipient, commencement address, 2007

04

CHAPTER

A Little Bit of (Intellectual) Entrepreneurship Goes a Long Way

Greg Lindsay
Centre for Independent Studies
(Australia)

Australia has been a peaceful and prosperous nation almost since European settlement in 1788. It is one of the world's most stable democracies. For much of the 20th century what has come to be known as the Australian Settlement drove government and policy. After World War II, the protectionism, labor market regulation, state paternalism and White Australia policy that were key components of the Australian Settlement vision were increasingly seen as ideas from another era. By the 1960s, when I was a teenager, the sense of anachronism was pervasive.

Looking at my early life, it would have been hard to guess that I would end up starting a major think tank. My background was solidly middle class, though by no means especially prosperous – my father died when I was thirteen. My life consisted of family (I was the eldest of three), school, Scouts, and part-time jobs in place of pocket money. I was more interested in bushwalking and skiing than ideas, and my first foray into university studies (in agriculture) was a dismal failure. Since I was on a teacher training scholarship, something had to be done with me, so I was shipped off to teachers' college to study mathematics, an area where I seemed to have some ability. Several faltering years later, I finally qualified.

My university years were politically exciting times for Australia. After 23 years of tired conservative government, the Australian Labor Party, led by Gough Whitlam, won the federal election in 1972, ousting Prime Minister William McMahon's Liberal/Country Party coalition. 'It's time' had been Labor's election slogan, and it truly was its time. But the Australian public were not quite ready for the government they got, which overspent, saw inflation rise, and ultimately ended in meltdown in 1975, when the opposition blocked supply in the Senate. In the ensuing constitutional crisis, the governor-general sacked Whitlam as prime minister and appointed opposition leader Malcolm Fraser as caretaker in his place. Fraser won the subsequent election in a landslide, but his government proved to be quite a disappointment to those seeking reform. It was at teachers' college that the world of ideas started to have an impact on me, but in surprising ways. The madness of the Whitlam government certainly provoked me into thinking that their way was a crazy way to run a country. Economically, the signs were less than promising. Inflation getting out of control was just one indicator.

One of my lecturers at college, the film critic Bill Collins, was a fan of Ayn Rand: he interspersed education theory with libertarian philosophy and showings of *The Fountainhead*. 'Now, this is something interesting,' I thought. 'What next?' I started reading, and entered the world of ideas about classical liberalism and freedom. Little did I know that world would shape the rest of my life.

But my immediate destiny was still to be a teacher. I had begun to wonder whether the organization and provision of education in Australia were consistent with my developing views about a free society and the role of education within it. As I suppose any 25-year-old teacher starting out with such ideas does, I decided that I should start an independent school.

A collection of pamphlets on education and the state began to fill my shelves. I also started to build my first freedom library, like so many others, by buying books from the Foundation for Economic Education in New York. Importantly, my reading included F. A. Hayek's 'The Intellectuals and Socialism', which first appeared in the University of Chicago Law Review in 1949, and had been reprinted by the Institute for Humane Studies (IHS). Strategically, this was the most important short article I was to read, because it set out the challenge to which the Centre for Independent Studies (CIS) still rises today: 'we can make the philosophic foundations of a free society once more a living intellectual issue, and its implementation a task which challenges the ingenuity and imagination of our liveliest minds . . . if we can regain that belief in the power of ideas which was the mark of liberalism at its best, the battle is not lost'.

In my earlier reading, I had discovered the Center for Independent Education (CIE) in Wichita, Kansas, which was part of the IHS. I began a fruitful correspondence with George Pearson, who ran it. That continued for many years – he remains a friend to this day. In 1975, my first year as a teacher, I traveled to Wichita and visited George and CIE (just a postbox, really), and it was at the Pearson home that I first came across the books of the Institute of Economic Affairs (IEA), about which I had previously known nothing. That lack of knowledge was to change within a short few months. A bigger picture of the world of ideas was emerging.

On that same 1975 trip to the USA, I met Murray Rothbard in New York, where I helped him and his wife stuff envelopes on their living-room floor – good training for running a think tank! Towards the end of the trip, I changed my mind about starting a school. I thought I could do something to remedy the problems that faced Australia, but it would require thinking bigger. I had to face squarely the task Hayek set in 'The Intellectuals and Socialism'.

The problems were intellectual . . . it was time for me to do something about them . . . CIE, IHS and IEA were all centers of intellectual endeavor . . . 'Forget the school,' I thought, 'this is what I should start!' By the time my plane landed back in Sydney, where I was ready to start my second year of teaching at Richmond High School, the die was cast.

That year, 1976, IEA founder Antony Fisher first visited Australia. He and a group of people were trying to start an IEA-style think tank here. When I found out where he was staying in Sydney, I called him and outlined what I was attempting to do. He wished me luck.

When Fisher returned in December of the same year, I met him at a small meeting he addressed. In October, I had already organized a seminar at Macquarie University with academics John Ray and Lauchlan Chipman as speakers. Chipman, a professor of philosophy, was the first academic I contacted to discuss my plans. It seemed to me that what Fisher was proposing was what I was already doing. I wondered how I could turn that to the center's advantage.

I spent the next few years on teaching, further university study in philosophy, and the first steps in building the CIS. In those years, I met some crucial people, including Maurice Newman, who had brought Milton Friedman to Australia in 1975, and Ross Parish, then a professor of economics at Monash University.

Many of the academic connections I had made came together to speak at a conference at Macquarie University in April 1978. The conference drew a decent crowd, including Paddy McGuinness, who was then the economics editor of the Australian Financial Review. Two days later, Paddy wrote a famous article about the conference, 'Where Friedman is a pinko', which gave our phone number and address. We were flooded with messages for days. It was a major coup for us.

While still a teacher, I had persuaded my school's principal to let me have some time off and attend the Mont Pelerin Society (MPS) meeting in Hong Kong in 1978. I became a member of the MPS in 1982, and was eventually elected to the board in 1994. In 2006, I had the honor of being elected the Society's president, which has truly been one of the highlights of my life. I followed as president some great people who have been my heroes – especially Hayek and Friedman. At the start of the 21st century, the MPS endures more strongly than ever as the pre-eminent organization dedicated to the principles of liberalism. Being a part of it has been of enormous benefit to the development of the CIS.

With the CIS building momentum, something in the other parts of my life had to give, so during 1979 I took leave without pay from my teaching job to try to kick the center into life as a full-time enterprise. It was another world for me, and a big risk. Still, my future wife, Jenny, whom I had met while she was still at university, was working, and two of the center's earliest supporters, Neville Kennard and Ross Graham-Taylor, were also providing some financial support, so we weren't entirely without income. Kennard remains a consistent and major supporter to this day. The group that had been supporting the efforts to start an IEA-style think tank decided that perhaps CIS should be supported after all, but nothing came of it right away.

Eventually, I identified Melbourne businessman Hugh Morgan as a key figure in that IEA effort. I rang him, told him I thought this institute business had stalled, and that it was time to stop the talk. A couple of days later, I flew down to Melbourne to see him, and he decided it was time to move on it. He mustered about AU$40,000 per year for five years, and with this small funding base, in 1980 we set up the CIS above Uncle Pete's Toys in St Leonards in Sydney. We stayed there for ten years; that office was where we set out to build our reputation and pursue our mission.

The Centre for Independent Studies celebrated its 30th anniversary in 2006 with a sell-out dinner. People who have been members and supporters from day one attended, and they were joined by others, including then prime minister John Howard, cabinet ministers and leaders in politics, business and other fields from across Australia and New Zealand.

Looking back, there have been many highlights. In the early years, we focused almost entirely on economic reform. And by the end of our first decade, in 1986, the impetus for that reform in Australia had been well established. We had a Labor government under Bob Hawke committed to reducing regulation and opening up free trade, and an opposition unlikely to oppose any such moves. It seemed that economic liberalism was the new orthodoxy.

That situation continues to this day, to varying degrees. A century of protectionism in Australia has given way. We are now one of the world's more open economies, with further tariff reductions scheduled within the next few years that will remove much of the remaining protectionism. For 30 years, governments at federal and state levels have privatized enterprises they have controlled for all of living memory. Banks, airlines, pharmaceutical companies, utilities and public transport have all made the transition, and the process continues. If you look at the early work of the CIS, you see numerous examples of published recommendations that became policy over time.

Our work was a key component in the environment for reform, but I can't claim that we were entirely responsible. Nevertheless, there are clear examples where a particular publication led to a policy change. The best known of these is the deregulation of shopping hours in New South Wales soon after we published *Free to Shop* by Geoff Hogbin: the reaction was visible and immediate.

Over the last ten years, we've had a growing interest in international and strategic policy, particularly with regard to China and the Pacific, in Indigenous issues and in health. And social policy has been a focus since the late 1980s. Much of the direction of our most successful work is the result of the contributions of key people. In our early work on economic policy,

Ross Parish's contribution was vital. Our currently acknowledged strength in social policy could not have come about without Barry Maley, Peter Saunders and the many younger people who have worked under their guidance. Helen Hughes has steered the way where Indigenous policy and the Pacific are concerned. And if I were to go through our entire list of past and present staff, I could think of some way in which they specifically contributed to the output and life of the CIS, and of the country.

We continue to produce a prodigious amount of material: our back catalogue includes probably over two hundred books and monographs. Our quarterly magazine, *Policy*, currently edited by Andrew Norton, has been going for 23 years; we have a series of almost one hundred Issue Analysis papers and have published thousands of newspaper articles and op-eds. When we have our weekly staff meetings, there is usually an exhaustive list to read out of all our staff's media appearances and mentions.

Seminars, lectures and conferences continue to be a part of CIS activities. The 2009 annual John Bonython Lecture was the 25th. Israel Kirzner gave the first of them in 1984 and since then we've had people including James Buchanan, Václav Klaus, Rupert Murdoch, Mario Vargas Llosa and Ralph Harris on the stage. The Acton Lecture on Religion and Freedom turns ten in 2008, and the CIS's flagship conference, Consilium, which attracts top-level people from the worlds of ideas, business and politics from around the globe, moves into its ninth year. Then there are all kinds of other events, such as our Policymakers series, where political leaders from both sides air their ideas in public, and the annual Big Ideas Forum, which attracts hundreds of people to hear debate on some of the most challenging and interesting ideas of the day.

Sometimes it's suggested to me that the CIS could start or become a university. This doesn't seem likely, but our Liberty and Society program brings together young people to hear about liberalism and the free society, sometimes for the first time, from liberal intellectuals. Some of those speakers are alumni of the same program, now academics – so we're having some success in bringing liberalism back into the universities. Liberty and Society harks back to that original impulse I had to start a school, and that mission to involve new people in an intellectual life where economic and personal liberty are key values is still an important driver for the center.

These past 30 years and more have been an incredible journey for me, and one that I've been privileged to be able to share with many others. All the institutes I know have stories about how they got to where they are, all different, and this is ours. There will certainly be others that will start on similar paths in the future.

For Australia now, however, I feel it would be more difficult for someone new to do what we have done without substantial start-up support. The CIS was the entrepreneurial endeavor of a young man (me) committed to doing something about the threats he and others saw to the free society. It was difficult enough back in 1976! I hope others will try nevertheless, and that they will have the clear vision and thick skin to succeed. Entrepreneurs in any field, as Israel Kirzner reminds us, are always alert to new ways of doing things and correcting what they see as errors. That's pretty much what I set out to do more than 30 years ago. I fully accepted the view Hayek and Keynes shared that ideas have great power to change the world for good or ill, even if that power is sometimes slow to take effect.

In 2004, an article by Diana Bagnall in The Bulletin, Australia's main news magazine, described me as the 'most influential man in Australia', saying that the Centre for Independent Studies had 'its fingerprints . . . all over this country's political agenda, on both sides'. Not bad, I guess, for an intellectual entrepreneur. Many of the ideas we've had about what governments should do and what individuals should do for themselves have increasingly become general practice in the past 30 years, but there is still a lengthy agenda of work ahead. The CIS exists to underpin the free society and its liberal democratic institutions. But it is a troubled world – I cannot see us being able to rest on our laurels any time soon. Australia and New Zealand are free and prosperous nations and Australia's economic performance in the last decade or so has outpaced that of much of the world, but the intellectual and policy wins that we have achieved can easily be reversed unless they are continually reinforced. Free trade, for instance, is subject to the whims of politicians and voters, and has always been so. Where those whims turn next will to some extent determine where we have to act to inform and guide the environment of ideas.

Passion for Freedom

Gerardo Bongiovanni
Fundación Libertad
(Argentina)

MOTIVATION

Since I was very young, I have always been attracted to public affairs. My family – farmers of humble origin – were very 'politicized' and in our home, there was always time for conversation and discussions on political and economic issues.

Aside from that, I have always been deeply interested in the study of history (particularly that of Argentina) and the personal story of my grandfather on my mother's side has always impressed and moved me.

Born in Italy at the end of the 19th century, he spent the early part of his childhood in poverty before his family decided to immigrate to Argentina in a quest for a future. He worked hard, very hard, and in a few years, he managed to achieve an economic and social position that was more than reasonable. This included, which was perhaps the most important to him and to many other immigrants, the chance for his children to have a good life, the opportunity to study and to become professionals.

What kind of country was Argentina in 1880 that permitted so many Italians, Spaniards and people from many other nationalities to reach such a state of development? What were the principles on which that society, booming and loaded with opportunities, was based? Who were the 'fathers' of this model and what were the ideas that made it work? I spent a great deal of my time between the ages of 15 and 17 trying to answer those questions. I read and re-read the history of my country from the mid-19th century until the 1930s until something caught my attention and shaped my life.

In fact, in a more general and even intuitive way, I started to become familiar with free market ideas and with the process that someone once said, allowed the building of 'a modern country in the middle of a desert.' I was also influenced by the free market model, which was reflected in the 1853 Constitution by the great jurist Juan Bautista Alberdi.

Some time later, at around the age of twenty, an almost accidental encounter allowed me to meet Mr Alberto Benegas Lynch (Sr), who encouraged me to develop my ideas and projects, and put me in contact with the Centro de Estudios sobre la Libertad de Buenos Aires (Center for the Study of Liberty of Buenos Aires), which was a reference for all of us who were engaged in free market ideas.

It was the combination of a family of entrepreneurial immigrants, an interest in the study of Argentine history during a time of peak development, as well as a relationship with small but active and committed groups of free market academics that was essential for what was going to happen next in my life: the decision to create a free market think tank that would promote the ideas of freedom as the driving force for the development of society.

HANDS-ON

Already settled into Rosario, the second largest city in Argentina, as I was studying economics and developing some small personal projects, with the encouragement of Alberto Benegas Lynch (Jr) and other friends from Buenos Aires, we started the slow and hard process of setting up a free market organization. The mere fact that our intention was to develop the organization in Rosario, a city in the interior of Argentina, would make this process even more challenging. In fact, in Argentina we say that 'God is everywhere, but he has his office in Buenos Aires.' As in most countries in Latin America, everything takes place in the capital city, so it is quite hard to achieve your goals and secure resources in the interior of the country. However, the free market and 'anti-privileges' spirit of our region could offset the effects of those drawbacks.

In the early 1980s, the international political context was far from ideal: the 'Reagan Age' was just beginning and his amazing results had not yet been seen and in Latin America, popular opinion was that this part of the world was doomed to leftist totalitarianism along the lines of what was happening in Cuba and Nicaragua. After a decade full of violence, in 1983, Argentina was coming back to democracy. Following the insensible actions of subversive groups, the military dictatorship imposed a savage repression that left thousands upon thousands dead or missing. Unfortunately, that was not all, in 1982, the insane governing military was being challenged in a war that was obviously being lost. (Some years earlier, while I was doing my obligatory military service, Great Britain had been on the verge of war with Chile, but thanks to intervention by Pope John Paul II, it was prevented).

The economic and political environment at this time was not the best. As was common practice in Latin America at that time, the major political parties were preaching populist ideas and they would slander free market ideas; blaming them for all the existing calamities in the country and around the world. Standing up for ideas such as economic liberalization, privatization, or deregulation would sound even more unusual. In general, these ideas were rejected not only by the population, but also by the academic world and policy makers.

Despite these realities, together with a group of young college students, we started to act. Our first task was to persuade some academics, professionals and entrepreneurs to join us, even if they could only make a humble contribution. At that time, I met two outstanding free market economists with great academic prestige: Rogelio Pontón and Antonio Margariti. Both of them were vital in Fundación Libertad´s development and they are still active today, in very prominent positions.

For the next three or four years we developed our activities in an 'informal' way; it was only at the beginning of 1988 that we gave Fundación Libertad a definite shape. However, in that period, while we were devoting ourselves almost exclusively to organizing courses on the free market doctrine for young college students, we set some criteria that ended up being decisive for the future development of the organization. These criteria included:

- Strengthening relations with organizations and groups or people with similar ideals, such as ESEADE (Escuela Superior de Economía y Administración de Empresas – High School of Business Economy and Administration) which had a special impact due to the group that it gathered.

- Developing a fundraising plan based on the strategy of having many donors, even if their contributions were minimal. We believed this strategy would give us more independence and institutional strength, something that would prove to be true.

- Applying the criteria of modern management to direct the organization.

- Committing to advancing free market ideas as a permanent solution for transforming society and avoiding focusing only on the short term. No one in our team was to have the expectation that Fundación Libertad would be a springboard for politics or public office. As a matter of fact and in spite of countless offers, none of the relevant members of the board or staff has accepted positions in the public sector; we have remained committed to working in the field of ideas.

Finally, during this time, we also began to understand the concept of intellectual entrepreneurs as a much-needed detector and mobilizing agent of human and economic resources.

On 3 March 1988, we incorporated this concept into plans and formally launched Fundación Libertad.

THE FIRST STEP

On several occasions I have been asked about what contributed to turning Fundación Libertad into a large and consolidated organization and when it happened. The answer is not an easy one; it has been a long and continuous process, in which numerous actions, people and circumstances were interacting. However, I believe that the years 1992–93 were a turning point in the course of our organization; it was the time when we began to 'go international.' As was the case on multiple occasions, the Atlas Economic Research Foundation played a key role in this achievement. After inviting me to a workshop in Punta del Este, Uruguay, at the end of 1991, Alex Chafuen gave us his support and, most importantly, provided us with access to his impressive network of contacts. Without a doubt, I can say that, of all the people I have met in the 'free market movement' (and to tell you the truth, I know a lot of people), I have come into contact with 80 per cent of them thanks to Atlas.

Making the most of these contacts is key for an institute in a remote country in South America, and we have certainly made the most of it. In the years to follow, Fundación Libertad invited seven economy Nobel Prize winners (including Gary Becker and James Buchanan), numerous intellectuals (including Paul Johnson, Mario Vargas Llosa and Jean Francoise Revel) as well as more than 200 lecturers from more than 50 countries in the world to Argentina. We also became members of different international networks and organizations, such as the Economic Freedom Network and Friedrich Naumann Foundation network, thus learning from our colleagues in a truly enriching process.

While working to expand our international exposure, we continued to consolidate the activities of our organization. Throughout the 1990s, during a time when another populist and mercantilist-oriented government was increasing public expenditure and calling it 'neoliberalism,' Fundación Libertad continued to grow and make three decisions of great significance:

- We created the Institute for Economic Research (IEE) that has allowed us to gather a team of high-level academics and researchers, who have been producing highly relevant studies and positioning Fundación Libertad as a generator of ideas and top-quality proposals.

- In an attempt to give our work a national dimension, we promoted the creation of think tanks in other cities in Argentina and, together with existing organizations, Fundación Libertad created Red Libertad (Libertad Network), a network which gathers fifteen think tanks throughout the main cities of Argentina and develops projects such as the *Index of Economic Freedom* and the *Performance Index of the Argentine Provinces.*

- Finally, in a very controversial decision, we decided to become directly involved in the communication media, not only through newspaper columns and electronic media, but also through our own radio and TV programs. We developed an area of considerable scale that has been producing a significant number of radio and television appearances.

THE SECOND STEP AND OUR CURRENT STATUS

In 1999, thanks to the generosity of a businessman on our board, Fundación Libertad moved its headquarters to an eight-floor building located in the heart of Rosario. This new office has allowed us to develop new projects that we had been longing to start and which we considered vital for the promotion of freedom.

On one hand, we created a Business School which, together with the ESEADE, offers post-graduate courses on economics and philosophy. This collaboration has made it possible for hundreds of young professionals in outstanding positions in private companies to nourish themselves with the principles of classical liberalism and the Austrian school of economics. On the other hand, the facilities in our new building have enabled us to create autonomous centers and institutes which, based on free market principles and the study and promotion of public policy ideas, have been instrumental in developing proposals in areas such as the environment, institutional strengthening, agricultural development, social and labor issues, entrepreneurship, fiscal and tax issues, art and culture, etc.

Currently, Fundación Libertad has twelve centers and institutes, many of which will hopefully become independent organizations one day.

We have also made progress at international level and have increased the number of networks and programs in which we are participating, and we continue to play a key role in the creation of FIL (International Foundation for Liberty), a free market think tank created in 2002 by representatives from Spain, the United States and Latin America, and chaired by the well-known Peruvian writer, Mario Vargas Llosa.

Finally, Fundación Libertad has decided to focus on its media presence by becoming a member of media partnerships aimed at strengthening the communication of the messages and values of a free society.

Today, a modest institute that began in the mid-1980s, fostered and fed by a group of young people in a small office, has evolved into an institution of 60 employees. It is currently supported by more than 300 private companies, and is active in coordinating a network of free market foundations throughout the country and in organizing numerous activities which attract over 500 speakers each year.

SOME ACHIEVEMENTS

Over the past few years, the development of the Republic of Argentina has been rather disappointing. This worries and saddens all of us who live in this country and, in particular, those of us who have devoted ourselves to the business of ideas and public policy. However, aside from admitting that there is still much left to be done, many people agree that Fundación Libertad has been relevant in several aspects:

- It is clear that we have played a role in what we call 'economic rationality.' It is no coincidence that the province of Santa Fe (where Rosario and the headquarters of Fundación Libertad are located) is practically the only province in the country that has no fiscal deficits or increases in its taxes.

- We have contributed to the strengthening of institutions through research and proposals, and have contributed to the improvement and performance of the judiciary and its independence.

- Our training of young people has been another important achievement. As has already been mentioned, thousands of young people have attended our courses in our business schools. They have been educated in the ideas of freedom and are, little by little, beginning to secure relevant positions in the political, economic and social sphere. In fact, a recent 'rebellion' in the Argentine agricultural sector against an attempt to produce an irrational and disproportionate increase in taxes has shown the extent to which this sector has been influenced by the ideas spread by Fundación Libertad.

- Lastly, it is not a minor achievement to have developed an institution whereby we constantly try to apply management criteria, exercise a self-critical approach, and develop a strong and close relationship with the donors and the targets of our projects and activities.

In conclusion, perhaps the most significant accomplishment of our institution is that it is seen by all of society, even by our harshest ideological opponents, as having a respect for seriousness, depth and openness. There is no politician, businessman or social or union leader who refuses a conversation or debate instigated by our institution, or who is unwilling to consider an idea or proposal made by us. In a country and a region where free market ideas are often slandered, we have managed to build an organization respected by everybody and admired by many. Interestingly, the city of Rosario has also been governed for many years by the socialist party, yet the mayor and his teams (much like the successive governors of Santa Fe province), regardless of their political affiliation, regularly attend our conferences and seminars. This was confirmed again during the remarkable seminar organized for Fundación Libertad's 20th anniversary in March 2008. Three hundred high-level international participants, attended, including six former Latin American presidents as well as prestigious Argentine intellectuals, political figures, businessmen and academics, and contributed to its great public impact.

OUR MANY CHALLENGES

Our challenges are numerous and varied. Apart from the usual ones related to the efficiency of the organization, fundraising or the marketing of our products, there are others related to the need to improve networking and boost our synergies with like-minded groups.

Furthermore, we know that the political and ideological challenges will not be small; we are aware that part of the academic world, and almost all of the political one, have decided to hold classical liberalism responsible for the international financial crisis. This will be a hard battle to fight as this politically correct – and blatantly false –explanation is very convenient for many, particularly for the politicians who broaden their powers via regulations and those from states that do not stop growing.

In Latin America there is an additional challenge: the so-called socialism of the 21st century. This socialism is from Venezuela and is trying to colonize the rest of Latin America with anachronistic ideas that aim to eliminate not only the continent's battered market economy, but also all vestiges of democracy by imposing a new model of totalitarianism similar to the one that has already failed all around the world.

Hard times await us; times that will bring about the sometimes violent confrontation of ideas. Yet these times will not be any harder than the ones that any intellectual entrepreneur faces when they start their project, nor harder than the ones we faced in the 1980s while starting the adventure of Fundación Libertad in Argentina. These are times that are worth living.

06

CHAPTER

Fostering Libertarianism in South Korea

Chung-Ho Kim
Center for Free Enterprise
(South Korea)

WE FOUND THE MARKET IN HAYEK

As I reflect on the establishment and brief history of the Center for Free Enterprise, I am reminded of something said by a former official in the Lyndon Baines Johnson administration: 'History never looks like history when you are living through it.' Sometimes, you don't realize how incredible some things are until you take a moment to reflect. In so many ways, it is remarkable that a libertarian think tank would be founded in South Korea and have had such incredible influence in such a short time.

Our story starts in 1994. At that time, Dr Gong Byeong-ho and I were resident researchers for the Korea Economic Research Institute (KERI). KERI was lukewarm in its defense of free markets, but at that time, they were the best we had. Dr Gong and I have the battle scars to prove it. We were regarded as heretics both inside and outside of our organization for refusing to yield to popularly held myths about the economy and government control.

Consider the context: in the early 1990s, most Koreans who discussed economic issues regarded chaebol (large conglomerates, such as Samsung, LG, Hyundai) as villains. They believed that chaebol needed to be tightly controlled in order to prevent them from abusing their power. This popular perception led to a number of shackles being placed on them. Regulations were constantly introduced to a welcoming public. Whether it was restrictions on chaebol business diversification plans or regulation over the amount they could loan from banks, it seemed that getting chaebol under control was the nation's priority.

Within that atmosphere, we argued that the fundamental problem with chaebol was not their excessive diversification or gigantic size. Rather, that the state rarely allowed them to go bankrupt. Those few times they were allowed to go belly-up, it was more likely to be revenge by politicians rather than decisions made based on economic principles. We argued that chaebol needed to be allowed to go bankrupt but we were dismissed as heretics.

KERI was like an isolated island adrift in an anti-capitalist ocean. Most people did not even consider whether our analysis made sense. They dismissed us as puppets of the chaebol because KERI was financed by the Federation of Korean Industries (FKI), a lobby group for these companies.

Shakespeare is often credited with the phrase, 'Don't shoot the messenger.' That dates back to ancient times in which messengers bringing bad news would be killed. As Sophocles declared in *Antigone*, 'No one loves the messenger who brings bad news.' However, our 'news' was actually good. There was no need to continue wasting valuable resources by propping up failing chaebol.

Our 'news' that seemed so bad was also good when it came to land issues. After extensively studying land and housing markets in South Korea, I concluded that prices were inflated because of a government-imposed ban on developing agricultural fields or forests for residential and commercial uses and restriction on high-rise buildings. Most people – citizens, as well as politicians – blamed an easy target: so-called speculation by investors. They assumed that land prices jumped because a few rich people owned too much land and too many houses. I refuted the myths in many articles, laying the blame at the hands of politicians intervening in the real estate market, but failed to make a considerable impact on policy decision-making. It was a frustrating experience.

Our frustration about the myths surrounding t chaebol and land issues motivated us to study human nature. We wanted to understand where the anti-capitalist mindset of so many people originated. We studied such diverse areas as anthropology, psychology and brain science in order to understand how jealousy affects human logical reasoning processes.

Then, in a case of serendipity, I came across Hayek's 'Three Sources of Human Values' translated into Korean by Professor Min Kyung-kuk who was, at that time, the one and only expert on Hayek in Korea. Hayek's conclusion that primitive instincts hard-wired in the brain conflict with the spontaneous order which evolves in the market provided a partial answer to my questions.

I recommended the book to Dr Gong. After a couple of weeks, he came to my office and made an unforgettable remark: 'Here, I see the market.' He meant that we could promote Hayek's ideas in Korean society.

We then launched into reading Hayek's other books and learned how to interpret social change through the concept of evolution. With Hayek as our mentor, we achieved our goal in 1996 by publishing a book entitled *Human Nature in Conflict*. Although it was not a commercial success, the publication helped us document the development of our intellectual journey.

GIVING BIRTH TO THE CENTER FOR FREE ENTERPRISE

Around that time, Mr Sohn Byung-doo joined KERI as CEO. He wanted to overhaul the institute. Gong became his de facto brain. There were few people who dared to say openly that Korea needed pure market principles. Although researchers at KERI were then the most market-friendly intellectuals in Korea, it would not have been accurate to label them libertarian. Their view was that although the market economy itself was superior to all known alternatives, pro-market policies should be introduced in a prudent manner given the possibility of market failure. Gong argued to Sohn that KERI must be overhauled to advocate the principles of the pure market economy in an open and aggressive way.

At the invitation of Jo Kwong of the Atlas Economic Research Foundation, Gong and Sohn participated in the Mont Pelerin Society's 1996 annual meeting. During the trip, Dr Gong finally succeeded in persuading

Sohn of the need to establish a libertarian think tank. After returning, the Center for Free Enterprise (CFE) was born under the umbrella of KERI. Gong launched the CFE with only five employees. Although I remained at the KERI as the division head for regulation studies, I implicitly agreed to join the CFE when the right time came.

Gong and I were eager to launch the CFE as a separate and independent think tank. The opportunity came at an unexpected time. In early 1997, Sohn moved from KERI to the Federation of Korean Industries (FKI) as its vice-chairman. We succeeded in launching the CFE as a separate organization with help from Mr Sohn and Mr Chae (then-president of both the FKI and the SK Corporation). Former Yonsei University president, Song Ja, joined us as chairman of our board. He did not hesitate in accepting our invitation although he clearly was too prominent for a start-up organization with just nine employees.

We knew we were going against the odds. Our motto: 'No Fear! No Compromise! Least Cost!' reflected our determination to promote the market economy externally without compromise, and internally to run the institute at a minimum cost. It would be very difficult to advocate free market principles in South Korea.

THE CFE AS A STRONG SUPPORTER OF LIBERTARIANS

Our mission was to foster libertarianism. We were determined to disseminate libertarian ideas in an organized and aggressive way. Under the theme of the 'Libertarian Series', we began to introduce libertarian classics to Korean readers, starting with the works of Hayek, Ludwig von Mises, Ayn Rand, Israel Kirzner, Douglas North, and James Buchanan. Up to September 2009 we had published 60 volumes in the series, including both Korean and foreign authors.

We also set out to publish a series of policy studies under the theme of 'Freedom and Reform'. The biggest hurdle was to ferret out scholars who could propose policy alternatives from a libertarian perspective. We offered research grants to university scholars with libertarian policy proposals. The result is that we published 21 books. In retrospect, the ideas were fairly mild and even flawed at times, but, nevertheless, they shocked readers and intellectuals. Park Dong-wun's *Labor Market Flexibility* and Kim Young-yong's *Medical License: Critiques and Alternatives* were especially controversial.

SPREADING LIBERTARIANISM VIA FAX AND EMAIL NEWSLETTER

Despite those academic successes, the CFE's main goal remained to spread the philosophy of libertarianism. All the research papers were produced with this goal in mind.. We made a series of booklets with easy and short writings on libertarianism for wide distribution to general readers, including the Story Handbook Series and the Free World Handbook Series.

We did not hesitate to go beyond the paradigm followed by the existing academic research centers. We launched massive promotional activities in public: we displayed our publications in bank lounges, and placed ads about CFE on the walls of subway stations and trains.

We started burning up our fax lines. Most research institutions mailed their research papers or held seminars to promote their achievements or viewpoints. CFE obtained fax numbers and email addresses of key opinion leaders and sent them weekly newsletters. We were lucky that it was May 1998 and not 2009. Today those tactics might be treated as push mail and we could be subject to penalties. We were the first in South Korea to do that, so naturally, we attracted quite a bit of attention. From August 1998, these newsletters became the most important communications outlet for the CFE. We also built a network of outside contributors, hosted research-paper contests for college students, and summer school for students and teachers.

SOLE FIGHTER AGAINST THE MINORITY-SHAREHOLDER RIGHTS MOVEMENT

Just eight months after the CFE was established in April 1997, the Asian foreign currency crisis erupted. With a number of companies and financial institutions at the brink of bankruptcy, the Korean economy was at a crossroads. Policymakers had to decide whether to use the cumbersome hand of government to protect the collapsing enterprises with state subsidies, or to let the invisible hand of the free market take care of them.

Debates started to heat up over the issue and the CFE was standing up for the free market. President Gong gained notoriety by vehemently supporting the free market in debates with interventionists, intellectuals and labor union leaders. Along the way, Dr Gong and the CFE gained attention, but critics again attempted to kill the messenger by charging that the CFE was a puppet for chaebol.

Another significant task for the CFE was to deal properly with civil rights groups. The start of democratization in 1987 had resulted in the creation of a number of civic groups. The People's Solidarity for Participatory Democracy (PSPD) emerged as one of the most influential organizations. In 1997, the economic democratization committee of the PSPD was chaired by Chang Ha-sung, a Korea University professor and internationally known activist. The politically popular PSPD launched a minority-shareholder movement.

Despite widespread support for their shareholder activism, we believed that they were wrong. Even though it was problematic that controlling shareholders dominated minority shareholders, shareholder activism would not solve the problem. There needed to be a free market in corporate control. We were convinced that the PSPD aimed at transferring corporate control away from existing controlling shareholders and to outside directors, who would be under the influence of civil groups. We began publishing monographs highlighting libertarian options for corporate problems.

No one dared to stand against the PSPD, which was portrayed as angels at war with nefarious business giants. The CFE was alone in arguing that the PSPD could be wrong. As time has gone by, a considerable number of intellectuals and journalists have come to agree with us. We just wish that more intellectuals would think with their heads rather than their hearts.

FREE MARKET EDUCATION

In May 2003, I became the acting president for the CFE, succeeding Dr Min who was the second president after founding president, Dr Gong. My first initiative was to reinforce our public relations activities, including email newsletters and educational functions. We began to send email newsletters four times a week to our list of 55,000 registered members. I also put our resources and effort into the education business. We launched a new project to establish classes on free market principles at universities during the 2003 fall semester. The CFE's role was to channel the FKI's fund into establishing free market lectures and it turned out to be mutually beneficial. It was good for universities because they could invite outside speakers without worrying about the financial cost. It was attractive for the CFE because a regular credit course would be the most effective way to teach free market principles directly to students and professors and we did not have to recruit students or rent lecture rooms. In the middle of the fall 2009 semester, there were approximately 3,300 students at 25 universities taking free market courses sponsored by the CFE. In 2006, the CFE was awarded the Templeton Freedom Prize in the area of student outreach.

CHALLENGES AHEAD

Although the CFE achieved a lot during its first twelve years, much more, to paraphrase Lenin, remains to be done. One main thing we need to do is to break the dependency that people of all income levels have on the government. This includes the firms that still look to the government to block competition, to low-income people who look to the government for income subsidies. In other words, the 'free lunch' that so many have become used to having must end. The biggest challenge associated with that will be ending the bad habit which so many politicians have of robbing the rich and middle-class to redistribute money.

In order to achieve such a fundamental social change, the CFE literally needs a different channel. I believe that now is the time for a broadcasting channel to reach the masses. In early December 2010, the CFE will be launching an Internet-based broadcast. Although we face many tremendous hurdles, the last twelve years are an indication that we can be successful. As I quoted at the beginning of this article, history doesn't always feel like history when you are living through it. But after twelve years of progress, we are confident that as advocates of liberty we are on the right side of history.

A Swedish Think Tank Punches Above its Weight

Billy McCormack
Timbro
(Sweden)

Sweden is a country that, in many respects, 'punches above its weight'. Despite a population of roughly nine million (only slightly greater than that of New York City) and tucked into the upper pocket of chilly northern Europe, Sweden has churned out a disproportionate share of billionaires and global corporate behemoths. It has topped the music charts and *The New York Times* bestseller list, exported top talent to the National Hockey League, and cornered the market on awards for scientific and cultural achievement.

Timbro, a free market think tank founded in 1978 in Stockholm, has followed in this noble tradition. On a par with much larger organizations, such as The Heritage Foundation in Washington, DC and the Institute of Economic Affairs (IEA) in London, Timbro has long shaped public opinion, groomed talent, and has been influential both at home and abroad. Timbro's alumni include senior members of the Swedish government, business world and media; the European Parliament; and influential members of the media and academia in the United States. It is without a doubt that its network, reach and influence extend far beyond Sweden's borders.

To grasp Timbro's current standing, and to appreciate the longevity of its relevance, one must first trace the organization's roots – to a Sweden doubtless unfamiliar to IKEA's customers in Moscow and safety-minded Volvo owners in Manhattan. As was the case in many countries, the late 1960s were a time of turmoil in Sweden. Student revolts and anti-war protests galvanized the political left and radicalized the political discussion leading into the 1970s. The powerful unions and their political allies were mobilizing. A chief goal was, by way of legislation, to force private firms to relinquish ownership to that of their unionized employees. Sweden stood at the proverbial crossroads. Yet, the business community slumbered and the political center-right dreaded 'polarization'. Rather than sitting at the table, it appeared as though capitalists were content just to be on the menu.

A few, however, recognized the fragility of the situation early on and believed that inaction would put the country on a slippery slope toward low growth, punitive taxation, high unemployment and a bloated public sector. One individual who ended up playing a crucial role in energizing the business community in Sweden was Sture Eskilsson, the mild-mannered communications director of the Swedish Employers Association. In early 1971, he began to set things in motion.

It all began with his now infamous 'secret' memo. Like a wartime general, Eskilsson's dry, eight-page memo to the governing body of the Swedish Employers Association methodically laid out a strategy he believed would impede the left's advances across all sectors of society. He recognized that successful advocacy work required serious investment. Books and magazines needed to be published. A greater presence was required on school campuses. The business community needed to begin articulating ideas and values, engaging in open debate. Business leaders needed to present arguments and convey messages with a sense of conviction and unbending confidence. Simply put, business must dare to voice an opinion, to stand for something.

It was, by today's standards, a straightforward memo sketching a three-year action plan aimed at achieving greater awareness and support for issues the business community held near and dear. However, when it was subsequently leaked to the left-leaning press, pandemonium broke out. The memo was heralded as a nefarious plan to brainwash the public – and Eskilsson was portrayed as Sweden's Svengali. Unwittingly, though nonetheless fortuitously, Eskilsson was thrust into the spotlight. The debate had begun.

The memo was a turning point – that was for sure. It challenged the notion that the left reigned supreme in the arena of public opinion. It brought new faces and new ideas into an otherwise homogeneous domain. Conferences were organized, pamphlets and other printed matter were distributed on school campuses, and communications campaigns were launched. But the battle was just getting underway and Timbro would not see the light of day until seven years after Eskilsson typed his 'secret' memo. Ironically, it would be the controversial and strident social democratic prime minister, Olof Palme, who provided the seed capital for the think tank.

In the early 1970s, Sture Eskilsson and political scientist Carl-Johan Westholm began extensively studying the emerging think tanks in Great Britain and the United States. Organizations such as the IEA and The Heritage Foundation were rapidly establishing themselves as policy shops for influential conservative politicians, and were neatly sewn into a growing patchwork of like-minded magazines and other intellectual outlets. It was there that Westholm and Eskilsson found the impulse and the inspiration for what would become Timbro. At a time when some in the business world wanted to tone things down, Westholm and Eskilsson wanted to turn up the volume.

In 1976, Olof Palme's social democrats passed, with the slightest of majorities, the Co-Determination Act, which was nothing less than revolutionary. It meant that business owners could not make any material decisions without first consulting the union. The rules were dense and complicated, so the government deemed it necessary to earmark 100 million SEK to be used for educating union members. The Swedish Employers Association received just six million SEK for similar activities aimed at business owners. Roughly half was used as seed capital for Timbro. In effect, Olof Palme was the unwitting benefactor of an organization that would seek to undermine him and fellow social democrats for the foreseeable future.

Timbro's job was to be an advocate in areas deemed unsuitable for the Swedish Employers Association. Sture Eskilsson and Carl-Johan Westholm began by recruiting the top names in academia to form the Ratio Scientific Council. In addition to Carl-Johan Westholm, the council was comprised of Rector Magnificus of Uppsala University, Torgny Segerstedt, nuclear physicist Tor Ragnar Gerholm, law professor Stig Strömholm, sociology professor Hans L. Zetterberg and economics professor Eric Dahmén. The group began in earnest by publishing books and organizing seminars. The first seminar, titled 'Anti-intellectualism in Sweden', as Eskilsson recalls in his memoirs, 'opened a new arena for discussions on an academic level in Sweden.'

The council decided that the first book to be published would be F. A. Hayek's magnum opus, *The Constitution of Liberty*. This tome, written in English by a native German speaker, proved to be quite a challenge for the translator: it took five years to finish the translation.

Timbro achieved its big breakthrough in 1980 with a translation of *Tomorrow, Capitalism* by a somewhat obscure French economist, Henri Lepage. The book, which detailed the economic doctrine that would be embraced and embodied by Margaret Thatcher and Ronald Reagan, ignited a ferocious debate in Sweden. The success of *Tomorrow, Capitalism* was due in no small part to the marketing strategy Timbro employed. It was released in paperback and sold for a paltry 20 SEK – a bargain even in 1980. The price and format gave financially strapped students an alternative to Chairman Mao's *Little Red Book*.

Between 1982 and 1988, Timbro published more than 150 books – many of them classics by thinkers such as Montesquieu, Weber and Berlin. Timbro continues to view the translation and dissemination of classic books as part of its core mission. More recently, Timbro has published the works of Adam Smith, Thomas Paine and Milton Friedman.

It should also be mentioned that during these early years, Timbro launched a newswire service that provided straightforward news on business and finance, primarily for rural media outlets that lacked the resources and personnel to cover such topics. The wire service produced around 7,000 articles per year. At the time, many papers saw business news as unessential, though many believe that Timbro helped to change this view. Timbro sold the wire service in 1993.

In the late 1970s and early 1980s, the unions were putting severe pressure on the social democrats to pass a law that would, essentially, force private Swedish firms to fork over ownership stakes to their unionized employees. The money would be placed into funds administered by the unions. The chief architect of the idea was Rudolf Meidner, a German-born socialist economist who viewed these funds as a method by which workers could incrementally assume control of the companies for which they worked.

These 'wage-earner funds' consequently galvanized and animated the Swedish Employers Association, Timbro and other interest groups. Under the astute leadership of the Swedish Employers Association's president, Curt Nicolin, a massive effort was unleashed to defeat the proposal. The campaign involved publishing books and newspaper articles, as well as organizing meetings and seminars around the country – all in an effort to raise awareness for a proposal that could have spelled the end of property rights as Swedes had come to understand them.

Their combined efforts bore fruit, and business owners from every corner of the country began to mobilize. This massive outpouring of discontent – culminating with 100,000 people protesting in front of parliament on the day of its opening, 4 October 1983 – gave the social democrats a colossal case of the jitters. However, Olof Palme's government grudgingly passed a watered-down version of the law on 21 December 1983. When Prime Minister Carl Bildt of the Moderate Party assumed power in 1991, the law was repealed irrevocably.

Compared to the 'soft tyranny', (as Alexis de Tocqueville so eloquently dubbed it) confronting Sweden in the early 1980s, the situation facing the Soviet Union's satellite countries along the Baltic rim was far grimmer. Timbro leveraged its network in direct support of dissidents, such as the future prime minister of Estonia, Mart Laar, and to bolster local activities. On March 19, 1990, the 'Monday Movement' appeared for the first time in a square in central Stockholm. For 79 straight Mondays, people gathered in this square to listen to speeches and to show their support for the oppressed peoples of the Baltic republics. In addition to the four main organizers of the Monday Movement – Gunnar Hökmark, Håkan Holmberg, Peeter Luskep and Andres Küng – Timbro's president at the time, Mats Johansson, was a driving force in this movement.

With the implosion of the Soviet Union – due largely to the combined efforts of Prime Minister Thatcher, President Reagan and Pope John Paul II – Timbro shifted its focus. Indeed, Timbro has consistently and deftly redeployed its efforts at regular intervals, always anticipating the next attack on people's core freedoms. While there are always new debates that arise which, at first blush, appear new, they more often than not boil down to the question of liberty. A think tank cannot survive, much less remain relevant, if its ear is not placed firmly on the ground.

Throughout the 1990s and into the 2000s, Timbro remained ahead of the curve on three main issues: free trade, public services and globalization. Of course, Timbro maintained a presence in other areas as well. Marie Söderqvist Tralau and Susanna Popova launched salvo after salvo into the debate on gender equality and state-sponsored feminism. Intellectuals such as Carl Rudbeck wrote extensively on cultural issues, religion and media policy. Economist Dick Kling called for the government to sell the state-owned companies and to give the proceeds to the people. And still others – too numerous to name – agitated against the social democratic hegemony, nanny statism, wealth destruction, monopolies, high taxes, media bias, restrictions on mobility, bad environmentalism and other threats to liberty. Timbro has also been blessed by an active board of directors, with luminaries from Swedish politics and business such as Janerik Larsson, Agneta Dreber, Lars Otterbeck, Marie Söderqvist Tralau and Anders Kempe.

Between 1999 and 2004, political economist Mauricio Rojas headed the Center for Welfare Reform at Timbro, which sought to shape an entrepreneurial narrative about the future provision of public services. Rojas produced an immense volume of reports and organized more than 60 seminars during this five-year period. In 2008, the equally energetic Thomas Idergard recognized that the debate on public services was about to explode again, and joined Timbro in 2009 to build on the work of Rojas. Idergard's assessment was indeed correct, and we have seen public services rise to the top of the agenda in the run-up to Sweden's general elections in the autumn of 2010.

The period in and around the new millennium was also heavily punctuated by debates on free trade and, of course, globalization. Under the leadership of Timbro president P. J. Anders Linder and his successsor Mattias Bengtsson, chief economist Fredrik Erixon and historian Johan Norberg stepped into the breach. While Erixon lectured and published on Doha trade negotiation round of the World Trade Organization, foreign aid and tariffs, Norberg mounted a fierce defense of globalization. The prolific Norberg, who had previously published well-received retrospectives on classical liberalism, penned in 2001 the bestselling book, *In Defense of Global Capitalism*. This was the first book to systematically rebut the claims made by the growing anti-globalization movement. Following an English edition by the Cato Institute, the book has been translated into more than twenty languages worldwide. The book catapulted Norberg into a new stratosphere of international notoriety.

However, Norberg and Erixon were just getting started. It is what they did next which perfectly illustrates Timbro's core values and aspirations. Rather than ensconce themselves indefinitely at Timbro, each has ventured out into the wider world. Erixon founded the influential, Brussels-based think tank the European Center for International Political Economy, and Norberg has gone on to make and star in several documentaries, publish numerous books and join the renowned Cato Institute as a senior fellow. It's safe to say that Erixon and Norberg have become stars in their own right.

More than any single book or project that I have been involved in since joining Timbro, my greatest joy has been witnessing the flow of talent that passes through Timbro year after year. The organization's current president, Maria Rankka, has worked hard to preserve and foster an attitude and mindset that has characterized Timbro since the days of Carl-Johan Westholm and Sture Eskilsson. In addition to serving as a platform for respected thinkers and doers, Timbro is also a talent factory and a laboratory where young people can hone their skills and challenge their ideas before moving on to bigger and better things. To this end, in 2003 Timbro created the Sture Academy, a year-long program which gives promising young men and women the intellectual knowledge and networks that open doors to new and exciting opportunities.

Every day I open the newspaper and read brilliant articles by men and women who once wandered these halls. I see them on television and listen to them on the radio. On my bookshelf I see Timbro books written by today's ministers, business leaders and top academics. Indeed, Timbro has touched the lives of many people of influence. Yet, Timbro is and never should be anyone's home for too long. Rather fittingly, this essay is the final piece I will publish as an employee of Timbro. Practicing what we preach, both president Maria Rankka and I are moving on after roughly five years at Timbro. It is time for new perspectives and a fresh outlook on the challenges that lay ahead. This, I believe, has been central to the organization's longevity and success. Timbro flows effortlessly forward, ferrying people and ideas to various ports, but never veering from the course leading to its final destination.

08

CHAPTER

20 Years of Fighting for Freedom in Slovakia

Ján Oravec
F. A. Hayek Foundation
(Slovakia)

INTRODUCTION

1989–2009. The dash between these two dates represents twenty years of a unique period: not only in the history of my region, but also in my country. It also represents a unique period in my personal and professional life. Transformational processes in former communist countries are thoroughly analyzed in plenty of studies with all their different aspects, nuances and peculiarities. The aim of this text is not to write another piece of that kind. Its goal, rather, is to tell a personal story. The story of someone who was privileged enough to have the opportunity to live through this exceptional period. And even more privileged to be active in all major sectors of society, including the think tank, government and private sectors, over the past two decades. In addition to this wide variety of professional experiences, I was lucky enough to have a small say in and a direct or indirect influence on several crucial transformation decisions in Slovakia, including privatization, tax reform and pension reform. The following is a story of the building of a free market think tank, its role in the transformation process in Slovakia, and its impact on the historical decisions of our time.

THE BEGINNING

After graduating from Commenius University in Bratislava in 1987, I started working as a young research assistant at the Institute of Economics of the Slovak Academy of Sciences. It was an exceptional and exciting time, when everybody wanted to contribute to necessary changes. I was no exception. Since free market thinking was extremely scarce at that time, I was looking for the most efficient way to accelerate our transformation towards the free market and a free society. The first step was to form an association of like-minded individuals, so in the early 1990s, we established the Libertarian Club. After several months, we still felt like we needed to take further steps to increase our impact. This prompted us to invite other market-oriented people together to establish an economic think tank called the F. A. Hayek Foundation in 1992. Its main mission was to establish a tradition of free market thinking and free market policies that were virtually absent in Slovakia before November 1989. None of us at that time had a clue that over the course of many years, the F. A. Hayek Foundation would become one of the most influential think tanks in Slovakia and would gain a high international reputation, as evidenced in cooperation with many distinguished institutions around the world.

In the meantime, history was taking giant steps almost every day. Due to differences in its industrial structures[1] Slovakia was disproportionately hit by the first reform measures[2]. Growing disagreements between Slovaks and Czechs over structural reforms, as well as monetary and fiscal policy, resulted in a well-known 'velvet divorce' within the Czechoslovak federa-

---

1   Dominated by heavy industry.
2   For example, while unemployment rates in the beginning of the 1990s were steadily
        below 2 per cent in the Czech Republic, they exceeded 10 per cent in Slovakia.

tion whereby the two split into two internationally recognised entities on 1 January 1993.

Back in 1993, there were many uncertainties associated with Slovakia due to its serious macroeconomic imbalances and microeconomic structural weaknesses. Many analysts predicted a drastic devaluation of the Slovak currency, and an early overall collapse of the Slovak economy. These extremely negative expectations did not materialize. Moreover, Slovakia successfully survived a risky period during the first years of its independent existence. It later learned from its painful lessons during the 1993–98 period of irresponsible macroeconomic policies and the lack of microeconomic adjustments, and surprized the world with courageous reforms during 2002–06. These reforms can be considered the most consistent and radical free market programs implemented by any developed country in the first decade of the 21st century.

Of course, there are many factors behind this development. There is no doubt that the small circle of people associated with the F. A. Hayek Foundation played a crucial role in the process. They had a significant impact in the public-policy-making process in Slovakia during its transition period, especially during its second half (after 1995). The foundation proved to be a very efficient vehicle, introducing innovative ideas into debates within the public-policy-making process in Slovakia. What was equally important, however, was its ability and capability to act also as the 'do tank' to make sure that these ideas were also implemented. Privatization, tax reform and pension reform illustrate the foundation's success in implementing these ideas.

PRIVATIZATION

Private property is not only a prerequisite of prosperity and higher standards of living for all; it is also the best guarantee of liberty, and a starting point for exercising other rights. In addition, the more extensive the privatization process, the fewer distortions can be expected from government actions. The economy too is more efficient. That is why we were campaigning from the very beginning for robust and fast privatization in Slovakia. We organized the very first privatization conference in Slovakia in early 1990.

Unlike in Poland, Hungary, or Yugoslavia, in 1989 almost 98 per cent of the economy (at that time Czechoslovakian) was state-owned. The first three years of transformation, between 1989 and 1992, which were also the last three years of the existence of Czechoslovakia, were utilized to establish the first foundations of the private sector and strengthen them further via three major privatization methods of that time: restitutions, public auctions, and voucher privatization.

The new government of the independent Slovakia led by Prime Minister Vladimír Meciar compiled a list of so-called 'strategic companies' excluded from privatization, including banks and energy-sector companies. However, the process of privatization was not stopped completely. On the contrary, most of those companies that weren't on the list of 'strategic companies' were subject to the privatization process.

The privatization process, particularly between 1996 and 1998, was not transparent, and foreign investors and most of the potential domestic buyers were deliberately excluded. Political allies, family members and friends were by and large openly preferred. This policy had serious consequences for Slovakia: it was excluded from all integration efforts and ended up in international isolation.

After the 1998 elections, a new reform-oriented government came into power in Slovakia, thus reflecting the frustrations that voters had with the bad policies of the previous government, which had brought the Slovak economy into a serious financial crisis. The new government promised to introduce changes into almost all policy areas, including privatization. One of its first measures was to cancel the list of companies that were excluded from privatization and to accelerate the process .

Transparent privatization, via open and international tenders, was used. This resulted in a complete privatization of the Slovak banking sector, which today is owned almost exclusively by foreign investors. Similar results were achieved in the energy sector.

In order to accelerate elaboration, implementation, and adoption of much-needed changes by executive power, some members of the Hayek Foundation decided to accept executive positions within the ministries, beginning in 1999–2002 and then later in a period after 2002.

In early 1999 I accepted an offer to become a strategy chief at the Ministry of Economy. Originally, I expected to complete my mission there within a period of three months, however, my expectations differed significantly from reality and I finally stayed there for more than three and a half years. I was responsible for laying down the foundations for corporate sector reforms, the preparation of the restructuring of energy sector companies and their subsequent privatizations, as well as improvements in the business environment. Thanks to my decision to take this position, the Hayek Foundation was able to have a direct influence on crucial decisions in these reforms and was able to accelerate and contribute to the biggest privatization in Slovakia's history: the Slovak Gas Industry, a company transporting Russian gas from Russia to Western Europe. All in all, 49 per cent of the shares of the electricity and gas production and distribution companies were privatized, and managerial control was handed over to foreign investors. Maneuvering space for politicians to exercise their control over the economy was significantly reduced. While in the beginning of the 1990s 98 per cent of the economy was owned by the state, today 95 per cent of GDP is generated by the private sector.

The transformation from a completely state-owned economy to a completely privately-owned economy[3] is one of the most impressive achievements of Slovakia's modern history, and I am glad that I was able to contribute to it.

TAX REFORM

Favorable conditions for any fundamental reform, including tax reform, rarely exist. This was also true in the case of Slovakia in the mid-1990s. The most important challenge of that period was to contribute to changes that would transform unfavorable conditions for tax reform into favorable ones.

In the mid-1990s, as a transition country, Slovakia was still struggling to get its fundamentals right, and was facing difficult challenges in the areas of price deregulation, liberalization, and privatization. Taxation was not one of the top priorities of that time. In 1993, Slovakia replaced its old tax system inherited from Communism, and adopted the standard system of a typical European country. This included the introduction of value added tax, excise duties and real estate taxes, as well as corporate and personal income taxes. Almost all the experts and government officials saw no reason for the introduction of any significant changes into the tax system that had been adopted only several years earlier. For a long time, the minister of finance refused to speak about the necessity of reform in the area of taxation. The only thing the government officials were ready to discuss was a 'fine tuning,' in other words, minor changes and adjustments.

Almost nobody seemed to understand that Slovakia was not able to afford to have a weak and inefficient economy which included a high tax burden that was financing an extensive welfare state, equal to that of an advanced country in Western Europe.

Under these circumstances, the most important challenge was to in-

---

3   With a few remaining exceptions such as the railways, forests, etc.

crease public awareness of these issues, and to persuade both the general public and experts that Slovakia needed a fundamental reform of its tax system. In order to increase public awareness of the growing tax burden and the need for reforms, in 1996 the Hayek Foundation decided to establish a specialized association called the Slovak Taxpayers Association, which focused exclusively on taxation. The association started to conduct polls on tax-related issues, initiate comparative studies of the tax systems in the Slovak Republic and other countries (OECD, European Union), organize debates on taxes and public expenditures, and launch an annual study called 'Analysis of Public Expenditures and Tax and Contribution Burden in the Slovak Republic'.

However, by far the most successful project of the association was its Tax Freedom Day project, which has attracted enormous media attention. It has demonstrated that official government figures have not reflected a true tax burden (a fact that was finally admitted by the government itself), informed citizens about a complex public policy issue in a simple way, successfully influenced a tax reform debate in favor of significant tax cuts, and opened discussions about the necessity of cutting public expenditure. These activities were preparing a fertile soil for more courageous ideas on how to change the tax system, including a flat tax idea.

Being a strategy chief at the Ministry of Economy, in 1999, I also brought this fight into the internal structures of the government. One of the documents developed by my team and submitted to government for approval included the introduction of a flat tax of 20 per cent. In 1999–2000, this proposal was potentially one of the most powerful measures to make the business environment more favorable for both domestic and foreign businesses. Since, at that time, the minister of finance, Mrs Schmognerova, was a representative of the left-wing party, our proposal failed. However, the first seeds were planted, and this venture brought its fruits several years later when the comprehensive 19 per cent flat tax proposal was implemented as of 1 January 2004. In my view this story proves that my life-long strategy of deliberately 'setting a high bar' or 'going beyond what is possible in a given time' works, and sooner or later pays off.

PENSION REFORM

In 1994, the World Bank published its famous report[4] that presented the first comprehensive and global examination of security in old age. This

---

4   (1994) *Averting the Old Age Crisis*, the World Bank, Washington DC.

report suggested, for the first time, three systems that were becoming well-known as the 'three pillar' architecture of the reformed pension system: a publicly and privately managed mandatory system as well as a voluntary savings system.

I read this report, and from the beginning, I had difficulties accepting this proposal. As a 'freedom fighter', it was impossible for me to accept the idea that the transition from state paternalism to individual responsibility would end up in a semi-paternalistic system, although I understood that complete transition still had a very long way to go. At that time, I was giving even more lectures and public speeches about the urgency of the pension crisis and the lack of awareness of these problems among the public, politicians, policy-makers and major media, as well as the necessity of taking immediate action to reverse an unfavorable trend.

Later, after becoming a strategy chief at the Ministry of Economy, I was able to influence two crucial decisions that were important for pension reform. First, I helped to block the wrong pension reform proposals of the labor ministry by the end of the 1998–2002 period. Secondly, I supported proposals to allocate the majority of the privatization revenues to financing future pension reform[5].

During this time, the Hayek Foundation adopted a strategic decision that brought us further towards increased involvement in the pension reform 'crusade'. It allowed us to prepare our own ambitious proposal for pension reform and to identify potential allies abroad that would help us to fight efficiently for the reform.

It was during the period 2000–01 that I first contacted José Piñera, an architect of the first successful privatization of the pension system in Chile. To cut a long story short, we invited Piñera to Slovakia and his visit became an important factor in helping pension reform receive the 'green light'.

We deliberately opted for our think tank to become a 'do tank' again. We decided to send our expert team to help the minister responsible for pension reform to implement the reforms from our campaigns. The F. A. Hayek Foundation's expert team became an important part of the pension reform team at the Ministry of Labor and Social Affairs during 2002–03. The introduction of private pension savings accounts was a huge success. One figure says it all: the total number of people switching to personal retirement accounts was more than 1.5 million, about 70 per cent of all eligible people in Slovakia.

---

5   SKK 65 billion of the SKK 130 billion from selling a 49 per cent stake in the Slovak Gas Industry was deposited at the central bank by the government, with an aim of financing an early stage of pension reform.

CONCLUDING REMARKS

I know from my practical experience that in order to succeed in the implementation of fundamental changes there need to be several factors in place: (i) an open crisis (in Slovakia we had it after the 1993–98 period of irresponsible macroeconomic policies and a lack of microeconomic adjustments); (ii) an appropriate inspiration and reform model (we looked to José Piñera and his reform efforts in Chile); (iii) a free market think tank and 'do tank' (we had the F. A. Hayek Foundation); and (iv) politicians ready and willing to implement the necessary reform steps (and we had open-minded labor and finance ministers).

Once again, all of these factors needed to be in place in order to make the radical reforms in Slovakia possible. I am sure the same can be done in every single country in the world. Hopefully, after reading this story, someone will become inspired and will make the first small steps on the same reform path in their country as we did many years ago in Slovakia. The most inspiring part of the experience of this country, which was once desperately lagging behind other nations, is that it was able to implement an ambitious reform plan that put it far ahead. If Slovakia can do it, other countries can do it too.

Ideas Have Consequences

Greg Fleming
Maxim Institute
(New Zealand)

CHAPTER

GREEN-CIRCLE WALLPAPER AND SHAG-PILE CARPET

Our office is a 1970s home, on a beautiful piece of land that juts out into one of Auckland's many harbors. It has been turned into office space, but the bathroom walls are still covered in retro wallpaper and the hallway is lined with shag-pile carpet. These quirky features are a daily reminder that fads have a limited lifespan. Both the fads of fashion and the fads of ideas can take a country by storm for a time, only to be found ugly, or worse in the case of ideas, destructive, at some point down the track. New Zealand is a remarkable little country, where fads often gain a foothold. Due to our size, ideas spread quickly, which is both a strength and a challenge.

THE LAND OF THE LONG WHITE CLOUD

If you haven't been to New Zealand you are missing out on one of the most spectacular little places on earth. We have an incredible landscape and a rich heritage, both from our indigenous Maori population and from our British roots. We were the last of the Western democracies to be founded. Captain Cook came to New Zealand and mapped the country in 1769 but it wasn't until 1840 that the grounds of New Zealand's government and nationhood were laid, when the Treaty of Waitangi was signed between Maori chiefs and the British Crown. Despite being a young nation, we have been at the forefront of a lot of development during the past two centuries, being the first country to introduce universal suffrage, the first to implement a modern welfare state and the first to adopt free trade – we were even the first to declare war in 1939. Internationally we are known as people of conviction. Many of the defining parts of our history have included protests. The two most famous such moments were the major protests over apartheid that took place when the South African rugby team toured New Zealand in 1981, and protests over nuclear testing in the Pacific.

Yet over the past decades, some of the foundations of our country have weakened, with post-modernity pushing us away from our earlier convictions towards ambiguity. New Zealand is instinctively quite a socialist nation. Because of that, when a banking crisis hits, the overwhelming reaction is to dismiss the working of markets. Similarly, there is a constant push to close income gaps for the sake of equality – to tax heavily and redistribute resources. With this dominant ideology shaping our country's decisions, there is a strong need for people to speak for freedom, justice and compassion.

Whilst the potential in New Zealand is great, we face some serious social problems. Family violence and child abuse in New Zealand are alarming. In 2008 alone, 'police were called to 86,000 domestic violence incidents' which is a significant number for a population of only 4.1 million people. Government has burgeoned, tax rates have climbed and welfare dependency has become the norm for various sections of our community. We have seen legislation passed quickly and poorly, in line with the latest trends, leading to a past prime minister, Sir Geoffrey Palmer, describing us as 'the fastest lawmakers in the west.' Maxim Institute came from the recognition that it was time to engage in this situation.

OUR STORY

In the early days of our marriage, my wife Kirsty and I did what many Kiwis do and headed overseas for the bright lights, high pay and opportunities of another place – in our case, London. We spent a few heady years there, living the good life. I worked contract jobs as an accountant, landed some great opportunities, got paid in pounds and flew to continental Europe for weekend ski-trips. Then we decided it was time to start a family.

It's amazing how the thought of a new generation motivates you to think about what really matters. We decided to come back to little New Zealand and to contribute to the country that we still loved. We wanted our kids to grow up here and we wanted to see our country do well. So I took a job as general manager of Parenting with Confidence (now Parents Inc), an organization that works with families, helping parents build skills to do their job well. Our first child, Harry, was born and we got into the rhythm of life in New Zealand.

But as my work at Parenting with Confidence grew, I started to see some real holes in the public life of New Zealand. While I valued the grass-roots work we were doing with families, we were often subject to the ebbs and flows of what was taking place in parliament or in the broader culture. Policy began to attract me, and some ideas were stirring. At this point, a significant meeting was called.

John Graham is an elder statesman of New Zealand, a man who commands enormous respect and has played a significant leadership role in our country. John is a former captain of the national All Blacks rugby team, and was principal of one of the most successful schools in the country for 21 years. When John speaks, people listen. So when he called a group of people who shared a common concern about New Zealand to come to his office at Auckland University where he was chancellor at the time – we obeyed. In that meeting, John challenged me and said, 'What are you doing to shape the future of New Zealand, Greg?' That question was a burning one that I could not ignore. In that meeting was another man named Bruce Logan, an experienced educationalist who had become increasingly vocal in the public sphere. Together, Bruce and I founded Maxim Institute on 12 November 2001. For four years we established the work together and in 2005, Bruce retired, leaving me as the CEO.

Our goal, right from the start, was to become an influential contributor to New Zealand's public policy and broader cultural debate. With a small team we started conducting research and began to write articles for newspapers. Momentum grew, the team expanded rapidly and we became a regular feature in the country's political and social commentary. It was an intense few years of fundraising, writing and speaking. Education was our mainstay issue, but we also broadened into policies affecting the shape of the family. We fought for more freedom for schools to choose their curriculum, for parental choice in education, for civil society, for limits on government.

Our biggest win during those early years was probably in regards to the issue of 'hate speech'. We were prepared for that battle and we fought it beautifully. We looked at the cultural climate, where civil freedoms were increasingly being curbed and made a calculated prediction that 'hate speech' would soon emerge in Parliament. We researched the subject and developed clear and solid arguments. Our policy manager at the time even did her Master's thesis on the subject. Sure enough a bill was introduced to parliament, pushing for 'hate speech' to be made illegal. We blew the issue entirely out of the water. It has not been raised since.

Despite this encouraging win, there have been other times when our work has seemed to fall on deaf ears. One of the major parts of our public communication during our early years was a journal called *Evidence*. We would publish it quarterly, with substantial articles that argued reasonably and clearly, backed up by research. Sometimes we would find that our work really challenged people, but often it seemed we were preaching to the choir. We would win our arguments, but people's foundational beliefs remained intact. They simply didn't care about what we were saying.

One of the most frustrating times I have had was a day spent in Wellington with our legal star Alex Penk, meeting members of parliament and speaking to them about legislation being introduced which would limit freedom of speech around elections. We spent significant time with them. Our arguments against the bill were solid. We were articulate and we even looked good in our swanky suits! But no impact even registered. This was a turning point in my mindset about the work we were doing. I began to realize that everybody, even people who defend the creed of pragmatism, are deeply shaped and governed by their assumptions. And for the politicians that we spoke to, those assumptions were already set in stone.

Over the past eight years, I have moved away from believing that you can win the public debates with good evidence alone. People's world views substantially shape their very reading of the data and their hearing of the arguments. Sometimes it's intellectual laziness, sometimes it's their die-hard framework, but either way it leads to them shutting out competing ideas.

COMPASSION

We got to a point as an organization where we were snookered. We had been quite effectively boxed as right-wing, and we were seldom speaking to people outside our natural, self-selected audience. Then, in 2006, we went to a conference in Washington DC and began to open our eyes to a new way of engaging with the challenges facing New Zealand. We met conservatives from think tanks around the world who were speaking about social justice in a way that was full, rich and inspiring. In a country like New Zealand, where the default setting is socialism, there is a need to speak in a language that is sufficiently broad and diverse to catch people's attention. Social justice, properly applied, is an accurate description of our work. We have found that from such a framework, we can speak with confidence and have real impact.

New Zealanders are, after all, a very compassionate people. Our national icon is a small, half-blind, timid, flightless bird totally incapable of defending itself. But our compassionate nature is what – in the absence of compelling alternatives in New Zealand – makes government the default provider for any social problem.

In a time in my country when impersonal government is being seen (increasingly across the political spectrum) as the answer to all of life's challenges, it's vital that the few of us who hold the hope for a truly compassionate way are found in the middle of the debate and not on the periphery. The framework of social justice has allowed us to participate in (and sometimes even lead) debates that conservatives are normally excluded from, on subjects such as educational under-achievement, welfare and criminal justice. We have been able to speak of opportunity instead of equal outcomes; community instead of government; redemption instead of fear. As we articulate the importance of relationships and community, we also try to practise this conviction, focusing on people in the way we work towards our goals.

IDEAS HAVE LEGS

Hanging beside the front door of our office is a quote by Boris Pasternak that says, 'It is not revolutions and upheavals that clear the road to new and better days, but someone's soul inspired and ablaze.' You do not simply win a public argument. Ideas are given life and limbs in people. This has been the greatest lesson of the past eight years of Maxim Institute, and this realization has shaped the work we now do. The ideas that we wrestle with, the policies we produce and the research that we do, must be intentionally seeded and nurtured in people.

My wife and I have five kids. I remember a few years ago, driving to the beach on a Sunday afternoon with the two kids we had at that point. I turned on the radio just as one of my policy opponents opened yet another front on an issue we were hotly debating. I complained to Kirsty that we could not compete with people who were able to work seven days a week, while I only had five. She patted me on the leg and said 'it's fine dear, in the end we'll win because we'll just outbreed them.'

While Kirsty's comment was a little troubling for a number of reasons, in a very strange way she was on to something. It's the relationships that we build, the people that we interact with, that shape the future. The way I interact with my children, the way that I treat my staff and our interns, is as significant as the research that we do. Ideas have consequences because people live out those ideas daily. Increasingly, our work has come to recognise this fact.

In 2005, I received the Sir Peter Blake Emerging Leaders award, and along with it, a grant. For a long time we had dabbled in running an internship and we wanted to expand this part of our work. So we used the grant to travel the world, scoping out internships to get ideas for how to strengthen and build our own program for young leaders.

We have run summer internships every year since 2002, taking on young leaders from a range of professional fields, helping them think through their foundational beliefs and giving them a chance to wrestle with the ideas our culture is throwing at them. For the past two years we have also run internships that last the full academic year, giving these young leaders a chance to go deeper in their thinking and to live together in a residential context while they study and work. We bring experts from around the world to the institute to teach interns. We use a Socratic method of teaching and are are strict about keeping the group size small. We believe we run a truly unique program that helps these young leaders develop into people of good character who confront the challenges life throws at them with wisdom and courage. This work has become one of our main hallmarks.

When I think about the fact that ideas have consequences in the lives of people, I am reminded of a young woman named Rebecca who interned with us about five years ago. Rebecca is an exceptionally bright young woman, who was studying law when she came to Maxim Institute. She had a vague sense of wanting to work for the cause of justice, but didn't know what that would look like. During Rebecca's time with us, she asked many big questions and wrestled seriously with the ideas she had learnt at university. Rebecca began to set clear goals for work and determined to hold on to justice as a vital principle, seeing it as relevant not only in the practice of law but also in a wider societal context. Rebecca went on to intern at the Supreme Court of the United States and now works as a judges' clerk at the High Court of New Zealand. Rebecca has become an integral part of the community that surrounds the institute, catching up with various staff for coffee and coming to our lecture events. As I watch the choices Rebecca is making and the clarity she has about what she wants to contribute, I am deeply encouraged.

OUR FUTURE

In many ways we are still young, trying to work out how to best make our mark. It is too early to know the full impact of what we do, but we are here for the long haul. We are busy changing the shape, the depth, the foundations of New Zealand's debates, by stirring the pot, throwing out questions and challenges, conducting solid research and offering credible alternatives to the anaemic visions that often seem to dominate.

Speaking into the world of ideas and investing in lives is a weighty thing to do, and it is never wasted. Our retro wallpaper and carpet remain as a daily testament to the weakness of fads, reminding us to push farther in our thinking, to challenge the rhetoric we hear and to provide something more than another catchphrase or hollow vision.

The men and women who work and intern at Maxim Institute are the whispers of a quiet renaissance taking place. People who are thinking deeply, who are growing in character and who are gently but firmly standing up and taking leadership; strengthening civil society, and working to help freedom, justice and compassion flourish. We work and wait with hope.

The War of Ideas: Thoughts from South Africa

Leon Louw
Free Market Foundation
of Southern Africa
(South Africa)

The course of events is a Hayekian 'spontaneous order'. Accordingly, its determinants are complex and obscure. A great diversity of people, institutions and interests try to influence the course of events, and invest substantial resources to do so.

Since the net effect of all this effort, ingenuity and wealth determines the fortunes of individuals, organizations, countries, regions, cultures, religions and life on earth itself, it is surprising how little scholarly analysis there has been on how best to influence outcomes. What there is tends to be in political science. Scatterings exist in sociology and psychology.

As one of the referees for this chapter put it, 'some of the so-called "think tanks" are disguises for certain individuals whose goal is not a better future for their country but rather that their photographs appear in the newspapers . . . they certainly show that in fact they could not care less about the principles of freedom (or, for that matter, principles of any sort)'.

For those of us who believe that one of the most decisive determinants of events is economic policy, there is virtually nothing on the subject in economic science. Policy analysts and 'activists' have sessions at conferences on 'strategy' which usually entail reports on what people are doing rather than analysis of what works.

In the first edition of *Waging the War of Ideas*, lifelong strategist and doyen of classical liberalism John Blundell made a unique and pioneering contribution to the subject – essential reading for anyone wanting to make a difference. My contribution to this edition has no pretensions of being scholarship. I have been asked for personal conclusions drawn from practical experience over forty years in the ideological trenches of South Africa's transition from apartheid, and my not insignificant experience in other countries combined with my modest role in the global war of ideas.

A crucial insight from our South African experience is that people fortunate enough to be doing the right thing in the right place at the right time often have decisive impacts. While there can never be certainty about causality, there are compelling reasons to believe that our work before, during and immediately after the transition in South Africa made a substantial contribution for the better. Curiously, convincing though the evidence might be, our role and even our presence are scarcely reflected in literature about this period.

The first decisive role we played was in masterminding the economic policies of one of South Africa's historically black homelands, Ciskei. We were invited into that role as part of a philanthropic contribution by the Anglo-American conglomerate towards 'development' in the region. They offered our services to the homeland government. The long story cut short is that we went to great lengths to secure support from the then banned anti-apartheid movement, and ended up formulating detailed policies that transformed the area into a free market enclave with predictably spectacular benefits. It became the only 'homeland' to increase revenue from internal sources, despite the fact that most forms of revenue were abolished or reduced substantially. There was, for instance, zero income tax on companies, apart from a 15 per cent withholding tax (on profits repatriated from the area).

Personal income tax was reduced to a flat rate of 15 per cent, starting at a threshold so high that 90 per cent of taxpayers ceased paying any tax at all. A multiplicity of other revenue sources, such as land tax, stamp duties, licensing fees and many more, were entirely abolished. The government was persuaded to implement this when we showed that the combined government–private cost of collection was nearly as high as the revenue itself, and more in some cases. Over 800 statutes were repealed and small businesses were exempted from most forms of regulation.

Apart from experiencing spectacular economic growth, Ciskei became South Africa's only homeland with an 'influx' problem ('white' South Africa maintained 'influx controls' to curtail the flow of black South Africans from other impoverished 'homelands' to 'white' South Africa).

Our second decisive, and historically much more significant, role was our influence on South Africa's transition from apartheid. We encouraged the apartheid regime to liberalize and privatize during its twilight years by divesting itself of much of its property and regulatory power before abdicating. Then we encouraged negotiating parties to adopt sufficient 'checks and balances' in the new constitution to protect people out of power sufficiently to ensure that they would submit peacefully to those in power. Finally, we encouraged the new government to replace its former socialist policies with pro-market policies that improved South Africa's score significantly on 'freedom', 'economic freedom' and 'competitiveness' indices. Predictably, the new 'left-wing' government was accused by the left of betraying the revolution and selling out to neoliberals.

It is seldom possible to say whether similar results would have occurred without the work of pro-market activism, but the coincidence in matters of detail between what we were propagating and what happened makes it probable that our role was decisive. The constitution, for instance, has provisions which, as far as we know, were uniquely propagated by us, and which are not found in other constitutions.

Lamentably, our courts have virtually interpreted our constitution out of existence. From this we learn at least two important lessons: first, the critical importance of precise unambiguous terminology and, second, that key actors need to operate within and fully comprehend the significance of a properly informed climate of opinion generated conterminously with the rule of law.

The following section summarizes the general lessons that can be learned from our local and international experience.

AERIAL BOMBARDMENT VERSUS TRENCH WARFARE

Participation in the war of ideas falls into two broad categories: that which is aimed at influencing the climate of opinion ('aerial bombardment'), and that which is intended to influence individual policies ('trench warfare'). The first great pioneer and exemplar of classical liberal aerial bombardment was the Institute of Economic Affairs (IEA) in London. Aerial bombardment entails influencing the climate of opinion within which policymakers work, primarily by way of research and publications. It is premised on the assumption that policies are a reflection of what policymakers regard as politically expedient for the time being, rather than objective evaluation of the evidence. If policies were the outcome of weighing the evidence objectively, there would be much greater international consensus.

Policymakers are, in truth, followers not leaders – they see where the crowd is going, get in front and say, 'Follow me.'

Aerial bombardment is, by its nature, a long-term strategy. It entails influencing society's intellectuals – academia, media, civil society, authors, consultants and advisers.

The climate of opinion was so thoroughly influenced in a classical liberal direction that it was presumed by many, most notably Francis Fukuyama, to have been entrenched permanently as the prevailing paradigm at 'the end of history'. It seems increasingly clear, however, that the price of freedom is indeed eternal vigilance, that there is no end of ideological history, and that power reasserts itself against liberty eternally, changing substantially in form, but never in substance.

There are no irreversible situations or 'laws' of history of the kind popularized as mistaken and dangerous old Marxist recipes. The outcomes in human affairs will always depend on what we are capable of doing every day. Paradoxically, communists and socialists who beat the drum of 'historical determinism' never thought they could leave history to roll in on the wheels of inevitability. Socialists in general work more diligently at influencing history than the supposed defenders of freedom. They take more seriously the dictum 'put your money where your mouth is', which is the main reason why most institutions that work to protect individual rights and property rights are insufficiently funded.

Two of the most ominous manifestations of dirigisme in new clothes are policies being popularized and adopted as the supposedly appropriate responses to both climate change and the 'war on terrorism'. Liberty is presently experiencing a profound setback, which is in sharp contrast with post-cold-war euphoria, when classical liberal activists seriously considered organizing an international 'victory celebration'. Their premature optimism is reminiscent of communist intellectuals proclaiming 'Victory is at hand!' during the 1970s.

I met an ageing classical liberal journalist, Robin Friedland, recently, not having read anything he'd written or seen him for 25 years. He said he was writing a book on what he regarded as the most important issue of modern times: climate change. 'Let me guess,' I said, 'you're skeptical about it.' Indeed he was – as are almost all people who favor human liberty.

Why are classical liberals so predictably skeptical? Is there a distinctive classical liberal climatology? Of course not. Their skepticism, and the equally predictable blind faith in the opposite direction of dirigistes, is not really about climate change, but about the fact that it has become the new weapon with which enemies of liberty subvert private property rights and legitimize a more invasive state through the amplification of collective control, which is the inevitable result of subjecting property to the 'tragedy of the commons'.

The second great issue, the war-on-terrorism erosion of civil liberties, entails a perplexing conundrum: the erosion of civil liberties to 'protect' citizens from the terrorist threat to civil liberties. Enemies in war become unwitting allies against freedom. Benjamin Franklin observed in 1759 that 'Any society that would give up a little liberty to gain a little security will deserve neither and lose both'.

The trench warfare approach tends to characterize activists and institutes in developing countries, leading examples being Hernando de Soto's Institute for Liberty and Democracy in Peru, India's Liberty Institute, and the Free Market Foundation in South Africa. Trench warfare entails such 'practical' and 'pragmatic' activities as submissions to government in response to published policy proposals, meetings, workshops, articles and media appearances – all dealing with a specific public discourse about an imminently proposed reform.

Developing countries have two distinctive features. First, they seldom have mature or even clearly identifiable climates of intellectual opinion. A greater proportion of policy development appears to be a direct ad hoc response to whoever happens, for the time being, to have the dominant influence, which is often highly contextual. Virtually any transient lobby that promotes its interests directly, if not obscenely, can have a policy adopted.

A colleague once observed how intellectually incoherent cabinet meetings are in most developing countries. Under agenda item 1, the minister for transport might recommend deregulating taxis and privatizing airlines. Agreed. Under item 2, the minister of finance recommends nationalizing banks and instituting price controls. Agreed. No one queries the contradiction. In mature democracies, on the other hand, policies tend to be consistent with the established policy paradigm of the ruling party or coalition. In other words, influencing the climate of opinion in developing countries may be easier in the short term, because there are fewer people to influence and they are more easily influenced, but doing so is less enduring and less effective, because the climate of opinion is not a significant determinant of individual policies.

Second, individual policies in developing countries tend to be the consequence of a much less rigorous process of evaluation and debate than in developed countries. Typically, policies are initiated by self-serving vested interests. The process tends to be accompanied by seductive rhetoric. Finding a developed country with a similar policy to emulate is likely to be disproportionately effective. Checks and balances taken for granted in mature democracies, such as the separation of powers, are seldom included. A crude pseudo-intellectual policy document claims that the measure is 'international best practice'. Vested-interest lobbying is usually accompanied by support in cash and kind for whatever cause policymakers nominate – which may, of course, be themselves.

Mancur Olson's theory of collective action is particularly apt in developing countries – namely, that small vested interests seeking highly concentrated benefits at the expense of the widely dispersed general public are more effective than large vested interests seeking dispersed benefits, such as low-income consumers. Trench warfare in these circumstances entails mobilizing countervailing interests, such as competitors, often at the proverbial eleventh hour. Where specialized vested interests are most effective (in developing countries), it 'cuts both ways', against and for classical liberals, who can, for instance, initiate rather than respond to policy development.

Sometimes trench warfare literally 'takes to the trenches', so to speak. In late November 2007, the Law Review Project worked on a high-profile march by residents of a historically black suburb, Alexandra, demanding restitution of land expropriated under apartheid. During the World Summit on Sustainable Development (WSSD, Johannesburg, 2002), we organized a 'freedom to trade' march on the summit by hundreds of South African informal sector traders, Indian farmers and US students. Which is better, aerial bombardment or trench warfare? The answer is that the former is better in the long run. Which is preferable? That depends on context and priorities. When a country, such as contemporary Nepal, is in the process of drawing up a new constitution or considering major policy shifts, intensive trench warfare is effective. When, as in most mature democracies, there is relative political and economic stability, and policies tend to be a reflection of prevailing ideas, aerial bombardment is best. For countries in between, like South Africa, both are appropriate, shifting towards aerial bombardment as policies stabilize.

RELEVANCE

Distinctions between aerial bombardment and trench warfare aside, an appreciation of which strategies and tactics in the war of ideas have been most effective historically is not necessarily instructive in the post-Cold-War world. Circumstances have changed so dramatically that previously effective strategies and tactics against ideologically explicit socialism, communism and fascism are unlikely to be effective henceforth. During the cold war, the war of ideas was clearly a clash of two readily identified titans, capitalism and socialism. The modern assault on liberty has different characteristics.

Liberty per se is no longer under explicit assault by people claiming that there are inherently superior alternatives (other than Islamists). The modern assault is more subtle and multifarious. Enemies of liberty do not define themselves as enemies; they often parade themselves as allies. Nobody of note propagates socialism, communism or fascism explicitly. People scarcely even propagate by name such once fashionable ideological concepts as 'the welfare state', 'social democracy' or 'the mixed economy'. That makes them harder to confront and protects them from being identified as enemies by the media and intellectuals. Protagonists of extreme regulation on a global scale see in climate change and terrorism opportunities for global feudalism. They are generally seen as benign and 'concerned', as wanting no more than to rescue 'the planet' from anthropogenic calamity – never as anti-liberty. They are latter-day Luddites in drag. That climate change must be harmful to man – whether or not it is – is a crucial ingredient, because it legitimizes global control of every aspect of life, from pop concerts to deep-level mining, from sport to packaging, and from room temperature to transport.

Enemies of liberty not only seize upon fashionable catastrophism to legitimize dirigisme, but mangle truth in extraordinarily convoluted, often obscure and seductive ways. They get away with false or creative claims. They caricature anyone, however scientifically justified they may be, who questions the slightest aspect of their dogma as reactionary 'deniers'. Even people like me, who do not debate scientific orthodoxy, and query only policy recommendations, are presumed to be deniers. I have, for instance, been the victim of sustained media slander for supposedly being a climate change denier. Yet none of the elaborate attacks has cited a single source for my alleged denialism.

The war on liberty has all the ingredients of religious fanaticism, including excommunication of supposed heretics, and heresy is, as with all fanaticism, failure to agree with every detail. The difference between the current war of ideas and that which preceded it is that the 1970s equivalent of 'global warming', which was 'the population explosion', had to be positioned within the socialism–capitalism dichotomy. Now it is the other way round. Advocates of liberty have to position themselves within the climate change and war-on-terrorism discourses.

The observation that the new anti-liberty bogeys are 'climate change' (left) and the 'war on terrorism' (right) does not imply that concerns about either are not fully justified, only that they have been hijacked to serve the ends of the enemy in the war of ideas.

Many classical liberals, justifiably distressed by the extent to which real or exaggerated concerns are regarded as excuses for curtailing liberty, debate whether there really is serious climate change or terrorism – they are 'deniers'. Some argue instead that these threats are real but insignificant. Others insist that climate change is catastrophic, but that it is inevitable rather than manmade, or that terrorism is a legitimate response to Western mischief, and that our responsibility is to 'understand them'. Another response is to produce elaborate theses to the effect that global warming is desirable, that it entails net benefits. And then there are those, like the International Policy Network (IPN), who argue compellingly that, regardless of the preceding debates, freedom and free markets are ideal policy responses. Those of us working for liberalization in developing countries are particularly concerned about the implications for the world's poor billions of the world's rich millions using climate change to vindicate 'eco-imperialism'.

While classical liberals remain deeply divided on empirical aspects of climate change and terrorism, enemies of liberty march resolutely towards an ominous world where fantastic pro-freedom gains during recent decades may become a romantic memory for those of us old enough to recall the Cold War and the advent of the 21st century.

Regarding the war on terrorism, classical liberals of a more conservative disposition regard post-9/11 terrorism as a cataclysmic threat, which vindicates everything effective. Those who are more libertarian agonize about the implications for liberty. Their concern is that measures such as intercepting communications and anti-money-laundering rules are an unwarranted erosion of fundamental liberties. They are obviously right to be concerned. Their great challenge is to suggest effective alternatives consistent with classical liberal values.

There are other dimensions to the war of ideas, such as the perennial 'consumer protection' shibboleth. This is an area where classical liberal warriors are in serious need of reinforcements. Old myths are being recycled successfully in new guises in most countries. The world, in which doing everything has become easier, cheaper and safer, is misleadingly called 'the modern complex world', and that imaginary complexity is paraded as justifying intensified 'consumer protection'. What this rhetoric has in common is the assumption that there are 'free lunches' – that consumer benefits can be gained by counterproductive regulation at no direct or indirect cost to consumers – and that regulation affords better protection than free competition.

It may be that the emphasis on 'competition' plays into the hands of the enemy. Von Mises pointed out that in truly free markets people collaborate rather than compete. Entrepreneurial rivals do not so much 'out-compete' as 'out-cooperate' each other. Adam Smith's celebrated observation was that competitors seldom meet without resorting to collaboration. The sport analogy of free markets is unfortunate, because it suggests mistakenly that people interacting with each other in the economy have, as in athletics, a single winner, whereas all people transacting in markets are, with rare exceptions, winners.

In short, in these great war-of-ideas battlefields, classical liberals face completely new challenges. We are still confined to operating within one or both of two broad strategies, intellectual aerial bombardment and tactical trench warfare, but cannot do so by simply recycling what served us well before. There is no longer a crude binary clash of ideas. It was easy and sometimes obvious to decide what to do when capitalism/liberalism fought communism/socialism. But now the arguments against freedom and markets are more obtuse and surreptitious. They tend to be from people who say they are for markets. To be relevant, classical liberalism now has to be advanced less as a fight of good against evil and more in terms of bona fide differences between kindred spirits in mutual pursuit of the good society.

There are many manifestations of this new foggy world of ideas, the most obvious being that the clear paradigm difference between political parties has all but vanished. The position the British Conservative, Labour and

Liberal Democrat parties, the American Democrats and Republicans, or the German CDU and SDP are likely to adopt on a given issue is no longer as predictable as it was before the 1990s. There are no more clear fault lines distinguishing them.

PROJECTS

One of the most effective projects in which the IEA and the Free Market Foundation (FMF) are involved is the production, with Canada's Fraser Institute playing the leading role, of the Economic Freedom of the World index. This, together with The Heritage Foundation–Wall Street Journal Economic Freedom Index (EFI) and Freedom House's Freedom Index, has enabled activists and decision-makers to identify the individual components in the complex policy mix of individual countries that enhance the likelihood of achieving policy objectives. Having noted the power of these indices to influence policymakers, we decided that the current world context needs something less overtly ideological which correlates a wide range of specific policy objectives (as opposed to such generic objectives as economic growth) more directly with individual policies (as opposed to baskets of policies). Accordingly, we took a pioneering step towards a fundamentally new approach, which we published as *Habits of Highly Effective Countries: Lessons for South Africa* (Habits), in the hope that in due course versions will be produced for other countries.

Habits builds on the positive experience of economic freedom indices but is fundamentally different in important respects. First, it is not informed by any philosophical concepts such as 'economic freedom', 'competitiveness' (World Economic Forum), 'freedom' (Freedom House), and so on. It is essentially an exercise in statistics. It asks what we call 'a policymakers' question', which is: 'Which policies in the world's experience coincide with success and failure at achieving individual policy objectives?'

Our thinking is that in a world in which there are no longer distinctive policy paradigms it will become increasingly important for classical liberals to fight the war of ideas in ways that appear overtly to be 'neutral'. This means that we will identify and publicize that which works in practice more than that which is morally or philosophically consistent with liberty. It is unfortunate for us to have to make this shift. We are more comfortable with and experienced at the defense of the principles of liberty. It is extremely hard work to identify and calculate empirical links between policy variables and outcomes. They are subject to sophisticated and complex debate and critique. Most importantly, it is very difficult to 'translate' complex statistical variables and correlations into language and forms that are readily understood by lay people. This, however, is what we regard as our challenge for the coming decades.

In Habits, now also available as a DVD video, we identify the policy characteristics of 'winners' and 'losers' with reference to all the major policy objectives of government. Which policies, for instance, coincide with higher or lower rates of crime, literacy, housing, health, sanitation, GDP or capital formation? By converting our message from being overtly ideological to being empirical, we believe that we will enhance our relevance as we move into the new circumstances of the 21st century.

CONCLUSION

The war of ideas must continue to be fought by aerial bombardment and trench warfare but, like all modern warfare, has to deploy new strategies and tactics. Research and publications, for instance, should embrace modern technology (concise and free to download). We have to confront new threats to liberty which are less obvious or readily classifiable than communism, socialism or fascism. We still need the right people doing the right thing at the right time in the right place, doing their best to understand what determines the course of events in the great spontaneous Hayekian order of ideas.

THINK TANK LESSONS

11

What Is a Think Tank?

John C. Goodman
National Center for Policy Analysis
(United States)

What is a think tank? What do think tanks do? Why are they important? These questions are more pertinent than ever in today's public policy environment.

THINK TANKS AS IDEA FACTORIES

A think tank is an organization that sponsors research on specific problems, encourages the discovery of solutions to those problems, and facilitates interaction among scientists and intellectuals in pursuit of these goals. A public policy think tank explicitly focuses on government policies, usually for the purpose of improving those policies or creating viable alternatives.

By their very nature, public policy think tanks are involved with the academic and scholarly world. In fact, the most important sources of political change are not politicians, political parties or financial contributions. Rather, they are ideas generated on college campuses, in think tanks and in other research organizations.

IDEAS THAT CAUSE CHANGE

Almost all important political change starts with an idea, which inevitably originates with people who spend a great deal of their lives thinking. Indeed, it's hard to point to any major public policy in the modern era that did not originate in the academic world. Here are some examples:

- When Chile became the first country to privatize its social security system, the architects were US-trained economists who looked to Nobel laureate Milton Friedman and his colleagues at the University of Chicago for guidance. Since then, more than 30 countries have followed Chile's lead.

- When Margaret Thatcher set out to privatize the British economy, she relied on the Adam Smith Institute and the Institute of Economic Affairs for key ideas that were later promoted in the United States by the Reason Foundation and others.[6]

- The idea of the flat tax, which has been adopted in Russia, in many Eastern European countries and elsewhere around

---

6   Pirie M. (1985), *Dismantling the State*, Dallas, Texas: National Center for Policy Analysis.

the world, was originally proposed by Milton Friedman and subsequently promoted by the Hoover Institution.[7, 8]

- Ronald Reagan's supply side economics came from Nobel laureate Robert Mundell, and was popularized by economist Art Laffer and *The Wall Street Journal* columnist Jude Wanninski.[9]

- Health savings accounts and Roth IRAs (Individual Retirement Accounts) are two of the numerous ideas generated by the National Center for Policy Analysis (NCPA).

Before the collapse of communism, underground copies of Milton Friedman's book *Free to Choose* were smuggled into Eastern Europe, where they introduced a generation of students and political dissidents to classical liberal economic ideas. This and other Western publications played a decisive role in bringing about the collapse of communism and later served as a foundation for countries' post-communist economic policies.

ORIGIN OF THE IDEA OF A THINK TANK

Ideas come from think tanks. But where did the idea of a think tank come from? It may well have come from Thomas Clarkson, an Englishman who co-founded the Society for the Abolition of the Slave Trade in 1787. By meticulously describing the condition of the slave trade, supplying diagrams of slave ships and combining factual inquiry with moral argument, Clarkson engaged in a war of ideas.[10]

Think tanks figured prominently in the 20th century. The Manhattan Project was a very focused think tank of sorts. The RAND Corporation, the Brookings Institution and the Urban Institute are other organizations that left their mark. Of special interest are organizations that sprang up in the latter part of the 20th century, often for the explicit purpose of defeating

---

7   Friedman M. (1962), *Capitalism and Freedom*, Chicago: University of Chicago Press.

8   Hall R. and Rabushka A. (1995), *Flat Tax*, Stanford, CA: Hoover Institution Press, second edition.

9   Wanninski J. (1978), *The Way the World Works*, New York: Basic Books.

10   Reed L. (2005), *A Student's Essay That Changed the World*, (Mackinac Center for Public Policy

collectivism, much as Clarkson sought to end slavery. Among these were the Hoover Institution, The Heritage Foundation, the American Enterprise Institute and the Cato Institute.

No single person was more important in encouraging the spread of think thanks than Sir Antony Fisher. A Royal Air Force pilot in World War II who went on to become successful in business, Fisher sought advice from Nobel laureate Friedrich Hayek on how to stop the spread of collectivism and encourage a resurgence of 19th- century classical liberal ideas. Don't go into politics, Hayek advised. Focus instead on the world of ideas.[11]

Fisher started the Institute of Economic Affairs in London, which later became Margaret Thatcher's think tank. Following that success, he helped start the Fraser Institute in Canada, the Institute for Liberty and Democracy in Peru, and the Manhattan Institute as well as the National Center for Policy Analysis in the United States. His Atlas Economic Research Foundation supplied modest seed money for these efforts and convened an annual think tank conference. By the time he died, Fisher had helped start more than three dozen think tanks around the world.

HOW IDEAS CAUSE CHANGE

Ideas tend to filter through a hierarchy. They start in the realm of intellectuals. The audience expands through conferences, speeches, briefings and reports written for lay readers. The ideas begin to appear in newspaper editorials. Special interests may find an idea to their liking and help it along. Gradually, more and more people become aware of it. Politicians are often the last to climb on board. Still, it's a process that has been repeated again and again.

But ideas take time to cause change. For example:

- It took twenty years from the time Clarkson started his think tank until Britain passed the first anti-slavery law and 26 more years after that until slavery was finally abolished throughout the realm.

- It took more than 30 years after Milton Friedman first proposed the idea of school vouchers and the idea of a flat tax for them to emerge as part of the national debate.

---

11   Frost G. (2002) , *Antony Fisher: Champion of Liberty*, London: Profile Books

- More than twenty years elapsed before George W. Bush campaigned on Social Security reform - an idea that the Cato Institute, the NCPA and other think tanks originally proposed.

- More than 15 years elapsed between the time the NCPA first proposed health savings accounts and the time they became available to most people.

- Even such popular ideas as the Roth IRA and repealing the Social Security earning penalty took a decade.

Bottom line: people who want important public policy changes need to be willing to make long-term investments.

HOW THINK TANKS FUNCTION

In general, think tanks that were formed before the emergence of the Internet tend to follow the 'one roof' model. The idea was to bring a diverse group of scholars together in one place, so they could interact face-to-face. One reason for this was communication. Forty or fifty years ago, the cost of communication from campus to campus was quite high, relative to what we experience today.

For think tanks formed in the classical liberal tradition, there was also another reason. When I was a graduate student at Columbia University in the early 1970s, the Reason Foundation attempted to compile a list of all the liberal arts faculties in the entire country who believed in free markets and personal liberty. The actual criteria were quite loose, including basically everyone who was not a socialist or a Hubert Humphrey liberal. The list was also very short. As I recall, there were only 15 or twenty names.

In those days, if you were a classical liberal teaching at a university, you were probably the only one on your campus. So places like the Hoover Institution (where as a young PhD economist I was employed) served a valuable function. They brought people together who would otherwise be intellectually isolated.

Today, things are different. The academic world is teeming with scholars (especially economists) who believe that markets work and are powerful engines of social change. In addition, the Internet has made communication cheap, easy and immediate. As a result, almost all younger think tanks are based on a different model: they are organizations without walls.

Think tanks without walls typically have no endowments and are less well-funded than older organizations that try to assemble everyone under one roof. To make smaller budgets stretch further, they economize by contracting with scholars at other institutions rather than employing them. This means that the university pays all the overheads and the think tank pays only the marginal cost of the research it wants. Against these greater efficiencies, the think tank may suffer an identity problem, however. For instance, a news story about a scholarly study may mention only the professor's or author's name and perhaps the name of the university that employs him or her – omitting the name of the think tank that actually funded the research.

THINK TANKS AS BUSINESSES

The NCPA is a non-profit institution, but it is run as a business. We invest in new programs and judge our success by the return on those investments. Other successful think tanks are also run like businesses, applying business techniques to the world of ideas.

When the NCPA was formed in 1983, there were older, larger think tanks already in existence. Our job was to find a market niche. Ronald Reagan was president and the existing right-of-center think tanks tended to focus on the president's agenda. The niche for the NCPA was all of the items that were not on Reagan's agenda: Social Security, health care, employee benefits and other 'social insurance' issues. As it turns out, these are the hardest areas to reform, not only in our country, but all over the world. However, by investing in these especially hard-to-solve issues, the NCPA built up expertise and institutional memory that could be brought to bear in later years when the body politic was ready to address them.

THE LOCATION OF THINK TANKS

In recent years, there has been a tendency for all organizations interested in public policy to move to Washington DC, if they were not already there in the first place. In my opinion, this is a mistake. There is enormous pressure on everyone within the Beltway to concentrate on what Congress and the current administration are focused on. To fail to do so is to risk being characterized as irrelevant.

My view is, if you want to think about what Congress is not thinking about (and is unlikely to think about any time soon), you need to do your thinking away from Washington. That, in any event, was the strategy followed by the NCPA, which opened a Washington office only when it was clear that Congress was ready to focus on some key NCPA proposals. The year was 1994, and the core tax ideas in the Republican Contract with America came directly from a pro-growth proposal generated by the NCPA and the US Chamber of Commerce.[12]

We continue to have an active Washington office, but its objective is narrow and focused: to provide Congress and the administration with NCPA's scholars' research, testimony and advice, and to conduct conferences and briefings on issues of direct interest on Capitol Hill.

THINK TANKS VERSUS UNIVERSITIES

Like think tanks, colleges and universities hire scholars, encourage research and provide a forum for scholarly interaction. So how are these academic institutions different from think tanks? Part of the difference is that the research of tenured professors is unmanaged and undirected. The object of research is up to the whim of the professor. The goal may or may not be to solve an important social problem. Think tanks, by contrast, tend to be very goal-oriented. They employ or contract with scholars to research specific topics, and encourage solutions to well-defined problems. Universities tend to be graded based on the academic prestige of their faculty members. Think tanks tend to be graded based on their success in solving real world problems.

THINK TANKS VERSUS ADVOCACY GROUPS

In recent years, there has been a proliferation of groups who openly advocate public policy changes (usually on a single issue). These groups, however, are not incubators of new ideas. They are better thought of as lobbyists for ideas. Often they receive financial backing from special interests. They may be very helpful in promoting needed public policy changes, but they are not staffed or led by intellectuals. In fact, they are typically anti-intellectual – resisting ways of thinking that are different from the narrow goals of their financial backers.

---

12   (1992), *A Strategy for Growth*, National Center for Policy Analysis and US Chamber of Commerce, January.

THE ROLE OF IDEOLOGY

To what degree do ideological preferences influence the output of think tanks? Among first-rate research organizations, ideology has no effect on findings of fact. If the economists at the NCPA, Urban Institute, Brookings Institution and the American Enterprise Institute calculate the government's unfunded liabilities under Social Security and Medicare, they are all likely to arrive at similar numbers. Where ideology matters is in deciding what problems to research and what solutions to investigate.

For example, the Brookings Institution is more likely to investigate unmet needs and ask what government programs could solve the problem. The NCPA is more likely to investigate how government policies are causing the problem in the first place and ask how the private sector can be utilized to solve it. Of course, occasionally we see eye-to-eye on problems and solutions.[13]

CONSERVATISM VERSUS CLASSICAL LIBERALISM

The NCPA is often called 'conservative' by the national news media. I have never been comfortable with that term and I avoid it whenever possible.

William F. Buckley once described conservatives as people who stand athwart history, yelling 'stop'. That may be an apt description of many people, but it is not a very good description of what most right-of-center think tanks do. For this and other reasons, Nobel laureates Milton Friedman and Friedrich Hayek avoided the term altogether and called themselves 'classical liberals'. Nineteenth-century liberals were not trying to conserve institutions. They were trying to reform them.[14]

The NCPA is in the classical liberal tradition. We are animated by the same desire to reform institutions that motivated Thomas Jefferson, Abraham Lincoln and other historical figures who worked to empower people and unleash the energy, creativity and innovative ability of individuals pursuing their own interests in competitive markets.

---

13   Goodman J. C. and Orszag P. R. (2004), *Retirement Savings Reforms on which the Left and the Right Can Agree*, National Center for Policy Analysis, Brief Analysis No. 495, December 1,.

14   Goodman J. C. (2005), *What Is Classical Liberalism?*, National Center for Policy Analysis, December 20.

THE FUTURE OF THINK TANKS

I believe that the NCPA is the youngest national think tank on the center-right of the ideological spectrum. By that I mean that ours was the last organization to enter the think tank marketplace successfully and address a wide array of public policy issues at the federal level. All of the organizations that have formed since that time have been state think tanks or organizations that focus on a narrow range of issues. I do not expect that to change. Today, our best think tanks are well-managed and so alert to market opportunities that potential entrants into the market are unlikely to find much opportunity.

Although I do not expect to see an increase in the number of organizations, I do believe the national think tanks are on the cusp of a virtual explosion of intellectual activity.

There is enormous untapped potential in the academic and scholarly world. As think tanks grow in terms of budget, skills and expertise, their ability to tap that potential will grow exponentially. The successes we have seen so far are not aberrations. They are the beginning of an intellectual revolution that will set the stage for the policy debates of the 21st century.

12

Awakening a Slumbering Elephant

Parth Shah
Centre for Civil Society
(India)

On my arrival in India in August 1997, after more than ten years of graduate studies and teaching economics in the United States, I resolved to be as self-sufficient in running my new Indian home as I was at manning my American apartment. Cleaning the bathroom and dusting the furniture were indeed more demanding here. When I spent more than half a day paying my first telephone bill, however, and several hours on the electricity bill, my resolve vanished into thin air. I felt utterly helpless; I hired a helper. The dehumanizing effects of government monopolies (telecoms and electricity) were no longer a theoretical speculation in the classroom.

But how did I manage to get a house and a telephone to begin with? Rent control and tenancy laws make it nearly impossible to lease any space without close personal contacts. Proprietors not only receive (legal) rents below market rates, but are also in constant danger of losing the property to their tenants. I was fortunate in finding a well-wisher with an apartment with a telephone and gas for cooking. Yes, cooking gas is also a government monopoly. Economically rational laws and the sanctity of contracts were no longer mantras to be recited at classical liberal gatherings.

Widespread abuse of political power, close ties between politicians and criminals, flagrant violation of even basic human rights, censorship of books, plays, films and works of art vividly demonstrated the government's control over not just the economic but also the social and cultural life of India. After her political independence from an alien state, India awaits her civil independence. It was to signify the necessity of economic, social and cultural freedom from the omnipresent Indian state that the Centre for Civil Society (CCS) was inaugurated on 15 August 1997, the 50th anniversary of India's political independence.

It is important to choose critical dates in the life of the institute with care. I capture here a few more observations and thoughts as I look back at the ten-year journey of CCS; it has indeed been a delightful and rewarding journey. Fortunately for me, I met my wife Mana through this work, and she is an even more uncompromising, enthusiastic and energetic champion of liberalism, pushing me as well as helping me to dream bigger and aim higher. Though I write this as a personal account, Mana and my former and current team members are all integral to and responsible for the achievements of CCS.

WHY THE CENTER FOR CIVIL SOCIETY? MAKING A STATEMENT THROUGH THE INSTITUTE'S NAME

It was clear to me that in India the message of liberty would need to be framed differently to how it is framed in the USA – within the historical and cultural context of India. The USA is rather unique in that being free from the state is generally seen as a virtue and accepted as a desirable situation. With the exception of political freedom, which is primarily practiced through ritualized frequent elections, statism is the main theme in India. The 'language of liberty', American style, would be too foreign to India.

Second, in the mid-1990s a philosophical battle began between classical liberals and the statists about who would claim 'civil society'. Central Europeans, who revived the idea of civil society in the second half of the 20th century, thought of it as the space between the family and the state. You do not choose your family and you must be a citizen of a state (at least as of now) and except for the obligations to the family and the state, everything else in life is voluntary. Voluntary action is the domain of civil society. In these theorists' conception, civil society included not only non-profit entities but also for-profit businesses. It was important that civil society be contrasted with political society, and not with business or capitalism. I decided to do my bit in this battle by choosing the Centre for Civil Society as the name of a classical liberal public policy institute in India.

Even though it was conceptually clear that in India the ideas of liberty would be best captured in the language of civil society and in the principles of subsidiarity and 'livelihood freedom', it took quite some time to articulate that approach clearly and consistently. The role of the state should be subsidiary to the role of the people and the government should do only those things that individuals and associations cannot do for themselves. Within the government, the first charge should be given to the local government, then to the state government, and only those tasks that cannot be done by the local or the state governments should be delegated to the central/federal government. This is the broad message that we tried to capture in various phrases. We oscillated among 'Working for a Freer India', 'Developing Ideas that Better the World', 'The Power of Ideas' and 'Social Change through Public Policy'. There is no doubt an apt tagline is critical in marketing and branding an institute.

THE ROAD TO SUCCESS: MODELS AND MODES

Everyone in our business has heard the story of F. A. Hayek and Sir Antony Fisher and the formation of the Institute of Economic Affairs (IEA) in London. Looking at think tanks around the world and my experience at CCS, it is clear that there are several different roads to success. These can be summarized in the following five models:

- Hayek-Fisher Model: this focuses on the second-hand dealers in ideas – professors, authors, journalists – and works through the trickling down of ideas. Judges are generally not included but they could be one of the most important transmitters of ideas since their judgments set precedents and change the course of legal reasoning. The main tasks embodied in this model are research, writing and dissemination of ideas. Prime examples of the approach include the IEA (London) and the Cato Institute (Washington DC). George Mason University's law and economics program has regularly conducted workshops for sitting judges in the USA.

- Read-Harper-Rockwell Model: this goes farther downstream than the Hayek-Fisher Model and focuses on students and young scholars. It bypasses the existing second-hand dealers in ideas by becoming the transmitter of ideas to the next generation. Fellowships, seminars, conferences and publications are the primary tasks. Several US-based think tanks are fine examples of this approach – the Foundation for Economic Education under Leonard Read (Irvington-on-Hudson, New York), the Institute for Humane Studies under F. A. Harper (Arlington, Virginia) and the Ludwig von Mises Institute under Llewellyn Rockwell (Auburn, Alabama). In a few cases, fully fledged universities have been created, such as the Universidad Francisco Marroquín in Guatemala and the University of Asia and the Pacific in the Philippines.

- Feulner-Bolick-Mellor Model: this focuses on lobbying policy/lawmakers directly through policy papers, legislative analyses, individual briefings, policy breakfasts and press meetings. Unlike in the previous models, the success is directly visible, even though one might find it difficult to take credit for the success publicly. People in the specific community, however, know why the bill got changed or how it got passed. The Heritage Foundation in Washington DC, which was founded by Edwin Feulner, is the granddaddy of this approach and a role model for many state-based think tanks in the United States. Judges are also lawmakers but typically it is illegal to lobby them directly on any specific case. Bringing properly chosen cases to court, however – if possible when the judges are likely to be sympathetic – could be a way to 'lobby' the judiciary. The Institute for Justice founded by Chip Mellor and Clint Bolick, based in Arlington, Virginia, has used this method very effectively and has brought about substantial shifts in the legal environment. The International Policy Network in London actively participates in formal meetings of international organizations such as the World Trade Organization and the World Health Organization to voice liberal positions from within. It brings outside pressure on these organizations through the regular publication of articles by local authors in the international media.

- Chicago-Eastern European Model: this approach does not worry about changing the larger intellectual and social climate; it attacks policies directly by securing positions of power or by advising those who are in power. The 'Chicago Boys' in Latin America are one famous example. The breakup of the Soviet Union created many opportunities for policy entrepreneurs to work closely with new governments, which lacked policy ideas and the experience and capacity to execute them. The Lithuanian Free Market Institute is one group that fully exploited such a situation; they not only issued policy ideas but also actually drafted bills and at times guided them through ministries and parliament.

- The Proletariat Model: different from the Hayek-Fisher Model, which targets intellectuals, or the Read-Harper-Rockwell Model, which focuses on young scholars; this model works directly with the proletariat. It mobilizes large numbers of people and groups directly affected by state policies, such as street vendors, taxi drivers, sex workers and unemployed youth. Their primary objectives are to help these people to organize, to provide meeting places and financial support and to conduct mass rallies and stage media events. The Free Market Foundation of South Africa has had good success with this model.

These five models offer a matrix to understand the work of existing institutes. More importantly, they can help guide new think tank entrepreneurs in determining the focus that would be most effective in their country.

The focus of a new institute could also be determined by a different approach – one that considers the type of activities or mode of actions undertaken by the institute. I can identify five basic activities: research, advocacy, campaigns, pilots and policymaking/writing. Research (along with writing and education) could be original or applied; this focus goes well with the Hayek-Fisher Model. Advocacy is not just passive dissemination but, rather, it takes the message actively, regularly and consistently to a target audience that generally includes politicians and policymakers, but could also consist of students, young scholars, lawyers, judges and non-governmental organization (NGO) activists. Campaigning involves bringing together a large number of affected citizens on a given issue and building a grassroots pressure group to implement change. Pilot projects take the policy idea a step farther by running actual experimental projects to demonstrate the feasibility of the idea and to generate statistical evidence in its favor. The last approach, policymaking, refers to drafting and implementing policy reforms by positioning oneself close to those in power. This could include building capacity within the government to undertake these tasks. The think tank's influence would come from the training and guidance provided to key people in a position to achieve change. The power center is generally the executive or the legislative branch of the government, but it could be the judiciary. Public interest litigations (PILs) in many Commonwealth countries utilize the judiciary for policy and institutional reforms.

One can imagine a single policy issue going through any of these five modes or different issues playing out in one or more modes depending on the ideological and policy context in a given country. Over the years, CCS itself has traversed these five approaches. Initially, we did research and advocacy through publications, policy dialogues, policy meetings for members of parliament (MPs) and members of the legislative assembly (MLAs), and student seminars and research internships. In recent years, we ran a Livelihood Freedom Campaign, which won a Templeton Freedom Award from the Atlas Economic Research Foundation, and a School Choice Campaign. To demonstrate the power of vouchers in offering school choice to poor parents and thereby helping to improve the quality of education, we are now conducting several voucher pilot projects. We are in the process of filing

PILs in the Delhi High Court and the Supreme Court to directly challenge some of the country's educational policies. Over time, CCS has moved from research and advocacy to campaigns and pilots, and now works across several of these modes simultaneously.

The objective for a think tank entrepreneur is to look at these five models and five modes/approaches and identify a more effective and efficient way to engage with the process of social change in a given country or area. It is not necessary to view these as distinct models and modes, which work only one at a time. Given the variety of circumstances in a country and the availability of financial resources and, more importantly, human resources, understanding these models can help to delineate an approach that is best for the entrepreneur and the location. The different modes could help differentiate the many issues of concern into the categories of research, advocacy, campaign, pilot or policy-making based on the overall intellectual climate and the policy options being considered by the government. More technical approaches and issues undertaken by the global think tank fraternity. I leave this task for some other day and abstract issues should be dealt with through research and advocacy (ie telecoms policy or insolvency law), while issues like the delicensing of street vendors and the legalisztion of sex work are more suitable for campaigns. Very concrete reform ideas could be promoted by developing pilot schemes. A triangulation exercise of issues, models and modes could provide a systematic method of determining the appropriate focus for new institutes or changing the strategy of existing institutes.

GET THE LETTERHEAD RIGHT: FIRST A GREAT LIBERAL BOARD OF SCHOLARS

Before and immediately after the formal launch of CCS, our primary focus was on identifying individuals who were classical liberal in approach, and respected and well known in their areas of expertise. Even though the think tank may be a new concept, there are usually several individuals in various walks of life who sympathize with classical liberal ideas and policies. We brought them together and created a Board of Scholars. Listing the names of these scholars on the letterhead opened many doors, provided credibility, and gave us a solid standing in the public arena. They also became our advocates when engaging with government bodies, the media and donors.

PLAN, PLAN; PREPARE, PREPARE

Initially, I wanted to start the think tank soon after I completed my PhD at Auburn University. I visited India in the late 1980s and met a large number of people, but the level of support was lukewarm. I realized that I needed to learn the tools of the think tank trade and, more importantly, save enough money to support my personal expenses for at least three years. It seemed possible to raise some money to support the work of the institute, but almost impossible to get support for myself. In India, only the wealthy are expected to engage in such 'social work', and even the law looks harshly on founders of non-profits who draw a salary from the organization.

While studying economics at Auburn University, I learned a great deal, first hand, by working at the Mises Institute on the campus. Later, while teaching at the University of Michigan-Dearborn, I was fortunate enough to be able to attend several excellent workshops hosted by the Atlas Economic Research Foundation, and I was inspired by Leonard Liggio and Alex Chafuen. I was also encouraged by the network of like-minded people across the world and by the work of institutes such as the Cato Institute (Washington, DC), the Institute for Humane Studies (Arlington, Virginia), the Foundation for Economic Education (Irvington-on-Hudson, New York), The Heritage Foundation (Washington DC) and the Mackinac Center for Public Policy (Midland, Michigan). The key person who got me to buy my one-way ticket to India, however, was David Kennedy of the Earhart Foundation when he promised to support the institute during its initial years.

I know that I was lucky. Sometimes the best way to learn to swim is just to dive in. As much as possible, however, one must plan, build relationships and learn the tools of the trade. While a spur-of-the-moment launch of an institute makes for a great story, it is not the best recipe for success.

FOCUS ON THE YOUTH: DEVELOPING OUR OWN SOLDIERS FOR THE BATTLE

We realized early on that it was quite difficult to find people to do public policy research and analysis from a classical liberal point of view. I had assumed that, by sheer statistical odds, there must be a few public-policy-oriented classical liberals in a country of a billion people. As we all learn eventually, statistical probabilities do not really work in the think tank arena. With the help of our scholars, we started to organize discussions on topical policy issues to develop human capital and establish our presence in Delhi. In addition, we immediately launched a training seminar for college students called the Liberty & Society Seminar (named after an Institute for Humane Studies program), a four-day-long residential program teaching them about classical liberal principles and policies. Along with the seminar, we also run a research internship program called Researching Reality, which allows students to experience and document the impact of public policies first hand. The indoctrination of the Indian youth, who came from a state-dominated education system, was a mammoth challenge for us. Our youth programs turned out to be a very effective antidote for many of the participants.

Over fifteen of the young people who participated in these seminars came to work with us full time and were responsible for most of our research and publications. In the process, they also discovered completely new careers for themselves in the fields of public policy and research! We actually thought of starting a one-year graduate program in public policy since such a program did not exist in India. We are still looking for someone to head this project! One CCS graduate (we call all those who have attended our student program CCS graduates) has started his own research institute, the Centre for Public Policy Research, in Cochin, Kerala, a state dominated by Marxists since the 1950s.

PUTTING A HUMAN FACE ON LIBERALISM: CHOOSING ISSUES AND STRATEGIES

CCS is a unique free market think tank in that it directly champions the causes of street entrepreneurs (vendors and cycle rickshaw-pullers), poor parents who can access only government schools, farmers and tribal peoples. Free market institutes are generally viewed as doing the bidding of corporations and the wealthy. We have consciously chosen issues that clearly demonstrate that the classical liberal approach is beneficial to the poor in urban as well as rural areas. Our 'Livelihood Freedom Campaign' talks about delicensing and deregulating street entrepreneurs and the 'Terracotta Campaign' successfully lobbied for giving forest land to tribal peoples.

The 'Duty to Publish Campaign' emphasized the government's duty to provide information suo moto (without citizens having to file specific requests for information), which became Section 4 of the new Right to Information Act. The School Choice Campaign advocates school vouchers to break the monopoly of the government on the education of the poor. The classical liberal approach does more for the poor than probably any other philosophy; we just need to find issues to drive home that message effectively.

NOVEL AND SUSTAINABLE SOLUTIONS

One reason why CCS has a strong appeal is because our focus is on solutions. We offer novel and at times even radical answers within the Indian context. Most non-governmental organizations (NGOs) spend their time and energy highlighting and magnifying problems. They hardly ever suggest solutions, and the ones that they do suggest typically deal with symptoms rather than the causes. In this NGO environment CCS stands out as the lone organization that is really concerned about the actual problem and the people being impacted. We contrast 'direct action' with 'policy action' and consistently show the power of addressing social problems through policy and institutional reforms – 'social change through public policy'.

The Chicago School mantra 'if it matters, then measure it' is the right approach to all issues, new and old. One may be philosophically skeptical of the phrase 'measurement is science', but for all practical policy debates, facts, numbers, case studies, tables and charts matter a great deal. One Indian company has a motto, 'In God we trust, the rest must bring numbers to the table.'

LEADING AND MANAGING: ARE YOU THE RIGHT PERSON FOR BOTH?

Like many intellectual entrepreneurs, I am an academic – not just by profession but, more importantly, also by nature. Researching, writing and talking about ideas excites me. This can be turned, though not without effort, into intellectual leadership. An equally important part of a successful think tank is managerial leadership. As with any start-up, the initial years run on adrenalin, but as the institute matures, high-quality management becomes critical for growth. At least after three to five years of existence institution-building must become one of the important concerns of the institute. When looking at the think tank fraternity, it is clear that those institutes that have had a sustained impact have been the ones with a team of two people at the helm. John Blundell has rightly emphasized the synergy between Ralph Harris and Arthur Seldon as a key reason for the success of the Institute of Economic Affairs.

Ultimately, ideas are the business of any think tank and ideas must be part of its team training and management. Reminding the institute's staff about the overall vision of the institute, about applying ideas to current issues and cultivating an attitude of critical inquiry, is crucial for the cohesion, motivation and growth of the team. The belief that 'ideas matter' should become a part of the organizational culture. We have tried different avenues over the years: luncheon discussions about the daily news, 'Coffee with Parth', guest speakers, annual planning workshops, human resources retreats and 'CCS Chintan'. CCS Chintan is an internal forum to engage team members in the philosophy and ideas that define CCS and how to apply those ideas to current issues. There is no one formula, but each member must feel that the power of liberal ideas can improve lives and society.

A LARGER, LONG-TERM VISION: INDIA A LIBERAL UTOPIA!

Along with the day-to-day policy work, it is critical to talk about an idealist social vision of the institute's work – particularly in engaging with the youth. We talk about the India of today where there is a long queue of Americans outside the Indian embassy in Chicago to pick up their visas to work in India! We ask ourselves: 'What then do we need to do to achieve that?' and 'What makes a good society? And then, how can we get there?'

For other audiences we predict that India could be the first fully and truly liberal society – a liberal utopia – that has bypassed the welfare state and has progressed from free markets to a genuinely free society. Here the institutions of civil society – for-profit and non-profit – not only produce all goods and services, but also care for the needy. Economic statism is losing its legitimacy, but welfare statism is still very dominant. Despite its perverse social and economic consequences, dismantling the welfare state in the West has proved to be a daunting challenge. Some progress has been made, but it is unlikely that the West would be able to convert its state-dominated welfare system to one governed by charity and voluntarism.

In India, the absence of welfare statism, coupled with continued high economic growth in a democratic political system, offers a unique opportunity to build a liberal utopia. Our approach is designed for this goal: define the right size of political society and rejuvenate civil society. Liberal think tanks typically focus on the former, but it is critical that we also look at how to build systems and institutions so that, as the state withers away, people will have the confidence and civil society will have the breadth and the depth to tackle social problems. Unless people see civil society alternatives working, they will be very reluctant to let the state withdraw.

The nature and extent of state intervention in India have been such that an ordinary Indian has little faith in the capacity of the government to do much good. Indians are very proud of the freedom movement that resulted in political independence from the British, and we talk about a Second Freedom Movement for economic and social independence!

Like many of you reading this, I find it hard to imagine doing anything else in life. It is a wonderful journey and a worthy challenge.

13

If it Matters, Measure it

Michael Walker
Fraser Institute
(Canada)

LET'S GO GET THEM

The Fraser Institute was founded in 1974 by Canadian industrialist T. P. Boyle with the advice of his colleague, economist and former Hungarian freedom fighter Csaba Hajdu, and by the direct efforts of Sally Pipes, John Raybould and Michael Walker. The two main differences that characterized the Fraser Institute's approach and its publications from other policy think tanks of the era were the empirical focus on very specific public policy issues of the day and an attention to marketing the studies to the broadest possible audience. The former attribute reflected my training as an econometrician, the latter the incredible energy and 'let's go get them' attitude of John Raybould and Sally Pipes. In particular, in the words of John Raybould, the Fraser Institute tried to lower the 'fog index' associated with its publications so that they would be accessible to the widest possible audience. (It is interesting to note that when he left the Fraser Institute to return to the United Kingdom because of family issues, John Raybould went to work for the Institute of Economic Affairs (IEA) where his job was the marketing of IEA publications.) Later we were fortunate to attract to our staff the libertarian Übermensch Walter Block, who for ten years was the dominant libertarian in Canada.

PEOPLE ARE NOT ENTITLED TO THEIR OWN FACTS

We rely primarily on measurement because we recognize that disputes about public policies are often based on opinions that have been formed without a careful consideration of all the facts. While everyone is entitled to their own opinions, they are not entitled to their own facts. It was and is our view at the Fraser Institute that, perhaps not immediately but in the end, many disputes about public policy can be resolved by the infusion of a generally agreed upon set of facts.

IF IT MATTERS, MEASURE IT

The Institute's motto, 'if it matters, measure it', also reflects the belief that through a program of careful measurement an institute can change the agenda of public discussion. Of course, the measurements have to be relevant and have to be related in some way to an interest that ordinary citizens have in a particular outcome. For this reason, we often say that the Institute's job is to think ahead a number of years to the public policy issues that will occupy the minds of the public and be ready with a publication that takes advantage of this natural demand for information, thus changing the public's view of that topic. The strategic idea here is that it is easier to fulfill a demand for information that already exists than it is to create a demand for that information and then to fulfill it.

IN THE BEGINNING

This forward-looking approach will only work, however, if the topic of concern is projected into the public's eye by the natural course of events.

So, for example, the first book that the Institute published dealt with the problems that rent controls would produce for tenants. We knew that, in a very short period of time, the existence of rent control would make it more difficult for tenants to find lodgings and that this would produce a demand for information about the rent controls themselves. Our assessment was accurate and *Rent Control – A Popular Paradox* became a national bestseller in Canada and found its way onto book racks in corner stores.

Our second book, *The Illusion of Wage and Price Controls*, was also a bestseller, and for the same reasons. Both books had the effect of destroying the credibility of the policy they targeted. In the case of wage and price controls, our book helped mobilize the trade union movement in Canada to fight wage controls.

THE KEY CHALLENGE – GETTING A SHARE OF THE PUBLIC'S MIND

By far the toughest job that public policy research institutes have to do is to create awareness about a public policy issue that has not already attracted public attention. Most citizens do not wake up in the morning asking themselves, 'I wonder what public policy is doing today?' The fact that most citizens are more focused on their own lives and parochial concerns explains why politicians often use emotional arguments and exaggerated claims to attract the interest of the public to their political position. Since public policy organizations are trying to encourage citizens to be more rational in their approach to public policy questions, it is obvious why we are often fighting an ineffectual rearguard action

MEASURE WHAT MATTERS TO THE PUBLIC

Having recognized this problem at an early stage in its development, the Fraser Institute has adopted a different strategy from most public policy organizations in approaching the problem of mobilizing opinion. Rather than reprinting classic masters like Frédéric Bastiat, Adam Smith and Friedrich Hayek, the Institute, as noted, sought to publish current economic analysis on topics related to pressing policy issues that were already in the public focus. But we also set out to provide measurements for public consumption that would address a deeper policy concern by mobilizing citizens' concerns about their own wallet or other direct impacts on their family circumstances.

One of the earliest projects of this kind undertaken by the Institute was the creation of the Consumer Tax Index and the associated calculation of Tax Freedom Day. The idea of the Consumer Tax Index emerged from the observation that consumers had a natural interest in how much they were paying for the goods and services they consumed and the monthly release of the government's consumer price index resulted in a lot of comments in the media. There was, however, almost no discussion of the cost of public services that were being consumed and the attendant tax burdens required to finance them.

HOW MANY DAYS DO *YOU* WORK FOR THE GOVERNMENT?

The Consumer Tax Index calculations were begun in 1976 and continue to be one of the most successful projects in the Institute's history. The annual studies that are required to produce the index include: calculation of the tax burden borne by families at different income levels; a comparison of the tax burdens in different provinces; a comparison of the tax burden with the cost of the necessities of life and how these comparisons have changed since 1961, the earliest date for which calculations can be made. The results of the tax studies make it possible to calculate Tax Freedom Day, the day in the year when the citizen with average income has worked long enough to pay the full tax bill owing to the various levels of government.

Tax Freedom Day has become one of the most widely known statistical facts in the country. The once obtuse provisions of federal and provincial budgets are now all reduced to the simple question, 'Will Tax Freedom Day be earlier in the year or later in the year?' During 2006 there were 475 media stories using Tax Freedom Day and the information contained in the Tax Facts book, which every other year compiles the calculations made to produce the Consumer Tax Index and Tax Freedom Day

BECOME A 'GO TO' SOURCE FOR RELEVANT INFORMATION

Apart from the direct media impact effect upon the climate of opinion, the Institute's work on taxation has made it a 'go to' source of information on a wide variety of topics related to government activities. As a consequence, the Fraser Institute is regarded within Canada as the most important force pushing governments to adopt a more conservative stance on public finances and the control of public expenditure. In Canada, the Fraser Institute is synonymous with fiscal probity, lower taxes and responsible fiscal conduct.

One of the spin-offs of our work on taxation and public expenditure has been the publication of our annual report cards on the tax, spending and debt management of the ten provincial governments and the federal government. These report cards are now so widely used by the public in Canada – particularly by those deciding whether or not to purchase government bonds – that even socialist governments within the country use their rating on the Fraser Institute's scorecard as a way of promoting their province when their score is good. A poor showing on a report card often produces telephone calls from provincial premiers and ministers of finance complaining that they have not been understood or that their position has in some way been misrepresented.

MEASURE THE ECONOMIC FREEDOM OF THE WORLD

It is often said that success begets success. This is the case with the Fraser Institute's focus on measurement as a way of achieving public policy objectives. Having observed the huge success of our tax measurement studies and Tax Freedom Day, the Institute began to apply the same strategy in other areas of public policy. One of the most outstanding results has been the Economic Freedom of the World Index.

In 1986, following a conference on the relationship between economic, civil and political freedom, the Fraser Institute decided, with the help of Liberty Fund Inc, to launch a program of study and discussion that would lead to the construction of a global index of economic freedom. The objective was to raise the level of discussion of economic freedom by journalists, politicians and the general public, by providing a league table that would make the concept of economic freedom more tangible. By 1986, we had had a decade of experience of raising the level of public discussion of fiscal issues using a variety of derivatives from the Canadian Consumer Tax Index. It was my hope that we would be able to accomplish for discussion of economic freedom what we had already done for the discussion of fiscal affairs. While we are a long way from achieving a satisfactory level of economic freedom around the world, there can be no question that the Economic Freedom of the World Index has made a material difference in raising the level of economic freedom. It has been effective, in part, because of the creation of the Economic Freedom of the World Network: a network of institutes in nearly 80 countries which collaborate annually in the publication and release of the

Index. Some of the members of the network have followed the Fraser Institute's lead and have created sub-national indices of economic freedom so as to encourage the discussion of variations between sub-national units such as provinces. Notable examples are India, China and Argentina.

FIND OUT WHAT FAMILIES ARE CONCERNED ABOUT AND MEASURE IT

While the Fraser Institute has been quite aggressive in using the economic freedom of the world methodology to encourage greater levels of economic freedom in Canada, it has also been using a variety of other measurements that have had a significant impact on public policy. While the constraints of the space available in this essay make it impossible to provide anything like a complete list of these projects, in the space remaining I will provide two examples that can be readily adapted to other countries.

Undoubtedly, the building of human capital is the most important aspect of both personal success and the prosperity of a nation. The development of human capital begins in the education system, yet it is an unfortunate reality that in most countries of the world this most crucial 'industry' is entirely owned by the government and funded by block grants from government. In many instances, this state education apparatus does not perform well and does not produce the kinds of additions to human capital that are commensurate with the large amounts of money which are spent to support it.

Notwithstanding this fact, in most countries the majority believe that the public education system is absolutely essential. The role of public policy research organizations is twofold: on one hand, they must document the quality of the public education system, and on the other hand, they must give an indication of the benefits of private education. A tremendously powerful tool for accomplishing both these goals is the creation and wide dissemination of report cards on the performance of public and private schools.

MEASURE SCHOOLS' PERFORMANCE AND MILLIONS WILL PAY ATTENTION

In 1998, the Fraser Institute began a project whose long-term goal is to publish comprehensive report cards on every high school in every Canadian province for which data is available. Currently, the Institute publishes evaluations of 5,700 high schools that provide education to 3 million children. These report cards have had a dramatic impact on the education debate and the choices that parents have been making about where to send their children for schooling.

The strategy behind the school report card program is similar to that discussed above. Parents have a natural interest in the welfare of their children and a curiosity about the quality of the schools they attend. The report cards feed this natural demand for information.

MEDIA COMPETE TO PUBLISH THE LEAGUE TABLES

The media have been quick to realize the interest that parents and grandparents have in the performance of schools. Consequently, in every jurisdiction where we are able to produce a report card, we have a media partner. The partner is usually a newspaper, but sometimes it is a news magazine, and it reports the results of the report card analysis. The media outlet also uses this as an opportunity to run a series of stories about education and a comparison of school performance. This comparative study, together with the reporting of the performance results, has made the annual release of the results of the school report cards the most important public policy development in education during the year.

In fact, the news magazine *L'Actualité* in Quebec, which has one of the widest circulations in that province, dedicates more than 80 pages of a special annual edition of its magazine to the report cards. Reader surveys by the magazine have ascertained that more than a million citizens read the results and use them as a means for assessing the quality of education. A competing publication, not sympathetic to the idea of assessing school performance, did, however, note that enrollment in private schools had increased by 30 per cent as a consequence of the wide availability of these measures.

But the most important effect that the report cards have had is to make school performance an issue for teachers, administrators, politicians and, most importantly, the parents of the pupils. In some provinces, such as British Columbia, the government has responded to the performance measures by enabling parents to cross enrollment boundaries to take advantage of schools that are better than the ones in the neighborhoods where they live. As can be imagined, this combination has produced increased pressure on the state school system and made performance enhancement more important for school administrators.

MEASURE HOSPITAL WAITING LISTS AND CHANGE PUBLIC OPINION ABOUT THE PUBLIC HEALTH MONOPOLY

A second area where the measurement of public services performance has had a beneficial effect is in healthcare. Seventeen years ago, realizing that the public ownership and operation of the healthcare system, and a lack of pricing signals to users, would lead to shortages and rationing, the Fraser Institute began a program of measuring hospital waiting lists. These measurements have shaped the debate and mobilized public opinion about the adequacy of the current healthcare system in Canada.

Most importantly, the waiting list measures have generated thousands of newspaper and television stories and have facilitated a general acceptance of the idea that the public healthcare system, as it exists now, has been failing citizens. Correspondingly, when the Supreme Court of Canada was asked to consider the case of a citizen who had waited a very long time for hip surgery, it concluded that the healthcare system as it presently operates is not answering the needs of citizens and that the prohibition of the purchase of private healthcare in Canada is a violation of their constitutional rights. These Supreme Court decisions have served to define the future outline of the discussion of healthcare in Canada and will undoubtedly lead to an increased reliance on private care and to less confidence in a monopoly public system.

The Battle of Ideas in Chile

Cristián Larroulet
Libertad y Desarrollo
(Chile)

INTRODUCTION

This chapter describes the key importance of ideas – and the institutions that promote them – in Chile's political, economic and social development.

During the 1960s and early 1970s, Chile was known for taking significant steps towards the socialist model. This process culminated in a severe economic, social and political crisis, leading to a virtual state of civil war. Thirty years later, however, Chile has transformed its economy in the direction of a free market system, opened its markets to the world, and advanced the welfare of its inhabitants (Buchi, 1993). It is also recognized as an example of a well-established democracy and a successful political transition from a military regime (which lasted for sixteen years).

Friedrich Hayek noted long ago that 'the only way to change the course of society is to change its ideas' (Blundell, 2004). Chile is a good illustration. Half a century ago, an agreement between the University of Chicago's Institute of Economics and Santiago's Catholic University brought free market ideas into Chile with clarity and force. In the generations that followed, these ideas were transmitted to economists, entrepreneurs, journalists and intellectuals, who have successfully influenced public policy (Rosende, 2007). Thanks to the work of other universities and research centers these ideas are gaining broad support and continue to be highly influential in contributing to the level of social and economic development in Chile (Larroulet, 2003).

The first part of this chapter describes the transformation process in Chile, specifically its free market reforms and their consequences. The second section describes the experiences of Libertad y Desarrollo (LyD), a research and educational center which, since the completion of Chile's transition to democracy in 1990, has consistently promoted free market ideas steeped in the tradition of thinkers such as Friedrich Hayek, Milton Friedman and Gary Becker. The paper concludes by noting key lessons from Chile's experience in promoting ideas in favor of a free society.

I have had the personal good fortune of being closely involved in this experience of national transformation, which some have called revolutionary (Tironi, 2002). After attending Chile's Pontifical Catholic University in the 1970s, in the 1980s I studied at the University of Chicago's Department of Economics, where George Stigler, Gary Becker and Arnold Harberger were among my professors. Later, I served in the Chilean ministries of economy and finance and helped to design and implement reforms in areas such as privatization, competition, trade liberalization, tax reduction and social programs for the needy. In combination with many other initiatives, these policies contributed to Chile's transformation from a socialist economy to a market economy and ultimately allowed the country to reach its current level of development. Finally, I had the opportunity to serve as executive director of Libertad y Desarrollo and help the think tank to promote public policies based on the ideas of a free society. As a result, over the past 27 years I have had the privilege of witnessing the impact of ideas on a country's transition process. I have also been able to affirm the importance of liberty. The rule of law, private property, free trade, competition and an auxiliary role for the state, among other factors, are essential conditions for development.

FROM A SOCIALIST COUNTRY TO A FREE SOCIETY

During the second half of the 19th century, Chile was one of the most prosperous countries in Latin America. This situation was the result of many years of political stability, clear institutional rules and a functioning market economy which was relatively open to the global marketplace. Within the political sphere, the ideas of the rule of law and republican ideology had been promoted by distinguished leaders such as Minister Diego Portales, President Manuel Montt and lawmaker Andrés Bello. Within the economic field, the French economist Jean Gustave Courcelle-Seneuil, who embraced the ideas of Adam Smith, was a powerful supporter of free trade in Chile (Couyoumdjian, 2008). He was also extremely influential in his capacity as adviser to the Chilean government, and taught economics at the University of Chile.

Beginning in the early 20th century, however, nationalist and socialist ideas gradually gained influence among policymakers, pushing them in the direction of greater state intervention. This process was accelerated by the depression of the 1930s, which severely affected Chile. Between 1929 and 1932, GDP decreased by 45 per cent. The impact of the crisis was dramatic, and, as is often seen in such circumstances, public opinion shifted towards greater state involvement and protectionism. Confidence in the private sector fell. Interventionist policies gained greater acceptance among the public and were viewed as necessary remedies. The so-called 'import substitution model', advocated by the Economic Commission for Latin America and the Caribbean (ECLAC), exerted a strong influence on policy. Import duties were systematically raised and numerous barriers to trade were introduced.

At first, increased protectionism and interventionist government policies resulted in growth in production. But the subsequent poor allocation of resources, lack of competition and low productivity rapidly diminished Chile's rate of economic growth. Prevailing socialist attitudes blamed individuals and the private sector for these failures, however, and insisted that there needed to be even more radical policies for increasing state involvement in the production and regulation of goods and services. Meanwhile, the higher public spending levels that resulted from this interventionism raised the tax burden and put an additional brake on the economy. The process culminated with the reappearance of high inflation rates.

In 1970, for the first time in Chile's history, a Marxist-socialist president, Salvador Allende, took office. Allende attempted to convert Chile into a socialist economy and placed most of the country's productive and service sectors into state hands. He continued to close the economy even further, and through a huge increase in public spending produced a massive macroeconomic imbalance (Meller and Larrain, 1991). The resulting political, economic and social chaos led to a state of civil conflict which the country's political leaders were unable to control. In September 1973, a military coup put an end to Chilean democracy.

The armed forces lacked confidence in the political class, which they held responsible for the crisis that had brought the military to power. They also lacked the economic expertise necessary to manage problems such as hyperinflation, food shortages, the falling investment rate and the balance of payments crisis. As a result, they placed their trust in a group of economists schooled in classical liberal thought.

Many of these experts had studied at the University of Chicago and were associated with Chile's two leading universities: the University of Chile and the Catholic University. They had been educated in the tradition of Frank Knight, Theodore Schultz, Harry Johnson, Milton Friedman and George Stigler. In response to the crisis situation of the early 1970s, they had prepared a manifesto now known as El Ladrillo (The Brick) (De Castro, 1992), which outlined the key economic and social reforms they considered necessary to end the crisis. This group, nicknamed the 'Chicago Boys', instituted a set of radical reforms to re-establish fiscal equilibrium, control inflation, open the economy by reducing tariffs and eliminating non-tariff barriers, and free prices in all markets except monopolistic sectors. The markets for capital and labor were liberalized and made more flexible. Numerous barriers to entry, which had restricted competition, were eliminated. Reforms were also carried out to allow private sector participation in a wide range of areas, including energy, telecommunications, basic and higher education and pension fund administration.

Another notable achievement by the Chicago Boys was groundbreaking reform in the area of social programs, which, in general, had not effectively served the poor (Larroulet, 1993). In response to this situation, policies were prioritized in favor of employment. Housing programs, healthcare, retirement insurance, education and monetary subsidies were targeted towards the most needy.

Of course, errors were made in the implementation of some of these reforms, but the final result was a profound transformation of the Chilean economy from a socialist-statist model to a more free market system.

These transformations were carried out amid sharp criticism from groups opposed to the military government, most notably all members of the leftist and center-left political parties. Thus, there was still widespread doubt in the late 1980s about the stability and viability of these reforms over the long run. This doubt was further reinforced when the reforms, owing to internal errors as well as external factors arising from the economic and financial crisis that plagued Latin America during the 1980s, were unable to show clear results in the form of increased wellbeing for the population. It should be noted that during this period per capita income fell by an average of 0.9 per cent per year in Latin America, leading many to refer to the 1980s as 'the lost decade'. This situation, which also affected Chile, did not promote the acceptance of free market reforms within Chilean society.

The transition to democracy began in 1988, when the military government lost a plebiscite, calling a presidential election in 1989. The victor in this election was Patricio Aylwin, the candidate of the center-left coalition called the Concertación. The transition process involved negotiations and agreements between the military government and the new authorities, most notably the consensual reforms to the Constitution of the Republic. The minister of the interior at that time, Carlos Cáceres, played a particularly noteworthy role in this process.[15]

The candidate with the second-largest percentage of the vote during the 1989 elections was Hernán Büchi. Having held several public offices, including minister of finance from 1985 to 1989, Büchi worked to reorient the country's economic policies in the direction of the free market. It is important to recall that in the years previous to his economic leadership, the country had experienced a severe crisis, leading to a 14 per cent drop in GDP in 1982 and an unemployment rate above 15 per cent in 1984. However, under Büchi's management Chile enjoyed an annual GDP growth rate of 8 per cent and unemployment was reduced to about 6 per cent by 1989.

15   It is easy to see how these five modes or approaches correlate with the five models discussed earlier. It would be useful to put the models and the modes in a table, understand their deeper connections and thereby determine a more effective focus of a new institute. Moreover, a great deal can be learned by taking all the institutes in the Atlas directory and classifying them into these models and modes. One can visualize a multidimensional graph or a matrix that captures the five approaches.

INTELLECTUAL ENTREPRENEURS:
THE CASE OF LIBERTAD Y DESARROLLO (LYD)
AN 'ENTERPRISE OF IDEAS' IS BORN

As previously mentioned, many of the economists and politicians of the new democratic administration in 1990 had been highly critical of most of the free market reforms implemented under the military government. Additionally, many free market supporters feared that the new authorities would return to the failed policies of the past. The idea arose to create a 'think tank' that would vigorously defend and promote public policies based on the principles of a free society. Thus a group of people assembled by Hernán Büchi set out to create Libertad y Desarrollo.[16] The new institution was defined as a study and research center specializing in public policies which was independent of any political, religious or commercial affiliation.

The organization was founded on three strategic pillars. The first, which is encompassed in its mission statement, is to defend the principles of a free society; that is, to promote individual freedom and to make individuals the central focus of public policy – in other words, democracy, market economy, rule of law and limited government. The second pillar is the development of strong technical expertise in identifying problem areas and designing public policies that will contribute to the country's development in the broadest sense of the word. This calls for significant investment in human capital in order to assemble experts who can address these tasks with the speed and rigor demanded by the rapidly evolving public debate. The third strategic pillar is the development of close ties with the leading institutions involved in the formulation of public policies. In other words, in order to have influence over public policy, it is necessary to establish direct relationships with the government, Congress, the judicial branch, the political parties, the communications media, the universities and other relevant institutions of civil society.

We began our work in March 1990 with a team of eight professionals. Our staff currently includes 29 experts from the political, economic, social, environmental and legal fields – all of whom are highly influential within the public policy debate in Chile. It is sufficient to note that during 2007, Libertad y Desarrollo or its researchers were cited on average more than 9.8 times per day in the media. Its website, lyd.org, has become one of the most

---

16   Currently chairman of the board of Libertad y Desarrollo; member of the Mont Pelerin Society and former minister of finance, 1983.

visited in Latin America, and over 600,000 copies of its reports and studies are distributed each year. While approximately 40 people currently work at the institute, LyD has made significant long-term investments in human capital over the past eighteen years, including supporting twenty young professionals in postgraduate studies at leading universities abroad.

From the start we were determined to develop close relations with think tanks in other countries that shared our concern for defending the ideas of a free society. Thus, we quickly became involved in the activities of the Atlas Economic Research Foundation, The Heritage Foundation and the Cato Institute in the United States; Canada's Fraser Institute; the Institute of Economic Affairs in England; and many others. We also decided that our institution should have a complementary profile to that of the already prestigious Centro de Estudios Públicos (CEP), which was founded in Chile in the early 1980s and had been extremely influential in spreading classical liberal ideas. In contrast to the work of the CEP, however, LyD's efforts are focused on the daily battle over specific public policies.

In addition to our work in Chile over the past eighteen years, we have undertaken a large number of international efforts, including contributing to seminars organized by the Atlas Economic Research Foundation Network, the International Policy Network, the Hanns Seidel Foundation and the Latin American Red Liberal (Liberal Network). In the same spirit, we have helped other think tanks in Latin America to obtain support and contributed to the creation of the Fundación Internacional de la Libertad (FIL), which unites people in Ibero-America and the United States who support ideas similar to ours.

We also train young people who will continue the work of defending and promoting public policies for a free society in the future. LyD organizes seminars and workshops for young university students and professionals each year, and awards prizes for the best undergraduate and graduate papers proposing private solutions to public problems. Moreover, we have created a special program to train young Latin Americans at Libertad y Desarrollo on how to become 'intellectual entrepreneurs', so they can apply their skills after returning to their home countries.

THE BATTLE OF IDEAS

It is impossible to describe fully Libertad y Desarrollo's influence on Chilean public policies. Its first achievement was to help prevent the country from turning back the clock on the free market reforms described above and to make contributions towards the country's progress, especially in key areas such as trade and macroeconomic policies. An illustration of that progress can be seen in the Index of Economic Freedom prepared by the Fraser Institute: in 1990 Chile ranked 26th among 113 countries, while by 2005 it had risen to joint eighth among 141 countries. In the case of the Heritage Foundation Wall Street Journal Index of Economic Freedom, the country was ranked fourteenth in 1995, rising to eighth in 2008.

One of our efforts with the most significant results has been the promotion of public policies supporting macroeconomic equilibrium. Achieving low inflation, a balanced budget and a limited state has been an ongoing concern for Libertad y Desarrollo. The fact that the country has reduced annual inflation to 3 per cent in recent years is a source of great satisfaction for the institute.

Another concrete example is our ongoing effort to increase the transparency of the national budget and to monitor and evaluate public spending. Each year, a team of about ten experts is assigned to evaluate public spending proposals and to participate in the debate over the current budget bill. Progress in this area has been enormous, as shown by the increase in Chile's score from 63.0 in 1998 to 87.5 in 2006 in the World Bank's fiscal transparency indicator. (This is the transparency index included in the World Bank's assessment of governance; it ranges from 0 to 100, with a higher value indicating greater transparency.)

Despite these achievements, there have also been tax increases. For example, rates of corporate tax and value added tax have risen. There have been reductions in personal income taxes and tariffs, however. The governing coalition, which is politically center-left, would like to increase the size of the public sector and the tax burden. Nevertheless, the relative size of the state has remained roughly stable in recent years, at 20.3 per cent of GDP.

Another area of satisfaction for us is trade liberalization. When Libertad y Desarrollo was founded, Chile's average tariff level stood at approximately 15 per cent. I remember that in one of the first seminars we organized, we proposed that the tariff rate should be reduced to 5 per cent, the average rate among our trading partners at the time. This idea took hold, and the economic authorities acted unilaterally to reduce tariffs: first from 15 per cent to 11 per cent in the early 1990s and later gradually from 11 per cent to 6 per cent by the end of that decade. In addition, the democratic administration decided to seek bilateral free trade agreements with the world's leading economies. Thanks to all of these efforts, we enjoy an average tariff rate today of only 1.6 per cent, thus making Chile one of the world's most open economies. In other words, the view that free trade is an effective tool for progress has prevailed, thus permitting the development of industries that could not have been conceived of 40 years ago. Therefore, the country is now not only a leader in mineral exports, but also in salmon, fruit, wine, forestry products and capital services. Chile is also increasingly becoming an attractive destination for immigrants.

A further high-priority area for our institute has been the promotion of private sector involvement in areas where it was not present before the 1990s. For example, in 1991 we published a book describing the potential benefits of private sector participation in prison services (Libertad y Desarollo, 1993). Studies were also prepared detailing the advantages of private investment in infrastructural services. We actively endorsed the changes implemented by the administration, Congress and the private sector to significantly expand private investment in infrastructure.

Not all of the efforts in the battle of ideas have been successful. Our country has moved backwards in significant areas of our national life, including education. Our proposals to increase freedom in education – to enhance demand-side subsidies to provide parents with greater choice in their children's education, to offer adequate and timely information about the quality of services provided by each school, and to increase the autonomy of individual schools – have not been implemented. Unfortunately, the tendency in recent years has been to limit freedom of choice, increase the Ministry of Education's bureaucratic authority and centralize key decisions on educational issues. Consequently, Chile's achievements have been limited to increases in educational coverage, not in educational quality. In fact, although public spending in this sector has quadrupled, the quality of instruction has remained stagnant. This is especially distressing since the performance of our students at the international level remains poor. Our struggle to move forward in the area of human capital is directly related to this situation.

Labor market regulation is another key area in which our ideas have not prospered as we had hoped. In spite of our efforts, the most influential ideas in recent years have been socialist concepts favoring controls that serve to make the labor market more rigid. This explains why the country's unemployment rate throughout the present decade has been 9.1 per cent, compared with 7.1 per cent between 1990 and 1997.

Nevertheless, we can conclude with satisfaction that Libertad y Desarrollo has played a prominent role in demonstrating that a developing country that bases its public policies on the ideas of a free society can make impressive progress. Today, per capita income in Chile has reached US$13,700

– eight times its level in 1970. Economic growth, job creation and targeted social policies have allowed Chile to reduce the rate of extreme poverty – which affected 45.1 per cent of the population in 1987 – to 13.7 per cent in 2006.

Our experience shows that a think tank promoting the ideas of a free society can achieve success if it has the force of conviction in its ideas and assembles a qualified team of experts. If it can combine solid principles, outstanding technical quality in its research and the ability to exercise influence through wide-ranging networks, its proposals will be taken seriously within the political system. If we add to this the qualities of perseverance and communication skills, I have no doubt that it can achieve a great deal.

Today, however, we must recognize that the battle of ideas can never be conclusively won. I mention this because public policies that lean in the direction of greater state intervention have come to the fore in Chile. Gradual changes have reduced the flexibility of markets, thus limiting the opportunities for entrepreneurship among individuals to flourish. This has reduced the dynamism of the country's economic development. In fact, while the growth rate averaged 7.4 per cent between 1985 and 1995, it managed only 4.2 per cent in the ten years from 1996 to 2006. As a nation aspiring to become a fully developed country, our performance in recent years has been disappointing. It is clear that the battle of ideas is never over and that the responsibilities of Libertad y Desarrollo will be even greater in the future. The challenges of a globalized world – and of the knowledge revolution – will demand even more from us. Consequently, we are determined to continue our active engagement in the marketplace of ideas and public policies with the independence and rigor demanded by this challenge.

REFERENCES

Blundell, J. (2004), *En el combate de las ideas no se puede tomar atajos*, Caracas: CEDICE.

Büchi, H. (1993), *La transformación económica de Chile: del estatismo a la libertad económica*, Santa Fé de Bogotá, Colombia: Editorial Norma.

Couyoumdjian, J. P. (2008), 'Hiring a foreign expert', forthcoming in S. J. Peart and D. M. Levy (eds), *The Street Porter and the Philosopher: Conversations on Analytical Egalitarianism*, Ann Arbor: University of Michigan Press.

De Castro, S. (1992), El Ladrillo, Santiago, Chile: Estudios Públicos.

Larroulet, C. (1993), *Private Solutions to Public Problems*, Santiago, Chile: Libertad y Desarrollo.

Larroulet, C. (2003), 'Políticas públicas para el desarrollo', Estudios Públicos, 91.

Libertad y Desarrollo (1993), *Modernización del sistema carcelario: colaboración del sector privado*, Santiago, Chile: Libertad y Desarrollo, Paz Ciudadana Foundation.

Meller, P. and F. Larrain (1991), 'The Socialist-populist Chilean experience: 1970–1973', in R.

Dornbusch and S. Edwards (eds), *Macroeconomic of Populism in Latin America*, Chicago: National Bureau of Economic Research/University of Chicago Press, pp. 175–222.

Rosende, F. (2007), *La Escuela de Chicago: una mirada histórica a 50 años del Convenio*, Chicago-Católica, Santiago, Chile: Ediciones Universidad Católica de Chile.

Tironi, E. (2002), *El cambio está aquí*, Santiago, Chile: La Tercera-Mondadori.

Launching and Building an Effective Think Tank

Martin Ågerup
Center for Political Studies
(Denmark)

15

CHAPTER

The Center for Political Studies (CEPOS), located in Copenhagen, Denmark, began its operations in March 2005. In the early days most of its work was centered on the topics of tax policy, public consumption and public finance. These are still important core issues for CEPOS, but it has gradually expanded its activities to also include labor market policy, retirement/pension policy as well as public sector production of services such as education, health care, care of the elderly and civil liberties.

In October 2003, around 40–50 conservative and classical liberal opinion leaders in Denmark – including myself – received an email from two renowned Danish journalists, Bent Blüdnikow and Samuel Rachlin. The email asked a question: could we conceivably establish a conservative think tank in Denmark? The email also invited us to a meeting a few weeks later to discuss that question.

That email turned out to be important. Those of us who turned up for that first meeting made the decision to establish an association with the end goal of starting a free market think tank.

The board that was elected during that meeting agreed to an ambitious 'make or break' strategy. The aim was to establish a fully functioning think tank with three years of guaranteed initial funding. This seed capital was to be obtained by persuading five donors to each commit to donating the equivalent of approximately US$200,000 per year for three years. The potential donors were told that the project would only go ahead if at least five donors were identified. Otherwise, the money that had already been donated would be returned.

The fifth donor came on board in September 2004 – slightly less than a year after the initial email went out. This was an amazing achievement by the board which was led at that time by the chairman and former Conservative Minister for Defense, Bernt Johan Collet.

There were 60 applicants for the job as president of the new think tank, which had already been named Center for Political Studies (CEPOS). I was one of the applicants and was offered the job. My first day of work was 6 December 2004. I was working from home because, at that time, CEPOS did not have an office. Tapping into my network and that of board members and others sympathetic to CEPOS, I started to search for suitable employees while also working with the board to devise a strategic plan for the organization.

As the name – Center for Political Studies – indicates, it was decided early on that CEPOS was to be a think tank dedicated to analyzing policy and formulating policy proposals. It was also decided that CEPOS' main focus would be on influencing the policy debate in Denmark rather than internationally – at least initially. Thus, the aim of CEPOS became to enhance freedom and prosperity in Denmark through a system of limited government and personal and economic freedom.

A policy-oriented approach needed to be pragmatic so that CEPOS could seek incremental change in the right direction. This implied proposing or supporting 'realistic' policy proposals that could be implemented in the medium or long term as opposed to 'unrealistic' but 'ideal world' policies.

We also decided that a policy-oriented approach would imply that we should focus more on 'consequentialist' arguments which support policies that produce good outcomes rather than those from an ideological standpoint which support ethical virtues. CEPOS takes both approaches, but puts more of an emphasis on consequentialist arguments. This is because certain policy goals such as economic growth and balanced budgets have wide political acceptance, whereas many – if not all – ideas about what constitutes justice or ethical virtue are more divisive and disputed.

Tax policy can be used as an example. CEPOS has argued that a high marginal tax rate has a number of unfortunate consequences. It lowers the incentive to work longer hours, thus decreasing labor supply and economic growth. It lowers the rate of education, thus decreasing the amount of human capital formation. It makes it difficult to attract highly skilled and highly productive foreign workers, and causes a 'brain drain'. And so on. While virtually everyone agrees that such consequences are undesirable, not everyone agrees that a progressive tax system is unjust.

This does not mean that CEPOS ignores all principled, ideological or moral arguments. The best example of this is CEPOS University, which teaches free market principles to young people. CEPOS also makes principled arguments in books, blogs and opinion editorials, but rarely outside the opinion pages of the papers. It is far easier to get media attention for an analysis of the consequences of the tax system than an analysis of the moral philosophy of tax reform.

Today, CEPOS plays a significant role in the policy debate in Denmark. Figure 1 shows the quarterly advertising value of the print media mentions that CEPOS has received between the fourth quarter of 2007 through the second quarter of 2009. After that period, we stopped subscribing to this service because it got too expensive. However, as described below, our total media hits have gone up since then and it appears likely that the same can be said for our total advertising values.

The figure below shows that advertising value has been steadily increasing. In the year 2008, the value exceeded 38 million DKK (US$6.6 million). While CEPOS' budget is confidential, this figure is several times the amount of our budget for that year.

In addition to the print media advertising value is the value from numerous appearances in the electronic media.

FIGURE 1. ADVERTISING VALUE OF MEDIA MENTIONS
– PRINT MEDIA ONLY (DKK)

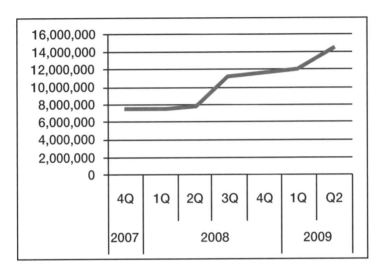

Source: Infomedia

As mentioned, the number of citations in the print media continues to increase. Looking at the number of citations in just the four main national newspapers (*Berlingske, Jyllands-Posten, Politiken* and *Børsen*) and excluding all other print media which cause an upward bias, we get an accurate picture of our development over time. In 2005, the number of citations in those four newspapers alone was 439. This grew to 606 in 2007 and 706 in 2009.

In its first year (2005), CEPOS published 21 policy papers. By 2009, the number of policy papers published had grown to 51. In addition, it produced six working papers: a new category of papers that covers new research, often at a standard that merits presentations at academic conferences and seminars and/or publications in peer- reviewed journals.CEPOS' analyses, policy proposals and its consistent presence in the media have had a significant impact on the climate of ideas, the policy debate, and on actual policy decisions in Denmark. Let me give some brief examples of these impacts.

Since its inception in 2005, CEPOS has produced a number of policy papers which have highlighted the damaging effects of high, top marginal tax rates and the benefits the reduction of the marginal tax rate would have on society. Every year, CEPOS hosts a tax conference that attracts some of the world's leading experts on the issue, including Professor Robert Barro and Nobel Prize winner Edward Prescott.

Figure 2 below shows a significant increase in the number of newspaper articles mentioning the top marginal tax rate which also coincides with the establishment of CEPOS in March 2005.

FIGURE 2: NUMBER OF NEWSPAPER CITATIONS MENTIONING THE TOP MARGINAL TAX RATE

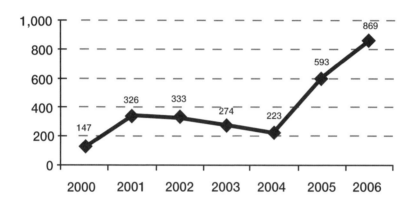

This suggests that CEPOS' focus on tax issues has had a direct effect in spurring the tax debate in Denmark.

In 2009, the tax debate culminated in a tax reform which reduced the top marginal tax rate by seven percentage points, from 63 per cent to 56 per cent.

CEPOS has recommended a freeze on public consumption growth since 2005. During its first few years, no economist, institution, organization or political party supported this proposal. Most economists argued that zero growth was impossible. CEPOS argued that continued growth was undesirable and impossible without intolerable tax hikes. In its 2010 economic recovery plan, the government included zero growth in public consumption for three years as part of its key policy goals.

During a labor market policy conference in 2006, CEPOS proposed cutting in half the four-year period during which unemployment benefits can be paid out. While this proposal did not receive any support from opinion-leaders or organizations, by 2010 it had been implemented by the government.

CEPOS was the first institution to point out that since the mid-1990s, contrary to popular belief, Denmark's economic growth and productivity growth performance has been poor compared to that of other OECD countries. The false perception that Denmark has had superior economic performance has been a major obstacle to policy reform for years. That obstacle now appears to be gone, admittedly aided by the current economic crisis.

CEPOS published a report and an article in a peer-reviewed scientific journal repudiating an estimate from the government's independent Economic Council claiming that outsourcing government activities to the private sector would yield relatively minor efficiency gains (to the tune of 2–4 billion DKK). The CEPOS estimate showed that the potentials savings were probably around 15 billion DKK.

CEPOS University started in 2006. Every semester we accept 24 of the brightest and most ambitious university students (out of approximately 60 applicants) and take them through a crash course in free market thinking and free market policies. This takes place during weekends in conjunction with their normal academic courses. CEPOS University has received accreditation from some university faculties.

I would not be surprised if in twenty years or so people equate CEPOS University with the early years of CEPOS and recognize its long-term impact on Denmark's ideological climate. As of now, approximately 200 students have taken courses through CEPOS University. Some of them are already in positions of influence: PhD students, political secretaries for high-profile Liberal and Conservative parliamentarians, elected local council politicians, parliamentary candidates, journalists or journalist interns at national media outlets, civil servants in ministries, and deputy chairmen of the youth branch of both the Liberal and the Conservative parties.

16

Advocating Free Enterprise

Alexandros Mantikas
Hellenic Leadership Institute
(Greece)

CHAPTER

Greece and many other Mediterranean countries seem to 'suffer' from a rather interesting paradox: although world-known for their entrepreneurial, free-enterprise spirit since antiquity, as manifested in a long tradition in shipping and international trade, this natural inclination somehow seems to be limited by the strong hold of an almost omnipresent and hypertrophic public sector.

It was based on the notion of facilitating dissemination of freedom ideas and thus interaction and entrepreneurial efforts – drawing from purely ideological affinities but also from personal experience – that the Hellenic Leadership Institute (HLI) came into being and embarked on a series of initiatives for the enhancement of civil society, rule of law, free enterprise, transparency and economic development.

Growing up in a family environment where both my parents and close relatives were firm believers of free enterprise ideas was the main reason I got involved with the think tank movement many years later.

My father, Marios Mantikas, was an entrepreneur for over 50 years; in fact he never worked for the public sector which he felt always hindered a man's creativity and passion for prosperity and personal growth. Working in the family business for three years when I turned twenty, I was lucky enough to experience the challenges and rewards of being part of the private sector. Besides the usual challenges that all entrepreneurs face in all parts of the planet – marketing, sales, HR, financial – Greek entrepreneurs have to face on a daily basis, the 'beast' called the public sector. This 'beast' could easily be compared to the one that Hercules faced, called Hydra, the beast that had multiple heads and the ability to grow new ones for every one cut. New taxes, the IRS, corrupt officials, to name a few, were the new heads that the public sector used to sap energy and resources in order to quench its thirst for money. I vividly recall many times when IRS officials would come for a quasi-control of the company books, only to ask for bribes a few minutes later in return for a clean report. My father never caved to these demands, and although he did pay a high price for not becoming part of this corrupt system, mostly through disappointment and stress, he showed remarkable resilience and stamina, and managed to think positively and stay energetic and creative throughout his career. Today, he is in his late '70s and retired, and he still feels blessed for making the right decision and becoming an entrepreneur against the common practice of most people of his era. You had to be a hero and fighter back then to work for the private sector, and even braver to have your own company, and I do admire him for that.

A second reason I became a free enterprise advocate was my good fortune of having relatives living in the United States. I was lucky to be able to travel there at the age of eight, and then to come back every year in the summer. Later on, from 1993 to 2000 I lived in New York, Baltimore, Maryland, and Washington DC for education and work. I received my Bachelor's degree in international business from Towson University, Maryland and an

MBA from American University in Washington DC, both with honors. I also received a scholarship to complete my Master's degree, another strong testament to free enterprise principles rewarding my hard work and efforts to excel. I then went to work in New York for two years (1999–2001) as an e-commerce analyst at one of the leading industry-providers of software and services for global-logistics execution companies at the time, Clear Cross. It was there that I experienced the benefits of the free cross-border flow of goods via Internet technology. These seven years allowed me to experience, firsthand, free enterprise at its best. I learned about the works of great free market scholars such as Milton Friedman's book, *Free to Choose*. I received a scholarship based on merit which rewarded my hard work and commitment. I was living in a society of choice where every individual was given every opportunity to reach his or her goals.

Upon my return to Greece in 2000, I joined the private sector again, and realized that despite the progress that Greek society had made over the years, the public sector was stronger and just as inflexible as before. It is a paradox, really, that when Greece became a full member of the European Union, bureaucracy became stronger than ever because of Brussels' string and its inflexible bureaucratic system. While looking for ways to fight against the 'beast' and make an impact, I was approached in 2001 by Anthony Livanios, an intellectual entrepreneur and a dear friend, who had been involved with the think tank network for over ten years, to join him and other entrepreneurs in creating an NGO (non-governmental organization) to promote freedom of choice and free enterprise ideas in Greece and the Mediterranean region. I soon became one of the founding members of the Hellenic Leadership Institute, and in 2005 I became vice-president of communications, where I was responsible for development programs in the Middle East as well as organizing conferences, roundtable discussions, networking events and fund-raising. In 2005, I also visited the Atlas Economic Research Foundation's headquarters in Arlington, Virginia: an eye-opening visit for me that introduced me to the world of international NGOs and the Atlas Economic Research Foundation's network. This experience, along with my understanding of the essence of intellectual entrepreneurs, was completed a few weeks later when I read the biography of Atlas' founder, Sir Antony Fisher. This book, which I firmly believe should become a must-read for every intellectual entrepreneur around the world, enhanced my understanding of the movement and inspired me to dedicate an even bigger part of my everyday life to promoting these ideas and looking for ways to make a difference in my country and other parts of the world.

The HLI started its work in 2001, to promote the values of democracy, civil society, free enterprise and economic development while utilizing local training, media campaigns and research as its preferred and trademark 'tools.'

The HLI has instigated and conducted development programs, which have included local training activities and various other events, such as conferences or exclusive meetings.

The institute has also focused on bringing together influential advocates of these ideas, forming the International Advisory Committee on Arab Affairs, to engage renowned personalities in the media, civil society and business sectors of the Arab world in public awareness campaigns.

Finally, we have made our first steps in publications – an area we look forward to developing – creating a quarterly newsletter, which celebrated its first anniversary in the fall of 2009.

ECONOMIC DEVELOPMENT PROGRAMS

The HLI promotes the values of free enterprise and open society, as well as international cooperation, through the planning and implementation of development programs in areas of the world where these values have not been fully embraced yet, or are seriously challenged.

Our programs are based on the principles of building local networks; initiating interaction with carefully planned conferences; facilitating transfer of know-how with capacity-building workshops; and maximizing message dissemination through media campaigns. Public-opinion research is one of our most widely used tools to gain specific knowledge for the countries and issues we work with. For the past few years, HLI has been active in the organiation, planning and implementation of successful development programs in Turkey, Serbia and Egypt.

'BUILDING LEADERSHIP' PROGRAM IN EGYPT

The 'Building Leadership' program seeks to promote the values of free enterprise, civil society, democracy and individual liberty. It focuses on the role of free enterprise and leadership development in Egypt, as a vehicle for sustainable development and democratization of the country.

Capacity-building seminars, research and media relations form the basis of the program, which aims to involve future leaders in the business, civil society and media sectors to reach a wide audience in Egypt and multiply advocates for change.

'PYRAMID' PROGRAM IN EGYPT

The Pyramid program (Pyramid I and Pyramid II) marked the beginning of a number of initiatives held in Egypt. It aimed to start discussions on civil society principles, based on a platform of common cultural heritage, which was welcome in Cairo and Alexandria. From that point on, the program evolved, engaging the media and discussing their role as active partners in promoting free enterprise, democratization and prosperity in the country.

'ENHANCING ENTREPRENEURSHIP' PROGRAM IN SERBIA

The 'Enhancing Entrepreneurship' program seeks to promote the values of free enterprise and individual liberty, the pillars of democratic society. It focuses on the role of free enterprise and leadership development in Serbia, as well as on the contribution of the mass media in advancing free enterprise as a vehicle for sustainable economic development.

The program aims to develop the leadership and communication skills of the participants through training seminars and workshops. The public awareness campaigns maximize dissemination of the core values to a wider audience in Serbia.

'YOUNG LEADERS' PROGRAM IN TURKEY

The 'Young Leaders' program enabled us to work in Turkey, cooperating with important members of the civil society network and the business and enterprise community. It was important for us to contact, train and discuss with young civil society representatives and young entrepreneurs. We focused on the role of the media in the promotion of civil society and enterprise values, and relied on research especially conducted to record and analyse the existing climate in the country.

NEWSLETTER

The HLI publishes the quarterly newsletter *HLI Communication* with regular updates on our upcoming projects and events, and recent activities and interesting developments in the NGO field, with featured articles by valued partners from civil society organizations. Our aim is to enrich this publication and expand its network of recipients in order for it to become a forum for the exchange of experiences and ideas on civil society issues.

TEMPLETON FREEDOM AWARD

In 2006, the HLI received two Atlas Economic Research Foundation Templeton Awards for its 'outstanding work in the field of international development and cooperation in the region of South Eastern Mediterranean', namely the 2006 Templeton Freedom Award and the 2006 Templeton Freedom Prize for Initiative in Public Relations. The Templeton Award is awarded to NGOs that play an active role in developing solutions to growth deficiencies and assisting the rapprochement of ethics and free enterprise. This has been a milestone in the development of the institute: a very important award for the recognition of the HLI and the promotion of its activities in international NGOs and the countries of south-east Europe.

NETWORKS

The HLI has developed a number of international partners all over the world within leading networks. Through the Atlas Economic Research Foundation network we have had valuable opportunities to cooperate with like-minded individuals and civil society organizations in various international projects. Through the Stockholm network we have had the opportunity to present our work and views in a number of articles and essays featured in various publications.

INTERNATIONAL ADVISORY COMMITTEE ON ARAB AFFAIRS

The Hellenic Leadership Institute has instigated the creation of the International Advisory Committee on Arab Affairs, which consists of selected prominent personalities in the business and media sectors of Egypt who will provide the necessary knowledge to approach the issues of free enterprise and civil society effectively. The aim of this committee is to contribute to the development of Egypt through the transfer of capacity building and education, capitalizing on the public awareness work already done in promoting the ideas of transparency and rule of law in the country. The members of this committee, leaders in their fields, also function as examples of principled leadership, facilitating HLI efforts to reach out to emerging leaders.

ADVOCATING FREE ENTERPRISE

The success of HLI activities so far has been a validation of our attitudes and beliefs: we believe in introducing free enterprise not only by training but also by example. We do believe that our way of operating itself serves as an example of free enterprise practices, and helps to show how our ideas are integrated in real life. When we approach often newly founded organizations in our areas of interest to present certain projects and establish collaboration; when we launch fund-raising campaigns and involve private companies and institutions; and when we launch media campaigns to communicate our projects and create a win-win situation for all parties involved, it is obvious that our audiences become acquainted with the ideas and practices of democracy, civil society and free enterprise and find themselves already 'supporting' them.

None of this has been easy. Our planning had to be backed with a lot of hard work, perseverance and adaptability. We had to find the proper balance between the force of our ideas and practices, and the level of acceptability in the societies we approached. We had to understand the viewpoint and experience of our target audiences, and adapt our ideas without compromising them. Our point was to be viewed as honest, unpatronising and therefore trustworthy project partners – and eventually, to be potential allies in our common quest for progress and prosperity.

As the judges of the Templeton Freedom Awards have commented, 'HLI gets the most credit for linking use of the media to social change and leadership directly to their strategic plan! They've also done an outstanding job of subtly wrapping social/policy issues into topics that are acceptable and useful in a part of the world with few free media outlets, very little public discourse, and a very thin marketplace for ideas. They've achieved remarkable visibility in credible force in a challenging region of the world for the concept of liberty'.

It is the HLI's ambition to continue and expand its work in the Mediterranean and other parts of the world through partnerships and networks. In a world where the relevance of democratization, free enterprise and civil society becomes more and more obvious, we believe that – having made a solid start these past eight years – it is important that we continue to develop our programs, improve our communication and thus enhance public discussion.

17

More than 30 Years of Fighting for Freedom and Prosperity

**Rowena Itchon and
Jason Clemens**
Pacific Research Institute
(United States)

CHAPTER

'There's no such thing as a new idea,' Mark Twain told his colleagues on an excursion to Washington DC. 'We simply take a lot of old ideas and put them into a sort of mental kaleidoscope. We give them a turn and they make new and curious combinations, but they are the same pieces of colored glass that have been in use through all the ages.'

Freedom and free markets are indeed timeless ideas, but during the 1970s they were not in vogue in the media, in academia, nor in the powerful publishing houses of New York. Someone outside those establishments had to give these proven ideas a new turn, and the Pacific Research Institute (PRI) took up the challenge. Founded in San Francisco in 1979 by Sir Antony Fisher, PRI first advanced freedom as a book publisher, providing scholars and writers of liberty with an outlet for their work.

By the early 1990s – due in part to the efforts of PRI and others – free market thinking saw a resurgence worldwide. Books and journals became widely available thanks to the innovations of the marketplace. PRI knew it couldn't rest on its laurels, and we had already seen the challenges looming ahead.

Books and journals alone could no longer keep pace with the new 24-hour news cycle. We needed a faster way to respond to the public's demand for information, a speedier way to communicate our ideas. Our answer? Transform ourselves into a think tank. Part publisher, part academia, part marketing and PR firm, PRI repositioned itself to excel in this new environment. Impressed with our response, the late Milton Friedman, an active supporter, called PRI 'one of the most innovative and effective think tanks in the world'.

New technology has enabled us to be even more effective. Today, the Internet has made it possible to obtain information with a speed and scale that no futurist could ever have predicted. Technological innovations have made it possible for almost anyone to establish a website, produce videos, and create interactive tools over the Internet. In this free-wheeling multimedia environment, PRI has been at the forefront. We have produced our own documentaries and videos, built an investigative news site, and designed online tools so that average citizens can easily access empirical data and draw their own conclusions.

These advances all build on PRI's 30-year record of policy achievement, which is perhaps most distinguished in the key area of the environment.

ENVIRONMENTAL RESEARCH

PRI was at the center of the movement to counter the widespread misperception that prosperity, progress, and free markets were enemies of the environment. Along with a handful of market-oriented groups, PRI altered the debate by proving to the world that it is the most prosperous countries that enjoy the cleanest air, the most pristine rivers, and have made the greatest strides in preserving the natural environment.

The 1992 release of *Free Market Environmentalism* by Terry L.. Anderson and Donald R. Leal was hailed as the starting point in advancing the case that economic prosperity and environmental improvement were inextricably linked. Now a classic, the book won first prize in the 1992 Sir Antony Fisher International Memorial Awards. But at the time, few efforts developed environmental indicators or reported trends in a useful way for the public and the media. PRI responded in 1995 with the *Index of Leading Environmental Indicators*, which did more than correct common environmental fallacies.

The Index took the environment out of the realm of prophecy and hysteria and brought the debate squarely into the realm of facts and information. It highlighted many measures of environmental quality and performance that have improved over time, but also showed areas where more data was needed, or where free market policies could reverse declines or accelerate improvements. The Index facilitated, indeed forced, a fact-based discourse about the state of the environment, the subject of a PRI film.

In *An Inconvenient Truth* (or *Convenient Fiction*) we took on Al Gore, Hollywood, the media, and environmental extremists. Starring PRI's own Steven Hayward, PhD, senior fellow in environmental studies, the film sorted out the sense and the nonsense on global warming. Dr Hayward surveyed the scientific evidence, called attention to the facts, and thwarted extremists' attempts to dominate the debate. *The New York Times* called the film 'the antidote to *An Inconvenient Truth*'.

HEALTH CARE

Another national issue in which PRI has held a prominent position is health care. Since joining PRI, Sally Pipes, president and CEO, has devoted much of her time to educating Americans on the problems of a government-controlled healthcare system. Her firsthand accounts of Canada's single-payer system and the enormous costs imposed on patients and citizens have informed millions of Americans.

Ms Pipes' first foray into the healthcare debate was in 1994 during the HillaryCare campaign – the first time the United States seriously considered overhauling the entire healthcare system. Her book, *Miracle Cure: How to Solve America's Healthcare Crisis and Why Canada Isn't the Answer* (2004) helped to educate Americans on the implications of importing single-payer health models into the US. Her second book, *The Top Ten Myths of American Health Care: A Citizen's Guide* was released in the middle of the national debate on ObamaCare. The book received wide acclaim and more than one million copies were downloaded from PRI's website.

While passage of ObamaCare was a setback for those committed to a market-based approach, Ms Pipes continues the fight to roll back ObamaCare. Her third book, *The Truth About ObamaCare*, was written in anticipation of the fierce debate in 2011 over the provisions of the new law. The book, like its predecessor, will outline in easy-to-read language what ObamaCare will mean to families, businesses, and the American economy, and why it will lead to shortages, increased costs, and fewer choices. But PRI's engagement in health care has not been limited to national policy.

PRI has been involved in a number of state-level debates. In 2007, for instance, California Governor Arnold Schwarzenegger pushed for increased taxes and more state spending on public health care. PRI spearheaded the opposition to this policy. *California Health Care Deforminator: Model ABX1 1* by PRI director of healthcare studies, John R. Graham, provided a strategic resource and helped avert attempts to push the state toward a single-payer healthcare system. Mr Graham also edited one of the leading books on state healthcare reform, *What States Can Do to Reform Health Care*, which serves as a handbook for legislators nationwide.

THE BENJAMIN RUSH SOCIETY

Ms Pipes' commitment to new approaches led to the founding of the Benjamin Rush Society, an organization that exposes the medical profession to alternatives to the current orthodoxy of government-provided health care. Currently, many doctors, medical researchers, and nurses have little knowledge of the contribution that free markets, innovation, and entrepreneurship has made to an American healthcare system that is second to none in the world.

Much like the 'Federalist Society', formed 25 years ago to challenge the legal profession's departure from the US Constitution's original concept of government, the Benjamin Rush Society challenges the medical profession to re-examine the current approach to medical delivery – and why it undermines the profession's commitment to the well-being of the patient.

In a little over two years, the Benjamin Rush Society has established about a dozen chapters at universities across the country and delivered debate programs at medical schools at Columbia, Harvard, George Washington, Stanford, and Texas A&M. The debates monitor opinions by tracking pre- and post-debate votes. As Ms Pipes has reminded colleagues, changing the minds of the next generation of doctors and medical professionals could very well establish the foundation for true and effective market-oriented, patient-focused healthcare reform in the future.

TORT REFORM

Another area of policy where PRI has made significant contributions is tort reform. Using the innovative approach of measuring differences between states, calculating rankings, and presenting the findings in an easily accessible format has allowed PRI to inform the public about costs and impact on the economy.

Several state legislatures have already proposed reforms based on the recommendations and analysis by PRI director of business and economics, Lawrence J. McQuillan, PhD. As recently stated by Mississippi State Representative, Greg Snowden: 'the Pacific Research Institute (PRI) is widely recognized as presenting the leading objective measures of how the enactment of specific tort reforms (or the failure to so enact) impacts the economic progress and well-being of various states.'

CALIFORNIA

PRI is also actively engaged in state-level policy research and education. Jerry Jordan, former chairman of the Federal Reserve Bank of Cleveland, noted that 'in the ten years I have been away from my native California, my one consistent source of good information and analysis of issues facing the state has been the Pacific Research Institute'.

California is a critical component of PRI's research not only due to our location but because on so many issues, California is looked on as a leader and innovator. California exports many of its policy successes – and failures – to the rest of the country. In the early 1980s this helped boost the national economy as the California tax revolt spread across America. Unfortunately, most, if not all policies from the state now weld negative effects on the nation.

More than ever, we need to fix California in order to lead the country away from debilitating and regressive public policies. Nowhere is PRI more active in state policy than in education reform.

EDUCATION REFORM

PRI's team is led by director of education studies, Lance Izumi, cited by Congressman Tom McClintock as the most effective education reformer in California's history. In a state dominated by the power of the teachers' union, PRI, through the leadership and vision of Mr Izumi, has achieved real success toward greater choice and effectiveness. The state's charter school laws (1993), for example, expressly recognized the power and achievements of school choice. In addition, a record number of education reform bills have been introduced in the state legislature over the last two years. The combination of electoral changes in 2010, coupled with the need to reform state government, may create an environment in 2011 for meaningful, lasting changes to the state's education system.

Mr Izumi's groundbreaking work on poor-performing middle-class and affluent schools led to the documentary *Not as Good as You Think: The Myth of the Middle Class School*. The film has been aired on Orange County public television more than 70 times. Sections of the film on Sweden's school choice system were also featured in *The New York Times* website. Mr Izumi, a strong proponent of film and video as a way to communicate to new generations, also appears in *Waiting for Superman*, a documentary by Academy Award-winning director Davis Guggenheim, and *Cartel*, a Moving Picture Institute film on New Jersey's school system.

In another cutting-edge project, PRI has provided parents with the ability to conduct customized online research on the districts in which their children attend school. Most parents do not have a clear or accurate picture of the funding schools receive each year. They are often misinformed about issues such as salaries and the distribution of funds but at the same time are expected to support schools through donations, local property taxes, and bond measures. PRI's California School Finance Center, developed by Vicki E. Murray, PhD, associate director of education studies, shows parents how well their own schools are doing with raising student achievement given the funding they receive. Parents can compare those results to similar school districts across the state and make informed decisions in their local communities.

CALIFORNIA PROSPERITY

The dire state of the Golden State is well known. Mindboggling deficits, unimaginably large pension and healthcare liabilities, poor public services, and high taxes have come to characterize what was, and should still be, the land of opportunity in the United States. PRI has been engaged ever more intently on California's fiscal problems.

Steve Forbes, in observing PRI's efforts said, 'Hope is on the way. Hope in the form of bold ideas for reform. Ideas based on practical reality and application of market principles to public policy. Hope based on the idea that you know how to spend your money and make choices for your family better than politicians in Sacramento. These ideas are coming from a gutsy policy center – a freedom-oriented think tank – called the Pacific Research Institute.'

PRI has launched an ambitious multi-year plan to inform Californians. *Taxifornia*, a study comparing California's tax burden and design with the other 49 states, has been widely covered across the country. More important, it is engaging Californians about the real effects of uncompetitive taxes. Indeed, policy makers increasingly recognize that California must reduce its taxes.

The California Prosperity project is a continuation of multiple efforts undertaken over the years on state fiscal issues. For example, Lawrence McQuillan was pivotal in the 2003 and 2004 review of California's Workers' Compensation system. His study, *How to Fix California's Broken Workers' Compensation System*, outlined a series of commonsense, practical reforms to make the system more effective and financially solvent while improving competitiveness. It resulted in a major overhaul of the system that has saved taxpayers billions, and restored soundness and competitiveness to the system.

While PRI achieved these economic, environmental and educational victories, we watched financially struggling daily newspapers forced to cut back on statehouse reporting and investigative journalism. Once again, PRI saw the need and responded in innovative style.

CALWATCHDOG.COM

PRI established CalWatchdog, a state news and investigative journalism website. Based in the state capital of Sacramento, CalWatchdog reports on government waste, fraud and abuse. Editor-in-chief Steven Greenhut, a prominent California journalist and former deputy editorial page editor of the *Orange County Register*, leads CalWatchdog's staff of experienced journalistic investigators.

Politicians and bureaucrats of every stripe and ideology now know that PRI's CalWatchdog is monitoring their activity and reporting it widely and objectively. As changes to the news business continue to unfold, CalWatchdog represents the frontier of news reporting and investigative journalism.

TOWARD A FREE AND PROSPEROUS FUTURE

More than 30 years after its founding, PRI continues to stand firm on its founding principles. While the modes of communication have evolved into new forms, we remain true to our mission: to ensure that the bright colors of freedom and free market ideals continue to shine on the next generations.

The path to greater prosperity and freedom is not linear, and PRI recognizes the advances and setbacks that occur in the ongoing battle for ideas. Looking back over the last three decades, however, there can be no doubt that PRI's work has made the United States a more prosperous and freer place. New and tougher challenges may be emerging, but PRI is committed to continuing the battle for a better state, country and world through continued research, education and outreach.

Opening Taxpayers' Eyes: an Uphill Battle Against Taxation in Japan

Masaru Uchiyama
Japanese for Tax Reform
(Japan)

CHAPTER

Margaret Thatcher, Britain's prime minister from 1979 to 1990, was heavily influenced by the thinking of Friedrich von Hayek. Hayek believed that economic prosperity could be achieved through a reduction in taxes, deregulation, a sound financial system and a decrease in government expenditure. In addition to Hayek, Sir Antony Fisher, who founded the Institute of Economic Affairs (UK) and the Atlas Economic Research Foundation (USA), was also a powerful catalyst for her achievements. I am profoundly grateful to the Institute of Economic Affairs for providing an institutional model for the Japanese for Tax Reform (JTR) – a foundation and grassroots organization that promotes lower taxes in Japan.

HISTORICAL REASONS FOR JAPAN'S HIGH TAX BURDEN

The growth in the size of Japan's government has its origins in Japan's democratization process. In accordance with the advice of Rudolf von Gneist of Berlin, Hirobumi Ito (Japan's first prime minister in 1885) established the Imperial Constitution in a way that prevented Congress from meddling in three areas: diplomacy, defense and the economy. Through this constitution, the Emperor became a 'demigod' and the elite bureaucrats working for the 'god' improved their standing. Dajyokan, the top bureaucrats, were able to obtain significant consular power. In 1945, the Emperor declared himself 'human' because of defeat in World War II. From this point on, bureaucratic organization became the responsibility of the person who held the highest position of authority within the government. Since the enlargement of bureaucratic growth and waste cannot be stopped, the tax burden keeps growing. The bureaucrats are also employed as board members of big companies, enabling the government to control the Japanese market. The current nominal national tax burden is 40 per cent of GDP, but the actual tax burden is much larger and is estimated to be over 60 per cent of GDP. Moreover, there are discrepancies between the government-issued data and independent studies, so the precise percentage is unknown.

LIBERTARIAN IDEAS AS A SOLUTION TO HIGH TAXES IN JAPAN

In September 1996, I organized a lecture for Grover Norquist, the president of Americans for Tax Reform (ATR). His simple message, which was rooted in libertarianism, resonated with me. A year later, while working as the chief operating officer of a small-to-medium-sized company in Gyoda City, in Saitama Prefecture, I established JTR as a vehicle for bringing those ideas to Japan as a way of addressing our large tax burden. Exactly seven years after founding JTR, I resigned from my job and dedicated myself exclusively to serving as the president of Japanese for Tax Reform. Using my retirement allowance for operating funds, I opened an office in Akasaka, Tokyo. JTR, an independent organization that does not receive any support from the government, believes in lower, simpler and fairer taxes. JTR considers this combination essential to Japan's economic revitalization, along with a limited role for the government in the economy and the promotion of economic freedoms. This is the basis of the tax-reduction movement that JTR has started. The JTR movement is a collaboration of think tanks, grassroots coalitions and educational institutions. JTR believes that the formulation of a social network to support these groups is extremely important.

CHALLENGES TO LIBERALISM IN JAPAN

Since I founded JTR in 1997, trends in the private sector, academia, the non-profit community, the media, parliament and education have been anything but supportive of liberalism. In the private sector, many large companies and members of the Federation of Economic Organizations are controlled by the central government and employ high-level government officials. In exchange for agreeing to the requests of bureaucrats, these companies receive benefits from bloated government coffers, which inflate the prices of commodities for taxpayers.

Since high-level government officials are now being criticized for accepting jobs within the private sector, they are flocking to academic positions at universities in Japan. There are numerous bureaucrat-turned-professors in Japanese universities, and these institutions are becoming increasingly dependent on government subsidies. This trend has led to an exponential increase in the number of academics known as 'Goyo Gakusha' (government scholars), who try to maintain and enlarge the vested interests of the government. Only Goyo Gakusha wield authoritarian powers and receive financial compensation as members of government consultative bodies and committees.

Of over 20,000 non-profit organizations which currently exist in Japan, 95 per cent receive funds and subsidies from the government and almost all non-profit organizations are under government control and subject to irrational taxation systems. There are many organizations that call themselves think tanks, but almost all of these think tanks are controlled by Kasumigaseki (the Japanese Central Government). Kasumigaseki controls them by providing their subsidies and human resources – there is little genuine competition.

The Ministry of Internal Affairs and Communications has the right to give approvals and issue licenses for broadcasting and reporters have to report exactly what the government announces. Moreover, the structure of bureaucratic organizations centered on Kasumigaseki diffuses into local administrative bodies. The nature of the Japanese taxation system makes local government revenues fragile. Local governments cannot operate without payouts from central government. They have very little financial autonomy and central government makes most of the decisions regarding the allocation of resources. In addition to the harmful effects of such a centralization of power, allowing government the freedom to exercise policy discretion creates economic paralysis.

Japan has a parliamentary system that consists of 480 members in the House of Representatives and 242 members in the House of Councilors. Ninety per cent of the bills proposed are government sponsored and lawmaker-initiated legislation is rare. Moreover, approximately 16 per cent of Diet lawmakers were previously administrative officers. Lawmakers preach 'small government' to taxpayers; only a few, however, sign our Taxpayers' Protection Pledge (page 167). In short, they align themselves with 'big government', which continues to increase taxes.

Compulsory education is conducted by teachers who are members of Nikkyoso – a communist trade union. While they make elementary schoolchildren learn calligraphy, composition writing and slogans, children are also indoctrinated with the idea that 'paying taxes is compulsory and that taxes make society better'.

JTR has been involved in a number of activities designed to address this situation. The following section briefly describes the most important of our initiatives before detailing the success of our Taxpayers' Protection Pledge.

SPREADING THE MESSAGE

TAX FREEDOM DAY

Tax Freedom Day is the first day of the year in which a nation as a whole has theoretically earned enough income to fund its annual tax burden. In 2008, we calculated this day to be 27 May. In addition, we also calculate the number of working days needed to generate enough tax revenues to pay for government expenditures and call it 'the day to think about the government expenditure'. In 2008, this day was 8 June. We post both of these days on our home page and in JTR News.

EDUCATIONAL LECTURES

We deliver speeches across Japan on Tax Freedom Day and throughout the year on the merits of lower taxes and smaller government. We believe that a transaction should start from the offer of 'Give me what I want, and I will give you what you want'. When both parties are satisfied with the trade, they say 'thank you'. Good trade makes people happy and can cross several borders: private, local and national. Nobody says 'thank you', however, when you pay tax. The wealth of the nation should be measured by the number of times people say 'thank you' rather than GDP. We also conduct quizzes and questionnaires via the Internet on these topics, and we are receiving a lot of feedback supporting our position of smaller government.

WEEKLY 'WEDNESDAY MEETING'

Beginning on 3 March 2004, we have held a meeting every Wednesday at JTR's offices for people who want to be free from political interference. We discuss the problems of big government and appropriate responses. These gatherings were inspired by the weekly meetings of Americans for Tax Reform.

MONTHLY STRATEGY SESSIONS WITH DIET MEMBERS

In addition to our Wednesday meetings, every month we work with the Leadership Institute Japan and the Institute of Public Accounting to sponsor 'strategy sessions' for Diet members of both chambers at the Diet Members Hall. Unfortunately, we had to suspend the strategy sessions owing to an anonymous document we received that contained defamatory statements about our activities and questioned our use of public facilities.

INTERNATIONAL MEETINGS AND PARTNERSHIPS

In July 2005, through the network of the Atlas Economic Research Foundation, we developed connections with think tanks and social entrepreneurs in a variety of countries. These connections helped to facilitate our membership of the World Taxpayers' Association and other networks. In 2007, we were awarded a Templeton Freedom Award grant from the Atlas Economic Research Foundation and gave a presentation on coalition-building at State Policy Network's Pacific-Rim Policy Conference in May 2007.

THE TAXPAYERS' PROTECTION PLEDGE

One of our most important activities is the Taxpayers' Protection Pledge. We ask incumbent lawmakers and candidates to sign a pledge that opposes any tax increases. They are also expected to maintain balanced budgets. In any democratic country, taxes are borne by taxpayers with the consent of an electoral majority. Budget deficits, however, result in a greater financial burden for future generations – children who may not have had the opportunity to consent to those taxes will be charged. No Japanese central or local governments can sustain budgets that supersede the tax revenue for more than 40 years. Unfortunately, the policy whereby taxpayers have a choice in taxes is now gone. The purpose of this pledge is to ensure that lawmakers promise voters 'small government' and that they advocate specific policies that support that objective. Once a year, on Japan's Tax Freedom Day, we publish a newsletter, JTR News, which is distributed to pledge-signers, interested individuals and potential donors. In 2007, we distributed 3,200 copies of JTR News.

The public accounting system developed by the Institute of Public Sector Accounting run by Dr Hiroshi Yoshida was crucial to this pledge process. This system helps pledge-signers to see the connection between the management of public finance and the tax burden on future generations and helps to identify the right person for making decisions about taxes. JTR asks pledge-signers to prepare an accounting statement in accordance with the accounting principles outlined by the Institute of Public Sector Accounting and the Taxpayers' Protection Pledge. The Institute's system prepares two balance sheets: the taxpayer's balance sheet and the governor's balance sheet. The public goods being provided are recorded in the taxpayer's balance sheet. The payment commitment by the governor is recorded in the liabilities of the governor's balance sheet and the source of the payment and other assets are recorded in the assets section of the governor's balance sheet. The difference between the assets and the liabilities in this balance sheet represents the future tax that will be charged to Japanese citizens.

FUKUMA CASE STUDY

The town of Fukuma in the Fukuoka Prefecture employed this system in 2002. In 1999, when the local government started the system, a taxpayer's future tax was 56,000 yen (US$467: based on an exchange rate of 120 yen to the US dollar). By 2005, it had become negative by 64,000 yen (US$533) as the budget had moved from deficit into surplus.

This proves that a capable person can maintain balanced finances. It also shows that if decisions about taxation and tax disbursement are the responsibility of an incapable person, then taxes will be utilized poorly. The Institute of Public Sector Accounting's system strives to explain this to the person in charge of taxes and encourages him to orient his daily activities in such a way that when determining taxation and tax disbursement, he strives for a balanced budget. This is analogous to the way a business manager expects an accountant to focus his daily activities on improving the company's profitability.

While JTR asks candidates who sign the Taxpayers' Protection Pledge to oppose any tax increases, this does not necessarily mean that all lawmakers have the ability to keep the pledge. This shows how valuable this accounting process is in providing accountability for pledge-signers by recording tax decisions.

EFFECTIVE POLICIES
ARE LIABLE TO MEET WITH HIGH RESISTANCE

Despite the effectiveness of this strategy in achieving JTR's goal of lower taxes, it has been met with high resistance. For example, on 10 December 2003, when asked by Tetsuya Kobayashi, a member of the prefectural assembly, about the proposal to introduce the Institute's accounting system, Kiyoshi Ueda, the governor of Saitama Prefecture, spoke favorably. Unfortunately, while this proposal would help to protect the assets of residents of the prefecture from bureaucrats who were planning to introduce new taxes, it has yet to be introduced into the assembly.

In 2005, the mayor of Ushiku City in Ibaraki Prefecture stopped employing this accounting system owing to 'political judgment', even though it had been recommended by a civic organization (loosely connected with JTR). Between 2006 and 2007, a pledge-signer, Chozo Nakagawa, mayor of Kasai City in Hyogo Prefecture, decided to employ the accounting system, but, for unrelated reasons, a no-confidence motion was submitted against him and the assembly was disbanded. Fortunately, he gained the confidence of the citizens and was re-elected. At the extraordinary session of the assembly after re-election, a budget was initially allocated before a no-confidence motion. After the session, Mayor Nakagawa learned from the section manager of finance that no budget was allocated for public accounting and that it was intentionally deleted by staff in the finance office. Despite this, Mayor Nakagawa continued to promote the system, saying: 'As an autonomous body in financial difficulties, it is more important for us to implement it ahead of other autonomous bodies by employing stringent standards that exceed those of the Ministry of Internal Affairs and Communications.'

These instances serve as evidence that useful policies are liable to be met with high resistance. Originally, this law was designed to protect the liberty of an individual from oppressive rules and restrictions by persons holding political power.

THE GOOD NEWS

In addition to these activities, I was instrumental in persuading a publisher to produce a Japanese translation of *Human Action* by Ludwig von

Mises, from the Liberty Fund version. It will be published prior to the Mont Pelerin Society meeting in Tokyo in September 2008. The Japanese translation has been out of print for many years. Professor Toshio Murata, who was a student under Mises at New York University in 1959–60, and who initially translated *Human Action* into Japanese, continues to fight for his beliefs despite old age. He is a great role model and has had a tremendous amount of influence on us.

The government's control over taxes takes away people's freedom. This should not be forgiven and should be minimized. We will continue to fight to promote this agenda and make sure taxes are simpler and lower across Japan.

19

From Small Beginnings

Madsen Pirie
Adam Smith Institute
(United Kingdom)

CHAPTER

The biggest asset of the Adam Smith Institute (ASI) – its name – happened by chance. It was 1976 when Stuart Butler, Eamonn Butler and I decided to found a think tank in the United Kingdom to innovate public policy ideas from a free market perspective. We wanted a name with worldwide recognition. We thought of calling it the Chatham Institute after the great British Prime Minister William Pitt, Earl of Chatham. That might have worked, but there already was Chatham House, dealing with foreign policy. The talk in 1976 was of America's Bicentennial, but there was another 200th birthday that same year, that of *The Wealth of Nations*, Adam Smith's seminal work on economics. So we chose 'Adam Smith Institute'- thereby unintentionally putting ourselves at the top of nearly every alphabetical list. When the media wanted a comment, they started with the 'A's at the top and called us first.

Now we had a name, but we did not have an office or any money, or anywhere to live. We guessed that if we wanted to influence policy, we would have to be based within a ten-minute walk from parliament and the main government offices.

Several problems were resolved simultaneously when a short-term lease became available on a Westminster apartment. We decided to use it as both an office and a dwelling. There were bedrooms for two of us, a living room that could double as a reception room, plus a room that could be used as an office. Unfortunately, there was no furniture, and we couldn't afford any, so we moved in onto bare floors with sleeping bags and used upturned tea chests as table and chairs. Although the place was not strictly zoned for commercial use, the apartment had previously been used as offices by no fewer than four commercial companies, so we hoped no one would mind if we were reasonably quiet and discreet. We moved in on the last day of August 1977, and the Adam Smith Institute was open for business.

I had relatives on the east coast of England who were prepared to give us some old furniture, so we hired a small van, loaded up at one house after the other, and took it on the ferry boat *Tattershall Castle* across the river Humber and thence to London. By coincidence that ferry boat is now moored at Westminster as a floating bar that we occasionally visit. We also had two electric typewriters that we had brought back with us from our time teaching at Hillsdale College, Michigan, perfectly suitable for office use. For a photocopier we rented the cheapest, single-copy Xerox machine we could find.

Told by the state-run telephone service that there was a fourteen-month wait to have a phone installed, we opted for a business line that took only fourteen days. They supplied a black, Bakelite handset with a rotary dial, designed in the 1930s. You could not buy these; you had to rent them from the Post Office (which also ran the telephone network) for £14.65 per quarter. The solution was obvious. We rewired the apartment ourselves (contrary to their rules) and used extra handsets brought back from the USA with adapters to fit UK sockets. Then we wallpapered the place ourselves, fitted curtains, and replaced the harsh fluorescent strip lights of our predecessors with something softer and more conducive to creative thought.

Our temporary solution to the problem of having no money and no backers was to run summer school courses for American students at Oxford and Cambridge. We rather grandly called this program the Adam Smith University, and took payment from students in advance, hoping to raise enough cash by the time the bills had to be paid. It was close, but it gave us cash up front and credibility at the bank, so we just made it.

The university program also enabled us to develop contacts with like-minded academics at British universities. We invited them to teach courses and in the process of developing relationships with them, most of them also ended up becoming ASI authors. Gradually we assembled a panel of scholars happy to be associated with us. We identified even more scholars by organizing weekend conferences in London on free market issues, modeled on the American courses we had seen run by the Philadelphia Society.

Money, or the lack of it, was a problem that remained with us for many years. The institute had no money with which to pay us salaries, so we had to earn it outside. I landed a job with the *Daily Mail* as a 'relief' leader writer, and went in one day a week, or whenever one of the other two leader writers went on holiday. Eamonn Butler secured a post editing the journal of the British Insurance Brokers Association. Both of these posts were part-time and could be combined with running the ASI. The other advantage was that they taught us a great deal about the media and the insurance business. Eamonn's brother Stuart had gone by now to take up a full-time post with The Heritage Foundation in Washington DC.

Things were beginning to lock into place. One of the bright young academics teaching our summer school programs, Dr John Burton, produced a paper for us on trade union power in British politics, and we had it printed and ready for publication in January 1979. That was right in the middle of the 'Winter of Discontent' when the unions paralyzed the country by opposing the Labour government's attempt to cap wage increases in the public sector. Every strike made the public angrier with both the unions and the government. The garbage collectors left Leicester Square with 30-foot high piles of hundreds of black garbage bags, and the municipal undertakers at Liverpool left the dead unburied and forced the city to resort to burial at sea. And a special mention must go to the ambulance men who, called out on strike over their radio, dropped their patient in the snow and went home.

John Burton's book, *The Trojan Horse*, introduced intelligent British opinion to the ideas of public choice and the rent-seeking behavior of labor unions. The *Daily Telegraph* saw our press release and asked to run feature articles summarizing the book on two consecutive days. The Adam Smith Institute had emerged for the first time into the public spotlight. Something else put wind into our sails, too. On 1 May 1979, the Conservatives won power in a general election, and a certain Margaret Thatcher, highly sympathetic to our cause, became prime minister.

While we maintained our academic respectability with the occasional publication on Austrian economics, we never took our eye off the ball of public policy. Our purpose was to change the way Britain was run, and to do it by pioneering policies which would make that possible in ways that could be attractive to the electorate and the political classes.

One member of parliament (MP) painstakingly gleaned for us a huge amount of information about the size and scope of the quasi-autonomous non-governmental organizations (quangos) which had a lot of power and consumed a significant amount of public funding. There were 3,068 of them, so we published the list on a single 12-foot long page which dropped out of the book as it was opened. Our aim was to dramatize their number and their growth, and we were successful.

Quango, Quango, Quango was an instant hit. The evening news on television showed 'the longest page in Britain' being printed, and nearly every paper carried a photograph of the MP, Sir Philip Holland, waving the page in front of parliament – taken, in our usual cost-conscious way, not by a professional photographer but by Eamonn with my old Zenith. By this time, the ASI had developed a house style for catchy titles in eye-catching covers and pithy press releases.

We knew that British governments often suffered 'ideas fatigue', that is, putting through part of their program in their first term, then coasting on autopilot through their second term (if they happen to win re-election). To address this issue, the ASI devised its Omega Project. We had 21 groups of five or six experts go through the responsibilities of each department of state, setting out programs of radical reform in each of them. We put a young Aberdeen graduate, Peter Young, in charge of the project.

The result was that when the Thatcher government did win re-election, we were able to bring out a series of reports with detailed proposals for each ministry. Many of the proposals involved the privatization of Britain's industries and services. Some pioneered the idea of internal markets in public services such as health and education, with power redirected from administrators into the hands of the public through their choices.

The Omega Project worked, and the government gratefully accepted hundreds of its ideas. It was quite thrilling to see a government even more radical in its second term than it had been in its first, and to watch the young people who took part in the Omega Project go on to be elected as MPs themselves, and then to become ministers to implement some of these policies.

By this time the Adam Smith Institute was a national institution, with many people supposing it had been founded by Adam Smith himself and had been running continuously for over 200 years! Members of our advisory panel appeared regularly on television, as did we, but the reality was that the ASI consisted of two directors with part-time jobs along with a gap-year student running the office. By now we were renting a small one-room office round the corner from our original apartment, but we still lived in dread of the monthly bank statements that showed the size of our overdraft.

Most outsiders probably imagined the ASI with a vast staff inhabiting some imposing corporate headquarters. The reality was that we were far smaller and more informal than that, and we kept our sense of fun and mischief. Our office rang with laughter every day – and it still does.

We accepted as many invitations as we could to speak at schools and universities, and built up a loyal following of young people. Our youth group, 'The Next Generation' (named after *Star Trek*) came to characterize our approach. It held receptions (as it continues to do, decades later) on the first Tuesday of each month, serving good wines and food, and with a ten-minute speaker timed by an alarm clock. Even cabinet ministers have to stop when the bell rings!

The ASI has always attracted young people. At our meetings, seminars and receptions, the average age is always years, even decades, younger than that of many other think tanks. And we are never short of bright youngsters joining us as interns or taking part in our activities. It helps to keep our thinking young and fresh, too, which is one reason why we are always launching so many new initiatives.

Eamonn and I have both kept one foot in the academic world, Eamonn through a series of books about economic giants such as Hayek, von Mises, Friedman and Adam Smith, and I by writing books on philosophy and logic. On the lighter side, we also co-authored a series of three popular books about IQ.

We finally got Adam Smith honored in his own country. Eamonn organized the construction and placement of a huge bronze statue of the great free market economic pioneer in one of the prime sites of Edinburgh, in the historic Royal Mile right outside St Giles' Cathedral. Supporters of Adam Smith from many countries contributed generously to bring it about. There was a big civic ceremony to unveil the statue, and it became an instant tourist attraction as Adam Smith fans from all over the world came to pay homage to the great man.

The fall of the 'Evil Empire' in 1989 was a watershed for us. It meant that we no longer had to fear that Britain might become a socialist state, as many 1970s intellectuals had wanted. After this event, we even ventured to put up our nameplate outside the office, something we were not able to do beforehand without asking for trouble! We then gradually went public with the word 'libertarian', adding it alongside our description as free market.

And now? There is no doubt that Britain still faces many problems – especially after the snooping and illiberal legislation of the recently departed but unlamented Labour government, coupled with the reckless state spending that multiplied the effects of the financial crisis for Britain (more than any other country). But we are a think tank that doesn't just think things – it does things. We are policy engineers, taking free market liberal thinking and using it to create practical policy initiatives, to change Britain and thereby provide models for the world. Today, Britain has a new coalition government actively looking for new ideas and solutions to problems, and the Adam Smith Institute is certainly going to help them; perhaps leading them more in the direction of liberty, free markets and free trade than they might originally have intended. That's what we do.

A WORLDWIDE BATTLE

20

Changing the Climate of Opinion in Turkey

Atilla Yayla
Association for Liberal Thinking
(Turkey)

Turkey does not have a strong cultural tradition of respecting individual rights, private property and free enterprise. Despite exaggerated claims that the country made a completely new start in 1923, when the Turkish republic was founded, little, if anything, changed, either culturally or in the way public authority was structured and used in social, economic, cultural and political life. The Ottoman Empire did not provide Turkey with full official and legal recognition of private property because it feared that strengthening private property holders and independent entrepreneurs could threaten the authority of the state. In addition, civil society institutions had not been aware of the need to limit the use of political authority. There were some developments in that direction during the last years of the empire, but they were interrupted by World War I and the empire disintegrated at the end of the war. When the new republic was founded, its leaders aimed to modernize and Westernize the country. This did not translate, however, into the new ruling elite establishing the rule of law, a free market economy, separation of powers, or a limited and constitutional government. The new ruling elite, in fact, attempted a social engineering project to reshape society. This is revealed by the words of the Tenth Year Anthem: 'we created 15 million youngsters at any age in ten years of the Republic'.

By the 1980s almost every intellectual believed in right or left versions of collectivism. Few believed in private property and the market economy. In the economics departments of Turkish universities, various types of collectivism and anti-market tendencies dominated the climate of opinion. The mildest form of anti-capitalist thought that existed was perhaps Keynesianism. Intellectuals believed in a strong state that would dominate society, take care of every citizen, create wealth and exercise social justice. It was almost impossible to find an article or book that defended private property, the free market economy, competition or free enterprise. The alternative was not to be a free marketeer; rather, it was fashionable to be a right-wing collectivist against left-wing collectivists or vice versa.

In the years that followed, this was bound to change. The story of the Association for Liberal Thinking (ALT) started with two young academics: Mustafa Erdogan and me. I had graduated from the Department of Economics in the Faculty of Politics at Ankara University and could be described as a right-wing socialist. Mustafa Erdogan graduated from the Law Faculty of the same university. We met in the late 1970s and by the early 1980s we had become close friends. As right-wing socialists we were unhappy, both with our ideological positions and the situation in our country. After months of debates and observations of our age group and country, we came to feel isolated and alienated from intellectual circles. We rejected the beliefs commonly held by other young people. These feelings were compounded by the fact that we exhibited a natural loathing for authority – especially arbitrary authority. We loved freedom, and this was what saved us from becoming true believers in anti-freedom. To get rid of our feelings of loneliness and to produce civilized solutions to problems created by this situation, we started reading day and night. Every day we learned something new about freedom, and we started to share these ideas with one another. This continued for several years. As the 1980s came to a close, we discovered what we believed in: individual freedom, private property, the free market economy, individual initiative and the minimal state. We then knew that we were classical liberals or libertarians.

While we were fortunate not to be alone in a country of 60 million, there were only two of us, and that was not enough. We were like a drop in the ocean, and it was crucial to change this situation. We spent the late 1980s thinking about what to do and decided to initiate an opinion movement. Eventually we got in touch with Professor Norman Barry of Buckingham University and paid him a visit in the summer of 1992. While in London, I visited the Institute of Economic Affairs and was given a scholarship to participate in the 1992 Mont Pelerin Society General Meeting in Vancouver, Canada. At that meeting, I met numerous defenders of the free market, including Milton Friedman and James Buchanan. This meeting was encouraging because I learned that our loneliness was limited to Turkey, not the rest of the world. We were inspired to go forward with our plan to defend and disseminate free market ideas under the roof of an organization.

Our group expanded by 50 per cent when Kazim Berzeg, a lawyer and long-time libertarian, discovered and joined us in the autumn of 1992. On 26 December 1992, we inaugurated our intellectual movement: the Association for Liberal Thinking. In the beginning, we had no office, no facilities and no legal status. Furthermore, at that time, it was dangerous even to use the label liberal. We had regular meetings for more than a year in a restaurant called Pigalle in the center of Ankara. Then Kazim Berzeg offered to let us use a dark and unoccupied room in his office near Pigalle as the ALT's base. He also allowed the ALT to use his phone, fax and typing machines. Shortly after this, I invited two of my talented students, Gozde Ergozen and Ozlem Caglar, to work part time for the Association. Thus the ALT had an office and communication facilities and a few months later, on 1 April 1994, it was registered and received its official status. Today, the ALT occupies two full apartments in the city center and has four full-time staff and many volunteers.

Over the years, ALT developed, step by step, into an institution. It started its publishing history with a little quarterly leaflet containing a few articles, book reviews and news items. In 1995, with a grant from the Atlas Economic Research Foundation (United States), we published our first book: F. A. Hayek's *The Road to Serfdom*. This was followed by numerous other books, and now our publications number almost 200. Liberte is the imprint for ALT's publications and they are distributed in bookshops and online at liberte.com.tr. ALT started its quarterly journal, Liberal Thought, in 1996, and over time it has become a prestigious academic journal. In 2002, we started a second quarterly economic journal, *Piyasa* (Market), but it was discontinued in 2005 to avoid splitting our readership. ALT was among the first NGOs in Turkey to have a website, and this features free market articles. We concentrated our efforts to strengthen the liberal position on electronic publishing and now publish daily commentaries from the free market perspective in a separate electronic journal, hurfikirler.com (free ideas).

To promote a tradition of classical liberal/libertarian thinking, books were indispensable to us. We had to work like an academy when training people in the ideas of liberty, because it was almost impossible for a person to hear and learn about these ideas in the faculties of Turkish universities. Since 1995 we have developed lectures on concepts such as the rule of law, individual rights, free market economics, liberal democracy and classical liberal/ libertarian philosophy. In the beginning we organized speeches every Friday evening and subsequently we have developed a series of seminars on these topics for a variety of NGOs, youth groups and political parties, which we hold in Ankara as well as other cities throughout the country. Currently, we hold regular weekend seminars under the 'Liberty School' title at our premises. These seminars are also held in numerous cities across Turkey so that they can include regional participants active in universities, NGOs, bar associations, trade chambers, business associations and local radio or television channels. Over 3,000 people have now graduated from 'Liberty School'.

Another aspect of our early activities included holding debates in different cities all over Turkey. We organized panel discussions in more than 30 cities on 'Political and Economical Liberalism', 'Islam, Civil Society and the Free Market Economy', 'Freedom of Expression' and 'Liberal Democracy'. These debates were either theoretical or addressed contemporary Turkish problems. The participation of local groups encouraged free-market organizations to expand and become centers of intellectual activism in their own area. Sometimes the local debates were enriched with weekend seminars, local TV appearances or workshops with local opinion leaders.

Apart from panel discussions, the ALT has organized almost twenty national and international symposia which served as important gatherings for interested partners. These have helped expose intellectuals, public policy experts, bureaucrats, decision makers, politicians, lawmakers and journalists to free market ideas.

The ALT, with its strategy of encouraging a classical liberal/ libertarian intellectual tradition, has helped to cultivate many young academics and thinkers. Our senior founders helped junior intellectuals in their studies and encouraged them to join academia. Today there are numerous senior classical liberal or libertarian academics and experts who can contribute to our mission. We now run an academic advisory service to help strengthen academic talents. We maintain a network of classical liberal intellectuals throughout Turkey and hold an annual 'Congress' to bring together academics, lawyers, journalists, bureaucrats, politicians, authors, free-market-oriented groups and promising young students to discuss liberal ideas. In these meetings the participants have the opportunity to meet other like-minded people and to explore areas of collaboration. People coming from all different parts of the country can feel that they are not alone in their thinking, as we were in the beginning. In addition to our annual Congress, each year the ALT holds a Freedom Dinner to bring together the defenders of liberty from all over Turkey and to reward a freedom fighter with a Freedom Award.

We have also established autonomous research centers to support independent studies and market-friendly solutions. They include centers for the study of educational policy, environmental issues, religion and liberty, and economic freedom.

From 2001 to 2003 the ALT conducted the biggest civil society project ever undertaken in Turkey. The project was on freedom of expression and was sponsored by the European Commission. It was very important for the ALT to contribute to this vital issue in Turkey, in terms of providing the theoretical principles required to strengthen legal protection. The project was very timely because at that time Turkey was in the process of meeting the Copenhagen criteria of the European Union and was engaged in some related legal reforms. The debates and the literature offered by the ALT were an important influence on the judges, public prosecutors, academics and intellectuals.

The ALT also completed a one-year project on religious freedom – another vital issue – in 2005. We brought together representatives of different Muslim and non-Muslim communities, as well as researchers and academics, to discuss relevant problems, and developed solutions based on the principles of individual rights, religious freedom, freedom of association, the rule of law and limited government. As a result of the remarkable success of this program, the ALT was awarded the Freda Utley Prize for Advancing Liberty from the Atlas Economic Research Foundation. The ALT is also very proud to have received the Templeton Institute of Excellence Award from Atlas in 2004.

The ALT has developed many international partners within the Atlas network. Through these international fellowships we receive many opportunities to collaborate with others to further develop our capacity and enhance our influence in Turkey.

Over time the activities of the ALT have expanded and gained stability. Today we concentrate on educational efforts, publishing and advising. When Professor Erdogan, Mr Berzeg and I started this intellectual movement, we never dreamed that the ALT would be so successful and influential. We have been sincere in our struggle and have desired freedom and prosperity, not only for ourselves, but for all our fellow citizens and all of humanity. Without a doubt, the strong ideas that we promote have been like a lighthouse for everyone and every group in Turkey. The classical liberal arguments we have offered have been utilized to legitimize the struggle of every individual or group whose rights have been violated. In the past fifteen years, we have advised various political parties, recommended free market economic policies to politicians and strived to improve freedom.

Throughout all this, we believed in the power of ideas. In our efforts we tried to combine professionalism with idealism. We did not seek positions in politics or bureaucracy and did not try to transform the ALT into a political movement. Instead we wanted to develop a strong movement of classical liberal/libertarian intellectuals.

While following this strategy we paid special attention to making sure that we maintained a constructive approach towards newcomers and were consistent in being comprehensive, pluralist, respectful and honest. We did not want to remain on the margins; rather, we worked hard to become an influential and 'dominant' intellectual group. We had to be a focal point for academics, media professionals, business people, university students and all other intellectuals. Since individualist thinking was so rare in Turkey, we needed to create a freedom movement to infiltrate into not only political studies and economics, but also history, literature and the arts.

We realize that we do not need to be the practitioners; as the transmitters of the ideas, however, we have to influence the politicians, bureaucrats and intellectuals. To maintain the autonomy and credibility of the ALT, we also remain alert to financial or political entanglements that could undermine ourToday the ALT has become the nation's most important intellectual movement. Without hesitation we can claim that, one day, those individuals who were brought up with the ideas that the ALT defends will run Turkey. After just fifteen years we can already see the fruits of the seeds that we have spread around the country.

21

CHAPTER

Advocating Freedom, Because Ideas Have Consequences

Rocio Guijarro Saucedo
CEDICE
(Venezuela)

In 1982, Timothy Browne (an Atlas Economic Research Foundation board member) introduced Sir Antony Fisher to Venezuelan entrepreneur Jesus Eduardo Rodriguez (CEDICE's president from 1991–1993). Mr Rodriguez was instantly fascinated with Sir Antony's work, and Sir Antony invited Mr Rodriguez to the Fraser Institute in Vancouver, Canada and to the Manhattan Institute in New York City. These visits inspired the development of the Center of Dissemination of Economic Knowledge (Centro de Divulgación del Conocimiento Economico), also known as CEDICE. When Mr Rodriguez came back to Caracas, he found out that freedom fighters Hayde Cisneros de Salas and Fernando Salas Falcon had convinced Oscar Schnell to promote free market ideas in the business community. Schnell was an important figure in Consecomercio (the Venezuelan Federation of Local Chambers of Commerce) and later became CEDICE's first chairman of the board. CEDICE was incorporated in November 1984. The inspiration from Sir Antony was crucial to this new institution in the same way that Alex Chafuen's inspiration has been in the twenty years since Sir Antony's death.

Modernism had not arrived in Venezuela as it had in most Spanish-speaking countries. It is important to remember that Western modernism was born as a consequence of four events: the decline of feudalism and its political and economic relations; religious reform; the Industrial Revolution; and the cultural and ideological revolution. These events did not transform the Spanish monarchy or any of its colonies (Latin America included), in the same way as it did in Europe and the United States.

Even now, we continue to see a mercantilist state with strong socialist ideas and vices. Tremendous wealth has been generated through natural resources, 'owned' by the government: revenues whose uses are decided by the president and executive power and which typically do not benefit the general population. Government wealth does not improve people's quality of life. Oil revenues have brought political power, with income distributed among the government's 'friends' and no accountability. Central government has been buying private enterprises with no managerial resources and no control.

In 1984, for the first time in twenty years, exchange control was imposed and the currency was devalued by more than 70 per cent. When some intellectuals started talking about economic solutions, Keynesian culture and communist ideas were dominant. The ideas in academia, the newspapers and throughout the media were oriented toward more government intervention. CEDICE's founding fathers found it to be a difficult environment to spread their ideas, so they decided to open a bookshop and convinced 40 businessmen to give them US$1,000 to start the institution.

The books arrived in early in 1985. Hayde de Salas and her assistant Rocio Guijarro started promoting them and looking for academics who would be interested in spreading the ideas about freedom. Despite the efforts of these two women, the institute experienced hard times. After a while, Hayde left for a job in the private sector and Rocio took her position as managing director. She is the only person who has been at the institute throughout its history, and has dedicated the past 25 years to battling the enemies of freedom and finding new friends to join in the fight.

Getting to know people and their work was the first challenge for the new institution. Promoting free market ideas, freedom of choice and equal opportunities to Venezuelan academics, students, entrepreneurs, businessmen, journalists, religious figures and the general public was the second challenge. Through the trial and error of using different approaches to segment the market, we were able to identify friends who supported our cause.

The first method we used was small group discussions. The groups consisted of no more than twenty people, half of them already supporters of freedom. Initially the groups consisted of academics only, but eventually included businessmen and journalists. The journalists were the most difficult to reach while the academics were the most receptive: they even started to give lessons on free market ideas. By the end of 1985, we had raised enough funds to launch a year-long program for young journalists, which has now attracted 1,300 people who have gone on to become the 'first-line warriors' against a regime that has spent the past ten years trying to impose socialism and dictatorship on the country.

Defending our values (individual freedom, free markets, property rights, equal opportunities and respect for human dignity) was the next step in CEDICE's growth. Student organizations were our target, so penetrating universities was the main goal in this program. Overall, young people have responded well: many have been CEDICE fellows and have been trying to defend values such as democracy, liberty of expression and honesty.

Since 2002, our main program has been our Property Rights Defence Program, which started with working on property rights issues with low-income people and has expanded to include rural property owners and homeowners in the city, which were both being attacked by the regime and its hordes. CEDICE's success can be attributed to the work of a team of founding members, institution members, academics, and friends, coordinated by Rocio Guijarro, whose effort, dedication, power, spirituality and kindness have been the main driver of the institution.

BATTLE AFTER BATTLE

CEDICE's life has been marked by difficulties, battles and great successes. The first challenge was to consolidate formally as an institution with our own space and identity, a participative team, a strong belief in its mission, and permanent funds for its operations. The Caracas Chamber of Commerce, currently known as the Chamber of Commerce and Industry of Caracas, is one of the oldest private sector business institutions in the country, and has been a permanent ally of the center. In 1985, its president rented an office for us for an extremely low fee, which we still occupy today.

Our Libre Iniciativa Bookshop and Oscar Schnell Library, located in our offices, are indispensable reference resources for any person interested in economic topics, public policy or liberty. People for and against classical liberalism are permanent visitors. Another difficult task facing our institute was to shake up Venezuelan public opinion with topics and ideas very new to them: why price control should be discarded, market-oriented interest rates, and the restitution of economic guarantees that were prohibited by executive-power decree in 1961.

Business associations support CEDICE's efforts in attacking these ideas and media enterprises have been our main supporters. Newspapers have been giving us space every week for articles, essays and interviews written by CEDICE staff and friends. Despite being a small organization, CEDICE has attracted a wide range of allies and intellectuals such as Emeterio Gomez, Carlos Rangel and Carlos Sabino who have contributed by writing and fighting for free market ideas. Newspapers from all over the country began asking for articles to be published and the general public began to be open to this 'new' approach. The need for new titles and written material forced CEDICE to expand its editorial work. We began by launching a series of short but concise essays (Monografias or monographs) by local or foreign figures such as F. A. Hayek, Sven Rydenfeldt, Carlos Rangel and Carlos Ball. To date, more than 100 titles have been published. We then produced *Clasicos Contemporaneos*, a collection of essays on social and economic theory. Books, magazines and short publications from CEDICE's team of experts and foreign authors are all coordinated by Rocio Guijarro, who is a member of several national and international editorial boards. These editorial works are a regular part of CEDICE's work and have contributed to creating a critical mass of material that understands the role of the free market as an instrument of integration.

FINDING LEADERS

In order to develop the institution and advance CEDICE's mission, Rocio has been expanding the institution's activities. She has developed new programs, is implementing new ideas, modernizing equipment and looking for new personnel. It was through a fellowship at the Atlas Economic Research Foundation that Rocio received training in think tank management and strategies for promoting new ideas, forums and institutes in many countries. This experience has helped her to network with like-minded foreign institutes, and with Venezuelan groups that were previously opponents but are now working together.

CEDICE has been very active in promoting public discussion on ideas through the organization of regular forums, congresses, seminars and workshops. Participants have included prominent international and national speakers, as well as members of the network of free market think tanks, of which CEDICE is a part. The work of CEDICE has made it possible for the Venezuelan community to have direct access to figures such as Sir Alan Walters, John Blundell, John Goodman, Michael Novak, Israel Kirshner, Gordon Tullock, Gary Becker, Richard Pipes, Juegen Donges and Robert Sirico. The vision and ideas they have presented have been a reflection of what happened in their countries during periods of major change. The contributions of Vitaly Naichul and Jiri Schwarz have been equally valuable in explaining what happened after the fall of the Iron Curtain during the opening up of the Soviet Union and Czechoslovakia.

These discussions have helped to educate Venezuela about contemporary economic, political and social topics and movements occurring in the world and how they are relevant to Venezuela. This includes increased public discussions on topics such as privatization, decentralization of public administration, political individualism, informal economy, leadership and citizen empowerment. In conjunction with these discussions, CEDICE has held training programs designed for students of journalism and economics and, more recently, has invited student leaders to participate in meetings and forums with classical liberal intellectuals. This training is paying off: former journalism students of CEDICE programs are now professionals who are taking advantage of opportunities to express their strong defense of freedom, their right to choose in a free economy and their commitment to a prosperous society. These journalists have also been the key factor in opposition to the Chavez regime. Our leader-training workshops have given men and women a vision of a free society and a libertarian culture, in their jobs in private enterprise, in municipal governments, business and professional associations, and as citizens of Venezuela.

Rocio and her team have been part of projects and programs such as the 'Sanitary Bureau', an initiative which has spurred hospitals to discuss how economics applies to their work. She has also initiated collaborations with the Citizen School of Venezuela, which has driven the management of citizens and the organization of individuals within urban environments. CEDICE also saw visible changes through the translation and promotion of

La Ciudad del Siglo XX, a publication from Indianapolis, Indiana, which is now the firsthand reference for many mayors in the country. She also linked innovating police chief William Bratton to the Metropolitan Caracas Council in order to enhance its efforts to fight crime and other programs with the Manhattan Institute. Rocio was also the promoter of the book *Building Consensus for a Free Venezuela*, an effort to unite the different factors opposed to the Chavez regime.

BATTLE IS MORE INTENSE

CEDICE has expanded and grown over the past 25 years, yet its daily efforts to impact Venezuelan history is not yet complete, and its performance and influence goes beyond being an institution that promotes the free market economy. CEDICE also runs the following programs: the Unit of Public Policy Analysis of the Informal Economy; the Ethics and Corporate Citizenship Center; the Center for Private Enterprise; the Country of Owner and Property Rights Center; the Health and Sanitary Bureau (now independent); the Center for Training in Free Market Ideas; the Economics for Kids and Youth program; the Publications for Freedom Unit; the Journalism Training in Free Market Ideas program; the Liberty Fund Colloquia; the Leadership Unit 'Liderazgo y Vision,' as well as a library and bookstore that includes freedom-oriented books by authors such as Hayek, Mises, Menger, Rand, Friedman and Infantino.

THE FREEDOM NETWORK

An important source of support for CEDICE's work is the network of freedom fighters around the world, including the Atlas Economic Research Foundation, Fundacion Internacional para la Libertad, Red Liberal de América Latina, the International Policy Network and the Economic Freedom of the World Project.

THE 25TH ANNIVERSARY: AN OPPORTUNITY TO DEBATE LIBERALISM VERSUS SOCIALISM IN VENEZUELA

In May 2009, CECIDE celebrated its 25th anniversary. Rocio and her team organized an international forum named 'The Latin American Challenge: freedom, democracy, property rights and fight against poverty', which brought together a marvelous selection of Latin American classical liberal intellectuals for a whole week. The forum was launched by a presentation by writer Mario Vargas Llosa, who was then followed by Plinio Apuleyo Mendoza, Jorge Quiroga, Enrique Krauze, Alvaro Vargas Llosa, Joaquin Lavin and Jorge Castañeda, Alejandro Chafuen, Gerardo Bongiovanni and Ian Vasquez. The presence of these individuals and others of equal importance resulted in the Venezuelan government creating a great controversy, including denying visitors entry into the forum and trying to block the international speakers from entering the country at airports. These angry reactions from the government resulted in journalists from all over the world coming to Venezuela with the sole purpose of knowing the regime's reasons for their actions. Their reports from the meetings, the actions of the Venezuelan regime, and Venezuelan freedom ideas made the front page of prominent newspapers all over the world.

CEDICE, now called CEDICE Libertad, is perceived as a strong democratic organization whose initiatives are publicly attacked by President Hugo Chavez and his regime. CEDICE Libertad has intensified its efforts to defend freedom in Venezuela, a society that is currently threatened by a totalitarian and socialist government.

Venezuela today has more difficulties than it did during the 1984 conflicts, and coercion, the control of autonomous powers, social differences, violence and the lack of freedom have all increased. To Rocio Guijarro, CEDICE Libertad and its officers, staff and institution members, the current challenge involves resistance to the persecution, attacks and threats. The institute's Property Rights Defense campaigns, which were designed to create awareness among citizens on the right to private property, have been censored. However, as with the 25th anniversary forum, this resistance has not only intensified the battle for freedom, but has also increased CEDICE Libertad's profile among the public. The institute's website has expanded, citizen support has increased, participation in its events has multiplied and the media have been covering its activities. The battle of ideas, tolerance and pluralism still exist, although no one would have thought that it would be so like Orwell's book, *1984*.

In conclusion, at CEDICE Libertad, we believe that even though modernism entered late into our Spanish-speaking world, there are two strong beliefs in our culture: freedom and intellectual openness. First, our societies have developed mainly against official cultures and unequal government legislation, and second, our societies have been creating their own rule of law and developing democratic ways to fight against dictatorial regimes. The Center for the Dissemination of Economic Knowledge (CEDICE) was founded in 1984 by 40 individuals who followed Sir Antony Fisher's vision and guidance. CEDICE Libertad is a non-partisan, non-profit, private association dedicated to the dissemination, research, education and promotion of philosophical, economic, political and social thinking that focuses on individual initiative, democracy, property rights and activities conducive to the better understanding of the free market system and free and responsible societies.

CEDICE Libertad carries out a series of activities and programs to meet its objectives, and its success has expanded CEDICE Libertad's presence and influence throughout Venezuela.

Freedom is Nomadic

Seyitbek Usmanov
Central Asian Free Market Institute
(Kyrgyzstan)

Kyrgyzstan has long been heralded as the bastion of democracy in Central Asia, yet this is not such a high bar given its surrounding neighbors: Uzbekistan, Tajikistan and Kazakhstan. However, Kyrgyzstan has the freest press and highest levels of freedom within civil society and among individuals. It is most likely these freedoms have allowed the people to topple two presidents, while in neighboring countries the Soviet apparatchiks are still in power.

Despite political change, the country remains in a dismal economic, political and social state. Kyrgyzstan consistently ranks among the most corrupt countries in the world in Transparency International's studies and the last in PISA's (Program for International Student Assessment) ranking of children's educational levels. Political change only happens as the result of *coups d'état*, not through the peaceful transition of power. The most recent political change process took place on the first anniversary of our institute.

HAPPY BIRTHDAY!

It was 11 p.m. on 6 April 2010. My four colleagues and I were leaving karaoke to celebrate the first birthday of the Central Asian Free Market Institute (CAFMI). It was not a typical celebration. My co-founder Mirsulzhan Namazaliev and I were on constant call with friends from the Talas region, where crowds were battling security forces to usurp the governor's office. At the same time, we heard that houses of the leaders of the opposition parties in Bishkek, the capital city, were being raided by SWAT teams. Mirsulzhan and I decided to see what was happening for ourselves and went to Vefa shopping center, adjacent to the house of Almaz Atambaev, a prominent opposition leader.

As we approached the house, crowds were standing on the streets and a small group of heavy-set people in civilian clothes (who appeared to be the police), stood on the various corners of the road. People told us that special forces had just broken into Atambaev's house and had taken him away to the building of the dreaded SNB, the successor of the KGB. Our curiosity led us to the SNB building. When we arrived, we saw people gathering at its gates. We feared that droves of security forces would soon arrive and bludgeon everyone nearby, so after five minutes, we left for home. As I lay in bed, I had a hard time imagining what tomorrow and the day after tomorrow would bring. My expectations were way off.

On 7 April, events unfolded very fast. Swarms of people descended onto the main square and on toward the White House, the presidential building in Bishkek. Sniper fire, automatic gunfire and tear gas did nothing to instill fear; people kept running to the gates. The special forces were there, trying to prevent the crowd from physically taking over the White House. As I stood there watching the scene I realized that April 7 would be 'Game Over' day for the current regime. Tomorrow would be the start of a new era. By midnight, the White House had been taken over and 84 people had lost their lives.

POST-REVOLUTIONARY OPTIMISM

As the faces of the country's new leadership came to the fore, there was a lot of hope for radical reforms. The government showed a determination to bring about reforms. Emil Umetaliev – owner of the largest tourist company, member of CAFMI's board and a long time advocate of free market economics – was selected to head the ministry of economic regulation. Among his first tasks was to call for the elimination of visa requirements for members of OECD states entering Kyrgyzstan.

CAFMI supported this measure in an open letter and prepared a policy brief on the necessity of this measure. Although we believed in abolishing visas to Kyrgyzstan for all countries, we saw this as a partial success in the fight for the free movement of people.

We hoped that this was just the first of many more free market successes to come. However, our hopes vanished because the reforms of the ministry of economy were being sidelined by other ministries. There was no cabinet-wide effort at liberalizing the economy. Emil was helpless against the other apparatchiks. The policy briefs that we prepared for him and which he forwarded to the country's leadership were dismissed as too radical. He was the lone fighter for free markets.

PEACE AND FREE MARKETS

Without free market reforms it seemed that political stability would remain a remote prospect for Kyrgyzstan. Indeed, the last five years have been the most restless period in modern Kyrgyzstan's history: two presidents have been toppled, three new constitutions adopted, and major ethnic clashes in the south of the country have taken the lives of some 3,000 people. The political tumult is a symptom of the lack of radical economic reforms within the last twenty years of independence. People are hungry and demand improvements in their living standards. Our neighbor, Kazakhstan, can provide improved living standards thanks to its vast mineral and petrodollars, while Uzbekistan and Tajikistan are simply suppressing any desire for change with an iron fist.

Since Kyrgyzstan can neither take an iron approach nor buy off time with petrodollars, there is an urgent need for economic reforms to avert political disaster and ensure peace. This is the chief ingredient for stability that Kyrgyzstan is deeply lacking. With this in mind, Mirsulzhan and I founded the Central Asian Free Market Institute in 2009.

CAFMI'S GROWTH

Although we are a young organization, just over a year old, we have shown enormous growth, and over 1,500 young people have participated in our programs. Events worth highlighting include week-long liberty camps (conducted in English and Russian), discussion seminars, a Free Market League (the largest debate tournament in Bishkek), a policy hand-book and surveys.

The life-changing event for most was the Liberty Camp for 40 intellectually-hungry youths, who stayed in a secluded, serene environment on the shores of Lake Issyk Kul. We invited international scholars Tom Palmer and Andrei Illarionov, as well as local experts Kuban Ashyrkulov and Uluk Kydyrbaev, to explain the virtues of free trade, individual freedom, and private property protection for Central Asia. In the evenings, participants debated the day's topics, thus distilling the garnered information. Our goal was for our alumni to emerge with a shift in their paradigms. Indeed, our alumni have provided us with glowing recommendations of the events. Rustam Gulov, from Hujand, Tajikistan, said, 'I learned more from this week than the four years of my legal education.'

Our camps achieved our desired results: providing a basic understanding of libertarianism and making our alumni sympathic to the cause. Some students opened free market clubs, while others interned for us and helped in our research work.

However, the outreach of our camps is limited. We want to expand the magnitude of our outreach to thousands, then tens of thousands, to impact upon the climate of ideas in Kyrgyzstan.

CAFMI'S OUTREACH

Gulmira Aidaralieva, CAFMI's program manager, attended a seminar on Promoting Liberalism Through Education at the International Academy for Leadership of the Friedrich Naumann Foundation. She learned new methods that would allow us to expand the outreach of our education programs. We are currently investing about US$5,000 on setting up the e-infrastructure for our student program, CAFMI University. CAFMI University will be accessible to everyone with an Internet connection, allowing us to educate thousands of students at a time with no additional marginal costs.

We are extremely excited about this project because it will allow us to become like a university, yet avoiding costly investments in buildings, licenses, administrative staff and full-time faculty members. Initially, we will offer basic courses on liberty, and then gradually expand to intermediate and advanced levels in different fields: economics, philosophy, politics, education and health care. There will be local course instructors, as well as international experts, working out of their offices at the Bishkek Business Club in Bishkek, Kyrgyzstan, or the Cato Institute in Washington DC, United States.

The technical infrastructure should be up and running by January 2011. The person spearheading the work will be my long-time colleague from the first days of CAFMI, Kamila Murazaeva. Kamila is responsible for the educational wing of our institute. A key benefit of having our own education system is that it will provide an audience to share our research work, which has been gathering quite a bit of momentum lately.

CAFMI'S RESEARCH

CAFMI's research provides the intellectual fodder to support the relevance of free markets and prosperity in Kyrgyzstan. The primary purpose of our research is to promote the ideas of free trade, free markets, minimal government and individual freedom. In addition, our research should increase CAFMI's reputation and recognition among Kyrgyzstan's expert community.

For this purpose our young researchers prepared a *Policy Reform Program* with the support of experienced local and foreign experts. It addresses pressing economic, social and political problems. The policy program consists of fourteen chapters, and it is the first comprehensive reform 'Bluebook' of its kind. It explains complex issues in simple terms because we want liberal ideas to be easily comprehensible to the general public.

Each chapter of the policy program is devoted to solving an issue that our country has been unable to tackle during the last twenty years, such as:
- Elimination of 'propiska' – the obligation to register place of residence
- Public private partnership (PPP)
- Reforming the education system
- Protection of private property

To facilitate reading and comparison, each chapter has the following structure:
- The ideal situation
- Problems to solve
- Ways to address the problem
- Results from reform

CAFMI is beginning to work closely with governmental institutions. We have signed a Memorandum of Understanding with the Ministry of Economic Regulation. Our work will ensure that the ministry fulfills Kyrgyzstan's obligation to the World Trade Organization (WTO), keeping them informed about changes in Kyrgyzstan's legislation that impact international trade. The work is very important because Kyrgyzstan has been a member of the WTO since 1998 (first in the Commonwealth of Independent States of former Soviet republics), and has never fulfilled its WTO obligations.

Also, we are currently working on two unique surveys on trade-related issues. The first survey seeks to estimate the economic damage of Kazakhstan's 43-day trade embargo after the April 7 revolution in Kyrgyzstan. The second survey will estimate the economic damage from the Customs Union by Kyrgyzstan's key trading partners, Russia and Kazakhstan. Once we have completed these surveys, we will provide policy recommendations on how to mitigate damage from trade embargoes as well as how to diversify Kyrgyzstan's trade partners.

THANK YOU!

The successes of CAFMI would have never been possible without the ardent support of two freedom lovers. Dr Tom G. Palmer of the Atlas Economic Research Foundation has been providing enormous (an understatement to be honest) input into our institute since day one. He gave us the idea of starting an institute when Mirsulzhan and I thought this was as likely as running two liberty camps in our first year of operation. In the end, both events miraculously materialized. Lots of miracles have happened thanks to the constant support of Tom.

Another strong supporter of CAFMI has been Sasha Tamm, who came to the modest opening of our office and has been a constant guest in Bishkek ever since. Thanks to the Friedrich Naumann Foundation, our staff have learned innovative techniques in how to educate (for example, Gulmira on e-education) and new political theories such as public-private partnership and decentralization. Most importantly, with the support of the foundation, we have organized camps, expert saloons, discussion seminars, and have opened a representative office in Tajikistan.

23

The Changed Mind is Changing the Country

Jaroslav Romanchuk
Scientific Research Mises Center
(Belarus)

CHAPTER

I was born in the USSR in a small town of 3,000 residents mostly of Polish origin. My father was an ordinary electrician, so he did a lot of odd jobs and my mother worked hard in a milk factory. The town used to be a Polish settlement but after the Ribbentrop-Molotov pact of August 1939 that triggered World War II, the Soviet Empire took it over. When I was a child I used to hear the words I could hardly understand, 'When we lived free before Soviet occupation'. Much later when I was sent to the Soviet army for two years as a conscript I heard from officers, 'Oh, you are a Pole, a potential enemy of our state. You and your compatriots should go to Siberia'.

I liked going to school. I devoured one book after another. I was leader of a school pioneer organization, captain of the volleyball team, and the winner of many contests on different school subjects (biology, physics, literature). I thought that you were born with certain things like the sun, the sky, the seasons, 'granny Lenin' and leader Leonid Brezhnev (leader of the Communist Party of the Soviet Union at that time).

The only kinds of ideas available at that time were communist ideas. But I was brought up in a Catholic family, which is why there was a kind of hybrid ideology, with some ideas borrowed both from communism and Catholicism. That is why even in childhood I was somehow confronted with a choice, either official propaganda or family values. At the same time people around me did not talk much about politics and the past. Much later I discovered that my grandfathers were sent to Siberia and did not survive. Only later I discovered that people were afraid to talk because the truth could bring you to prison or to a psychiatric clinic.

I was lucky to have great teachers both in high school and at university, and I wanted to be different and to challenge the communist environment. As a child I rebelled in a few unusual ways. People drank heavily in the Soviet countryside . So I decided not to drink and smoke at all. I was also different from the people around me as I listened to hard rock music, had long hair and did all kinds of sports. There was very little information available about the outside world. The Iron Curtain was so tight that it effectively blocked any 'unauthorized' news. My friends and I were typical victims of the Soviet brainwashing machine. We thought that we were lucky to be born in the freest country in the world.

As a teenager I began to listen to so-called 'enemy voices' over the radio ('Radio Liberty,' 'Voice of America'). They described a very different situation about the world and talked about 'wild capitalism',as well as the inhumane treatment of black people in America and poor people in Western Europe. I started asking questions and I asked them basically wherever it was possible.

With all 'A's from high school and a gold medal, I entered the Belarusian Linguistic University. I studied English and American literature, Polish and French. My first degree is in linguistics. Not a single professor in Belarus ever mentioned Ayn Rand's name. I graduated from the university on the top of the list again with all 'A's and I was proud to get a teaching job at my alma mater.

Those were the times of dramatic historic change. The Soviet Union collapsed. I took part in my first demonstrations against the August 1991 *coup d'etat* held against Mikhail Gorbachev. Being an anticommunist young man at that time I was a strong supporter of capitalism. Much later I discovered what capitalist ideology really is.

The salary at the university was about US$30 a month. That was the time of change and I changed my life. In the early 1990s I became general director of a foreign company. Essentially, I was in business. I enjoyed it and devoured the knowledge of entrepreneurship in the same way as I read my first books in my life. Those were the times of chaotic liberalism in independent Belarus. However I did not enjoy this degree of freedom for a long time. The tax police came to us and told us how harshly they planned to treat our business. Many more state bodies also began to exercise their powers over private business. In addition there were gangs of criminal groups that wanted to control every business. You were given the choice of working either for the state or for the mafia. I hated these two options. I was ready for another major change in my life. The decision to stop doing business and to take up an intellectual career came easily. By that time I had learnt one name that was the key to my intellectual career – Ayn Rand.

In 1992 I arranged 'People-to-People' tours during which Americans visited Belarus and studied life there. I met Suzanna and Charles Tomlinson, a family of private foresters from Alabama. They talked about rather controversial things such as the morality of capitalism, the benevolence of entrepreneurship and self-esteem. They later sent me *Atlas Shrugged*. I did not know the author but the recommendations were powerful and I began to read. Each page of the book increased my desire to fly high and to promote the ideas I had just discovered. The feeling was sensational. I was short of superlatives. The problem was nobody around could share my joy of intellectual discovery. Nobody had even heard of Ayn Rand, to say nothing about other libertarian thinkers I discovered later. I decided to make Rand ideas and the ideology of capitalism known in Belarus and in all of the Russian-speaking world. I ordered more and more books. Mises, Hayek, Rothbard, Friedman, Menger, Bastiat – I discovered a goldmine of ideas!

I began my intellectual crusade by joining the first think tank in Belarus – the National Center for Strategic Initiatives 'East-West'. This was the first organization in which I could really deal with ideas on a professional level. I learnt and I taught. I started writing articles and published them in Belarusian independent newspapers. At that time, I began to speak and write, principally on themes of individualism versus collectivism, and analyzing the situation in Belarus from that perspective. The reactions were interesting. One future friend of mine, who didn't know me at that time, read an article of mine and thought, 'Who is this guy? He must be 50 years old with these sort of thoughts.' When we finally met, he turned out to be something like 23, and I was only about 27.

I was determined to spread Rand's ideas and promote the ideas of capitalism. In order to do so I needed books. I ordered books from US libertarian organizations. I also discovered that another enthusiast from Saint-Petersburg translated all major Ayn Rand novels into Russian and published them. I bought most of these and gave them to intellectuals and entrepreneurs in Belarus. Later on the same person who supported the first Rand translation into Russian (Glenn Cripe) helped me to get more Rand books in the language.

My launch of libertarian ideas in Belarus almost coincided with one political event that had a far-reaching effect on our country. In 1994, due to lack of reforms and a coherent opposition, Alexander Lukashenko was elected first President. A new era of Slavic chauvinism and neo-planned economy dawned on Belarus. The person who strongly believed that the break-up of the Soviet Union was the biggest tragedy of the 20th century ruthlessly turned Belarus into a small totalitarian state. From that moment, for me, the battle of ideas was coupled with the fight for lost liberty, against another reincarnation of socialism.

The new Belarusian ruler did not care about such 'trifles' as the division of power, the rule of law, human rights, freedom of expression or private property. In November 1996, he fudged a referendum and dissolved the legally elected parliament where at that time I was a senior economist of the Commission for Economic Reforms. I could not just do 'business as usual'. My insatiable appetite to innovate in the world of ideas and to promote libertarianism took the shape of both think tank and political-party activities. In 1994 I became one of the founders of the Civic Party which in 1995–96 was part of parliament, but was then thrown out by the Belarusian dictator. People in a democratic opposition party in an authoritarian environment are not bureaucracy- and political-career-oriented but rather value-oriented. After six years of active participation in the party I became its chairman, and persuaded my colleagues to take a comprehensive libertarian platform as a party program. The access to such a network enabled me to enhance my advocacy considerably.

Since 1993 I consistently increased my presence in the independent media. In the later 1990s I even became executive director of the leading Belarusian weekly *Belorusskaya Gazeta*. Covering economic policy, business and international relations, I had a chance to explain in detail what policies are truly liberal (in the classical tradition) and why interventionism is immoral, inefficient, corrupt and therefore doomed.

In 1996 the authorities banned the activities of the think tank where I was senior fellow because it did not support the *coup d'état* staged by the authorities. In 1997 my colleagues and I decided to set up another think tank – 'Analytical Center Strategy'. That was the platform that I used to challenge the theories and ideology which underpinned communism and different forms of interventionism. I got a chance to take part in scientific conferences, to hold youth seminars, and to share the experience of transforming a centrally planned totalitarian state into a free market, democratic country.

By the end of the 20th century I had introduced thousands of libertarian books into Belarus. I found strong support among active students, university teachers and many NGOs (non-governmental organizations) which saw that we offered a real alternative to the policies of the government.

In order to increase the effectiveness of libertarian advocacy, I decided not just to criticize the current policies of the government and the European mainstream, but also to propose concrete laws, concepts and programs of economic and institutional reforms. A few areas of activities are worth mentioning.

Firstly, I devised a course of lectures called 'Foundations of capitalism' and delivered it at the European Humanities University. I constantly provided teachers and students with books, data, audio and video materials. We managed to lay the foundations of the Austrian school of economics in Belarus. Since the end of the 1990s we have trained and educated at least twenty university teachers who now spread the Austrian economic tradition and who are powerful multipliers of libertarian traditions.

Secondly, I took the initiative and authored the following draft laws and concepts: 'On budget', 'On taxation', 'On privatization', 'On social security reform', 'On pension reform', 'On administrative reform', 'On business environment reform', 'Youth platform' and 'On healthcare reform'. The innovative proposal was the 'economic constitution', which provided concrete quantitative restrictions of the size and performance of the government (general government expenditures – 30 per cent of GDP; inflation – maximum 3 per cent; zero budget deficit; general government debt – maximum 20 per cent of GDP; trade tariff – maximum 3 per cent). In 2009 some of the principles laid out in this work were integrated into free market legislation in Georgia. In late 2008 the Scientific Research Mises Center that I had set up in 2002 presented an anti-crisis program, the 'New Economic Course. First 100 Steps'. We were the first in the country to offer a comprehensive reform-package based on ideas of liberty and free market solutions. In 2009 I undertook an anti-crisis tour around Belarus (32 cities) and advocated free market reforms and freedom. I published books, working papers, brochures and leaflets on various aspects of economic policy and used the growing freedom network inside the country. We were very active during political campaigns (presidential and parliamentary elections), distributing over one million of pieces of information.

Thirdly, I find it important to network and cooperate with potential beneficiaries and stakeholders of liberty – entrepreneurs and private business. Starting in 2006, Belarusian business associations and my think tank jointly worked out the National Business Platform. It is the document that provides concrete recommendations for the government on the issues of the greatest importance for business (property rights, taxation, market entry and exit, licensing, trade regulation). The coalition of free marketers and advocates of private business interests managed to galvanize interest in comprehensive market reforms. As a result of active campaigning, the government set the goal of entering the list of the top 30 countries of the world in the Ease of Doing Business Index, designed by the World Bank. The government was forced to acknowledge openly that strategically, Belarus should move toward free market institutions and solutions.

Among the biggest victories we enjoyed as a result of our advocacy, I should mention the introduction of a flat rate of personal income tax (12 per cent). It was introduced in 2009. My campaign for a flat tax began in the late 1990s. First it was vehemently rejected by the overwhelming majority of policy makers and Belarusian economists. Gradually the idea was put on the agenda of the business community. Flat tax recommendation was included into the National Business Platform (NBP). More than 100,000 copies of the NBP were distributed each year in 2007–2009. Dozens of seminars, roundtables and business club meetings were held with national and local authorities. Finally even the authoritarian Belarusian government could not ignore the strong case for the flat tax.

Another campaign that I initiated was to abolish the legal tool, 'golden share'. It resembled the US 'eminent domain' but it was much more damaging for the national economy. The government had a right to introduce a 'golden share' into any privatized company or any company even when 99 per cent of the shares belonged to a physical entity. It was a kind of an axe that hung over the heads of any entrepreneur including foreign ones. My colleagues and I agreed with the business community to make it one of our advocacy priorities. Numerous articles, letters to the government, appeals to the president, and statements from the opposition United Democratic Forces eventually forced the government to reconsider the 'golden share'. Finally, after ten years in existence, it was abolished in 2008.

The peculiarity of free market advocacy in Belarus is that we cannot address deputies of the parliament, because the body called 'parliament' is simply appointed by the president – the elections are forged and staged with 100 per cent certainty of the result. We also cannot use public media, and television and radio in particular, because they are both under strict control of the government. Belarus is among the bottom twenty countries of the world for political and media freedom.

After more than fifteen years of campaigning I realized that libertarian ideas worked. They win the hearts and minds of the people. Even hardliners on many occasions grudgingly admitted that we were right (for example on taxation, privatization and investment, climate change). In 2008 I decided to test libertarian ideas among the general population. I ran for parliament. Unlike three previous times, the authorities registered me and let me campaign in a very limited way (no access to TV, denial to meet voters at big factories). Holding 40 pickets, distributing over 100,000 leaflets and newspapers during 40 days of active campaigning ensured my de-facto victory. Opinion polls and the real vote count (after the elections it is done by government intelligence) gave me 59 per cent of the votes in the first round. The authorities were not ready to accept such a result and officially gave me 32 per cent of the vote which was the highest of all democratic candidates for the parliament. Such a result would be impossible without a great team of like-minded libertarians and freedom fighters. I invested much of my heart and energy in the campaign and received further evidence that ordinary people support ideas of liberty if we deliver them in a friendly, simple, open-hearted manner.

And finally the books: *Atlas Shrugged* opened the world of libertarian ideas and I wanted to write not just articles but books. My colleagues and I published our first book, *National Interests of Belarus*, in 1998. Then we published one or two books a year every two years since 2006. The most important books are *Belarus: Road to the Future. Book for the Parliament* (2005), *Belarus: Transit Zone* (2009), *Belarus: Choosing Economic Future* (in Russian), *Business in Belarus: In Circle One* (2006), *Economic Constitution of the Republic of Belarus* (2008), *In Search of Economic Miracle* (2008), *Liberalism: ideology of a happy person* (2007) and *Libertarianism: Easy and Simple* (2009). I distributed my books through the large social network that covers all of the country. My contribution to the development of the

Austrian school of economics and to the wealth of libertarian ideas made our think tank a leading intellectual organization in the country and in the region. Our web site liberty-belarus.info and my blog are both the source of information and data for a growing number of people, and a discussion ground to challenge statism in ideology and interventionism in economic policy making.

Apart from political, intellectual and media activism, the Mises Center and our events are great fun and a joy to attend. I have been holding economic salons for eleven seasons. Sunday movie evenings have been held for two years. Our great project, the Language of Liberty Camp, has been a summer hit since 1999. Expert classes for in-depth analysis of the most burning issues of economic policy and transforming the economic system were held for seven years in a row. Mises center holds up to twenty weekend schools a year, and we have more applications than we can accommodate for these flagship events.Belarusian libertarians are active on the Internet. They initiate and moderate ideological debates, and launch campaigns to advocate education reform. They are active in the capital and in all the regions. They set up their own clubs, centers and circles to have intellectual fun and to share the minds and hearts of the people who will become decision-makers in our country in the near future.

One of my favorite mottos is 'Use your mind. It does not hurt!' I used my mind to change my life many times. Change is great. Change for liberty is divine. And it is irresistibly attractive to me that in the hearts of Belarusians, the desire for change and liberty is sure to come.

24

Hong Kong: Milton's *Paradise Lost*?

**Andrew Work
and Simon Lee**
Lion Rock Institute
(Hong Kong)

CHAPTER

WHY WOULD ANYONE START A WAR?

When we started the Lion Rock Institute (LRI) in 2004, we were often asked 'Why do we need a free market think tank where it is already the freest economy in the world?'

After all, as Milton Friedman once said 'if you want to see capitalism in action, go to Hong Kong.'

SO WHY START A WAR FOR
FREER MARKETS IN HONG KONG?

Hong Kong has no effective trade barriers to the movement of goods. The burden of taxation is extraordinarily low by any standard. The government and people of Hong Kong genuinely support the principle of rule of law. Hong Kong is consistently on the top of the economic freedom indexes. Capital controls are non-existent and monetary policy is sound and almost entirely beyond political control.

However, in 2003 'creeping socialism' seemed to have taken root in Hong Kong. The government post-July 2003 was driven by the urge to please a discontented public, soured on feckless decision-making in the face of two economic downturns in six years. Interest groups soon realized that public discontent created an opportunity to push for progressive policies. Serious government intrusions into the market such as minimum wage and antitrust laws were proposed, along with more technically populist moves such as taxes on plastic bags, and consumer subsidies for incandescent light bulbs were advanced.

One month before his death, in 2006, Milton Friedman authored an article 'Hong Kong Wrong' in *The Wall Street Journal*, criticising the Special Administrative Region government for abandoning positive non-interventionism – a term popularized in the 1970s to describe the government's previously hands-off approach.

It seemed that this was Milton's *Paradise Lost*. It was against this backdrop that the Lion Rock Institute was born.

A STEP BACK IN TIME: UNDERSTANDING THE HONG KONG
OF TODAY THROUGH ITS PAST

To understand how we arrived at the 2003 policy environment, one needs to take a step back.

Policy generation effected in Hong Kong did not arise from the familiar Western ecology of universities, think tanks, community groups and political parties. Far-away policy boffins in London, whether in the Home Office or British members of parliament riding their personal hobby horses, would send edicts to Hong Kong that the local administration would attempt to implement, ignore, or find a compromise between the two.

For example, turn-of-the-century hygiene edicts resulted in the British trying to raze tenement housing. The resulting riots and pushbacks saw the British abandon their efforts. Local Chinese worthies saw the underlying cause for concern as it affected the spread of disease and founded what is now the Tung Wah Hospital Group to improve hygienic standards in the community. Bans on opium trading, considered distasteful in Britain, saw up to 70 per cent of 1930s' government revenue in Hong Kong listed as 'miscellaneous' in reports back to Britain.

Some exceptions included the commitment to tackle corruption in the 1970s, resulting in a transformation of society as police powers were reduced, the civil servant risk-reward balance was changed and a ruthless anti-corruption program was executed.

Public housing was another such example and one that was to have a massive impact on how the people of Hong Kong saw the role of government.

The government has been intervening progressively and massively since the 1970s but the real starting point goes back to the public housing program in the late 1950s. Currently, half the city's population is living in government-subsidized housing, making the Hong Kong government the world's biggest landlord with over 3.5 million people in Housing Authority and Housing Society accommodation. Nations and city states alike have their peculiarly favourite form of government intervention – housing is the signature of Hong Kong's social policy.

At the beginning, public housing in Hong Kong was merely a measure to move citizens from squatter huts to dwellings of relative safety, out of concerns arising from illness, hill fires and mudslides that inflicted massive hardship – and death – on thousands of the millions of refugees from China's communist rule.

Public housing estates were built close to factories where people could find jobs. Flats were spartan and functional. Residents, especially those newly arrived from mainland China, were grateful for what the colonial government provided.

Just like all government initiatives, the public housing program eventually expanded both quantitatively and qualitatively. In the 1970s, the Home Ownership Scheme was introduced to encourage people living in public rental housing to buy apartments, at a discounted rate, to free up the rental units for the incoming population. Income from selling off these low-cost apartments then went to fund the building of more public rental housing.

As the expanded public rental housing program came into being, the city was becoming more prosperous. The colonial government imported the concept of 'satellite towns' from ambitious town-planners in London. Unfortunately, the more grandiose ambitions of emboldened bureaucrats did not match their results.

The new towns were gigantic but located farther away from where people could find jobs. Unemployment rates in these newly created districts were abnormally high, as were crime rates and other social problems. Beginning in the 1970s, public housing projects came with commercial facilities, and were managed by bureaucrats, in order to create local employment opportunities, but the dream of creating local employment clusters was never realized. For many years, gratitude for a roof over their heads and the distance of policy makers meant that the objectives of Whitehall dreamers never clashed with the reality of public housing dwellers in Hong Kong as they did in Britain.

As the transportation network became more established, social issues in new towns gradually diminished. Remaining in the collective memories of 1980s' Hong Kong residents was an illusion that public housing lifted many from poverty. People had forgotten how tortuous was the path to prosperity.

HANDOVER: THE NEW HONG KONG

As mentioned, the ecology of policy making in Hong Kong was relatively barren in 1997 and made more so by the withdrawal of professional policy makers in the UK. In its stead, special interest groups pushed their agendas on a government with no solutions. Predictably, government response to demands for 'action' meant spending public money. The reckless spending resulted in Hong Kong running deficits, an event not seen since the 1920s.

Discontent peaked in July 2003 when half a million people marched on the streets demanding change. The economy was a shambles. The city was recovering from the SARS epidemic, 9/11 and the 'dotcom' bust. People were infuriated by Article 23 – the government proposal for anti-subversion legislation. The march, while peaceful, was unprecedented in its size and emotion, with one in fourteen Hong Kong residents participating. In the following two weeks, almost 20 per cent of the cabinet resigned.

With this state of disarray prevailing, three young men began to explore options to provide policy solutions to halt the part-accidental, part-deliberate slide into socialism.

ORIGINS AND OPERATIONS: THE BEGINNING

In the beginning, the three young men sought outside help to understand the nature of policy influence and were supported through advice and support from key people at organizations such as the Fraser Institute and the Atlas Economic Research Foundation. Atlas directed LRI founders to the Mackinac Center for Public Policy who introduced us to concepts such as the Overton Window of Political Possibilities – the concept that there are a limited range of acceptable policy solutions in society – and our role was to influence that range towards productive and helpful free market solutions.

Again, remember that without an established playing field for policy advocates to play on, no one understood what we were trying to do. There was one other think tank focused on environmental issues and democratic reforms. Government policy initiatives consisted of hiring Harvard professors to launch quick studies for big bucks to produce policy solutions with no roots and ultimately no impact on actual policy implementation. The Harvard Report on Hospital Authority Reform in 1999 is a perfect example of this.

The institute quickly established some operating principles that have served to help explain to a querulous public what we were doing, how we were structured and what our aims were. It was important to explain we were not a PR firm for hire, consultant professors or foreign agents such as Greenpeace or Oxfam.

THE RULES OF ENGAGEMENT

Wars often have rules of engagement. Given the founders were almost unilaterally trying to create a novel form of policy debate (for Hong Kong), we needed to establish rules of engagement. While they are followed by many similar groups around the world, their articulation may be new to some and our local adaptations may prove a useful example to others. They are:

Policy, not people – Policy is what matters, not the people advancing it. A sound philosophical and economic underpinning for a common approach to ideas ensured intellectual honesty and prevented resorting to unproductive mudslinging. Vigorously disparaging the details of a policy proposal is encouraged; disparaging people, their motives or their backgrounds is forbidden. Indeed, today's enemy may be tomorrow's colleague when policy interests align.

Hong Kong only – An early guide to our focus kept the institute focused on its mission for change for Hong Kong policy. It also helped to keep our public image clear as thoughtful, committed, long-term thinkers. It helped us to avoid the pressure to step into issues related to China and other Asian jurisdiction issues where we have no chance of impact and a high risk of alienating Hong Kong supporters.

Economics only – We chose to keep our focus strong on economics – broadly defined. This also allowed us to avoid 'third rail' topics such as democratic structure for Hong Kong, and to avoid social causes where, for example, conservative Christians and atheist libertarians might work together with mutual respect toward common goals.

'2 x 2' prong approach – Given we knew what we would not do, how did we decide how and where to focus? Some think tanks work on influencing technical discussions in parliamentary committees, some solely on public opinion and some only operate in the shadowy side corridors of government halls. The Lion Rock Institute chose the '2 x 2' approach to changing policy direction in Hong Kong. The institute targets people at two levels and in two ways:

Policy makers and influencers -The institute directs certain reports, events and information to policy makers (senior bureaucrats, legislators, cabinet members) who have a direct impact on legislation. Policy influencers are a group of people involved in community groups, NGOs (nongovernmental organizations), business and professional organizations, and others who are directly engaged as part of a strategy to change the thinking of those who have a voice beyond their immediate circle, through their positions of influence, or well-regarded opinions.

The general public – The institute currently makes up to 40 media appearances a month (not including the Internet) to speak to the broader public about the issues currently targeted by the institute. Television, radio, print and Internet are all part of the strategy and help us to explain broad principles and specific policy positions to the people of Hong Kong. The most brilliant policy ideas will never take root among a broad and vocal population (which Hong Kong certainly has) unless care is taken to argue issues intelligently, passionately and forcefully.

THE OTHER AXIS: SPECIFIC POLICIES AND BROAD ECONOMIC EDUCATION

Specific policies are approached with policy papers, references to external research and experiences in other jurisdictions. The institute seeks specific outcomes related to specific policies.

Broad economic education is undertaken to explain the underlying principles of free market thinking to a public that may have some, none, or considerable experience with economic ideas. The best policy proposals will never be accepted if requisite understanding of underlying principles is not held. Without a basic understanding of common ideas, such as the law of unintended consequences, people may blithely accept smooth-talking populists with the latest snake-oil-lubricated government solution to their concern of the day.

One example of this approach in action includes our work on a proposed competition law.

COMPETITION LAW

Competition law had been mooted in Hong Kong for many years but seemed to take hold of government imagination in the mid-2000s. Populists were using it as a staging tool to bash elites as a vote-winning strategy, regardless of the lack of support for their economic accusations in actual economic realities. The institute launched a massive campaign targeted at the general public through op-eds in newspapers and other popular media. Policy makers in the legal sphere were reached through a cover story in Hong Kong's leading legal journal, *Hong Kong Lawyer*. This led to invitations to public debates in front of influential groups. Some even asked for our help in drafting their position papers after hearing our representatives debate competition law in public.

While much of the general public did not have the time nor inclination to listen to detailed arguments from obscure academic economists and legal theorists, they did enjoy engaging in discussions about fundamental principles of the rule of law and how competition law would fit with their notions of Hong Kong's adherence to that principle. Broad economic principles matter to the well-educated population of Hong Kong and they are willing to engage.

As the city came to understand the underlying principles against competition law and the falseness of specific cases, pressure built for the government to answer questions being raised about potential abuse of power contravening rule-of-law issues. Leaders of groups that could influence policy became more and more vocal in opposition as they came to understand how it could damage their interests. Finally, law makers had to announce they were retiring the proposal on 'technical issues'. The bell was rung and victory declared.

THE REAL, NEVER-ENDING WAR

This is one example of a small victory by a group with only a few years of history. However, governments have massive budgets supporting legions of bureaucrats who do not necessarily need to justify their jobs year to year, and can lay in wait for the coast to clear before reviving bad ideas.

Competition law seems to be making a revival and will need to be put down again. Fortunately, many groups who were ambivalent or pro-competition law now have official positions against it and are ready to revive their activity.

While the LRI has been successful in stopping the introduction of competition law and other initiatives like the Goods and Services Tax (GST), at some point, greater operational capabilities will be necessary to tackle fundamental issues holding Hong Kong back – such as the aforementioned housing situation.

To reform a public housing system with over 3.5 million people will require a broad campaign to inform the public about how it hurts their interests (no legacy for their children, powerlessness in choosing where they live). The campaign will explain to policy influencers how changing the system will not result in chaos and how it can move Hong Kong forward, with extensive research in Hong Kong's specific situation and a broad understanding of its principles. It will transform a mythology of government intervention into an understanding of how it held our city back. Such a campaign of research and education would hopefully transform 3.5 million government wards into millions of property owners and their inheritors.

That's a war worth fighting.

25

Planting Freedom in the Ashes of a Failed Communist Experiment

Veselin Vukotic
Institute for Strategic
Studies and Prognoses
(Montenegro)

The Institute for Strategic Studies and Prognoses (1998) and the private University UDG (2007) are two institutions in Montenegro that I created with my close associates as a result of my own idea.

How was the idea born, and what is the essence behind the idea? Institutions have always been created as a result of an individual's idea (more often than a collective idea) and concrete historical circumstances (the spirit of the time). Individual ideas seek the market, but also create the market for their realization in concrete life and historical situations. The development of an institution is an indicator of the maturity of the idea behind it. Thus, in order to understand the nature of an institution, one needs to understand its driving force – the idea behind it as well as its roots. My experience taught me that liberalism is sustainable only if you continuously develop new ideas and create innovations. An idea is the most valuable currency in the free market world.

Two events from my childhood might have provoked my unconventional understanding of the world. I was born into a politically tormented family, which caused people to look at us differently and constrained our freedom. I had a different view on the official Communist Party postulate which assumed that all people live in justice and equality. The other important event that shaped my way of thinking was in the form of an answer from my neighbor to my question of why he sold all his land (his main source of income). 'I need money to pay my son's school!' he said. This was a shock for me. I thought, 'If you want to succeed – read. Be yourself. You have to think differently from the masses and you have to fight!' As time passed, I was growing and becoming more mature. I realized that the way of thinking for every individual – the way we understand common, everyday events – is the key to our life and our success. A person's way of thinking is their lighthouse. The problem arises when that lighthouse is placed in the wrong direction. In order to succeed, the mental lighthouse must be in the right place.

Shortly after, while I was a student, I started to notice that my colleagues did not see or understand the nonsense embodied in the behavior of people in universities and in society. At the time, one of my older colleagues started a student newspaper and, as a first-year student, I became a part of the editorial staff. I thought that our writing would change people. What a delusion – these activities branded us as 'revolutionaries' and we were threatened with trial and imprisonment!

At that time, my experience had already made me realize that a certain group of people with a similar view of the world must spread their ideas. As an assistant professor at the State University of Montenegro, I started the institution named the 'University Tribune', a form of political work allowed by the Communist Party. Around 50 students were involved in the roundtable discussions that we organized and 500–800 students participated in public debates, to which we invited well-known Yugoslav intellectuals to be our guest-speakers. Young people involved in the activities of the University Tribune became key figures in the political scene in Montenegro in the last two decades. After Yugoslavia crashed, this group fell apart as well.

In the meantime, I was a member of the government of Montenegro (1986–1989) and a member of the last Federal Government of Yugoslavia (1989–1992). In the federal government, as a minister responsible for privatization and entrepreneurship, I had extensive communication with people from Western countries, especially with Professor Steve Pejovich. The reform concept pushed by the federal government soon failed, Yugoslavia fell apart and the terrible era of nationalism started. I came back to the State University and founded a postgraduate studies' program in entrepreneurial economics. As the dean of entrepreneurial economics I got the same freedom and privileges that I would have as the dean at a private university. This was my silent agreement with the authorities not to enter politics. I had all the independence I needed in creating the program and selecting the lecturers, and the studies were financed by student tuition fees, not the state budget. These studies were the first program that the University of Montenegro students paid for, and the first program conducted in English. Experience taught me that the madness of war would end and I knew then we would need people fluent in free market ideas and with knowledge of foreign languages.

The postgraduate studies' program in entrepreneurial economics is theoretically based on the Austrian school of economics, but also respects the culture, tradition and informal rules that exist in Montenegro. Many famous professors from the region and abroad have lectured in the program. We received enormous help from four great professors: Steve Pejovich, Enrico Colombatto, John Moore and Leonard Liggio. Although it was a time of war and hyperinflation, we had a solid start.

In order to spread free market ideas invisibly, we also founded the institution: 'Christmas Discussions on Economics'. The discussions are held on Christmas Eve (6 January in the Eastern Orthodox religion) and they start at 9 p.m. and finish around 4 a.m. The discussions are still being organized by the entrepreneurial economics program and they attract 300–400 participants. This institution gave birth to many important ideas, one of which was the foundation of G-17, a group of Yugoslav economists who would spread free market ideas. This group also created an economic platform for the well-known student demonstrations that began in Belgrade in 1996.

At that time, the movement for independent Montenegro and its separation from Serbia started to grow. In 1998, the ruling coalition split into two parts, and the pro-independence wing won the following elections. This wing was and still is headed by Mr Milo Djukanovic, my former student, who entered politics through the University Tribune in 1980. He understands the importance of the free market spirit, private property and its protection, and the openness of the economy. However, achieving political and state independence for Montenegro was his primary goal. The attitude of the international community toward Montenegro as part of Yugoslavia (Serbia and Montenegro) was changing. At the end of 1997, after almost ten years of isolation, a high-level US delegation visited Montenegro for three to four days. Government officials told me that the delegation wanted to meet with me and were asking me to join the government. 'No,' I said, 'If they want to talk to me, they should come to the university.' As a result, the seven-member delegation came and met with myself and a few of my associates for three hours. They were surprised by our free market logic and our view on Montenegrin economic problems and solutions. It differed significantly from that of the people they had previously talked to. After three hours the head of the delegation started to thank us for our time and I said, 'No, we are not finished – I have a question for you', and I presented to them the idea for our mini-project: the development of the Institute for Strategic Studies and Prognoses (ISSP). I elaborated on the idea and we had a long discussion about it. As a result of these conversations, we founded the ISSP and applied for the grant. At that time, the ISSP functioned in a rented apartment and the staff consisted of three recent graduates and a few post-graduate students.

In the meantime, in the political realm, we successfully explained that the idea of economic liberalism, free market economy, and the national treatment of foreigners are not only the key driving forces of Montenegro's development, but also the cornerstones of our independence from Yugoslavia, since Yugoslavia was founded on the postulates of state property and interventionism. A better quality of life for every individual was possible only if we turned to markets and free trade, and only if we turned to private property and foreign investments. The struggle for political and state independence would be meaningful only if citizens realized that it would bring them a better quality of life. This was the time when our post-graduate students were starting to become key figures in society.

During the period from 1998 to 2006, when independence was regained, the ISSP, with the assistance of foreign experts, developed all the relevant economic policy documents in Montenegro. My book, the *Conceptual Basis of the New Economic System in Montenegro*, was the starting point and the foundation for the government's economic policy, and also served as the platform for political negotiations in the relations between Montenegro and Serbia. At the same time, we were also reforming the customs system which led to the decrease of average tariff rates from approximately 30 per cent to 2.9 per cent. Montenegro abolished visas for foreigners. The ISSP worked on the project named 'Privatization in Montenegro', which was theoretically founded on the principle that any economic entity can be privatized and that it should be done as soon as possible. In a few years, around 80 per cent of Montenegro's economy was privatized. It was the students of the post-graduate studies' program in entrepreneurial economics who carried out this process. The ISSP published a monthly economic journal, *Montenegro Economic Trends – MONET*, which spread free market ideas in public.

The ISSP also initiated the debate on the change of the official Montenegrin currency. In 1999, after long discussions, the ISSP's proposal to replace the official currency (Yugoslav dinar) with the Deutschmark was accepted and implemented (the Deutschmark was replaced by the euro in 2002). Even though Montenegro is not part of the European Union, we still use the euro as the official currency. The ISSP successfully carried out expert discussions in Brussels which aimed to prove that Montenegro needed to keep the euro as its official currency. In our opinion, the introduction of the euro was of historical importance for the development of Montenegro. The introduction of the Deutschmark/euro brought economic sovereignty to the country and thus laid the foundations for political independence. I firmly believed that Montenegro would never have become independent without the introduction of the euro. As with the founding fathers' creation of the United States, Montenegro is an example of a country where liberalism has brought political and state sovereignty.

The results of a survey conducted at the end of 2000, the period of the strongest political divisions in Montenegro, showed how crucial the currency has been in waking up individual rationality and personal interests. The question about future relations between Montenegro and Serbia was being discussed at that time and prevailing opinion held that Montenegro should remain with Serbia. Despite this, when we asked about the currency and whether they wanted to bring back the Yugoslav dinar as official tender or to keep the Deutschmark, around 86 per cent of respondents said they wanted to keep using the Deutschmark. When, among other things, an individual feels personal sovereignty through a strong currency, then political independence is just one step ahead. True to what Mises wrote, 'Money is the measure of personal sovereignty', that is the message from Montenegro's experience.

The ISSP team works on many projects. The most important one is the implementation of our concept, 'Montenegro – micro-state'. Essentially, the idea is based on the reduction of government administration; that is, decreasing the government to only five ministries (instead of today's twenty); reducing the presidential political system; making English the official language; abolishing conscription; and opening up the economy to free markets. The concept 'Montenegro – micro-state' was discussed at an international conference with around 200 participants, including distinguished speakers such as Richard Rahn, Dan Mitchell and Mart Laar. A large public campaign against both the ISSP and myself started. This was supported mainly by 'experts' from the European Union in Montenegro. This campaign, along with the difficult and unpleasant discussions about the euro, and the opposition to the European Union's idea to abandon the euro as legal currency, are the reasons for the cold relations that still exist between Montenegro and the European Union. The concept of the micro-state has not been accepted, but it is alive. Discussions about this concept undermined the prevailing thought that the state is from God and that the state is God. This opened the door to other ideas about liberalism.

After Milosevic was overthrown in Serbia (2000), Europe started discussing the idea of an independent Montenegro. This began a time of bitter debates, which aimed to prove that Montenegro should finally take over the responsibility for its own destiny and development. The ISSP worked on many studies, including one entitled, 'Construction Mistakes of the Federation', which had special importance and served as the platform for negotiations. ISSP members and associates presented results from the analysis and the surveys in public, which was hazardous at the time, but could be considered as an act of personal courage.

We worked on other projects such as tax reform and pension-system reform. The ISSP coordinated the work on the Agenda of Economic Reforms 2002–06 and the Agenda of Economic Reforms 2002-07. We proposed the Agenda of Economic Reforms 2007–11, which contained the outlook for the Montenegrin economy and society until 2025. After minor changes, these were adopted as official government documents.

Until Montenegro's independence in 2006, the ISSP had been the key institution that gathered together all relevant foreign economic consultants. It has always been, and still is, the source of young, successful professionals and many ISSP researchers cover important positions in Montenegro, including serving as government ministers. In addition, around 250 graduates from our postgraduate studies' program on entrepreneurial economics, now hold important positions in areas such as business and politics, and promote free market ideas. All this time, the ISSP received no donations or money from the government of Montenegro and we remained independent from government, despite our close cooperation on projects. The acceptance and implementation of our ideas were the highest 'earnings' and recognition we would receive!

The referendum on Montenegro's independence took place on 21 May 2006 and 55.5 per cent of the vote was for independence. Earlier, the European Union had made the requirement that at least 55 per cent of the votes had to be in the affirmative in order to recognize the results.

The ISSP is still the most important research institution in Montenegro, and is now managed by young people who have received professional experience at the institute. Our goal is to strengthen the research function and human capital of the institute farther, and to aim to develop professional, economic research. The ISSP generates its revenue from its projects and we cooperate with many international research organizations.

Achievement of a certain goal, such as independence of the country where you were born and live, represents an ideal opportunity to make a new turn in life and to realize a new idea: an idea that promotes the development of free markets, free trade, private property and the protection of contracts.

Thus, I started to implement the idea I have had since I founded the postgraduate studies' program in entrepreneurial economics. Since postgraduate studies played such an important role in educating the people who have carried out these ideas, I had the idea of starting a private university. I ended up founding the university with a colleague of mine from the State University, Professor Dragan Vukcevic. The implementation of the idea started with the construction of a 17,000m^2 building, which now provides conditions comparable to those of most modern Western universities. The building is six kilometers away from the center of Podgorica and is located in the growing business district. The university is called the UDG and it is becoming very popular among young people. It is widely recognized through the sentence 'Ah, they're the liberals...' Today, two years after opening the university, we have educated 1,500 students within our five schools (School for International Economics, School of Finance and Business, Law School, School for Information Systems and Technologies, Humanities Studies and the School of Arts).

The UDG is financed solely by the market; we generate our revenues primarily from tuition fees and our students do not receive education vouchers from the state. At this time, when the majority blames free markets (economic liberalism) for the current crisis, we are facing severe criticism from interventionists and social democrats. Despite this, this year we enrolled 20 per cent more students than last year. While most of our students are from Montenegro, we also have students from other regions, including Nigeria and Egypt.

The school year starts on 4 July (Celebration of Victory Day in Montenegro) with the race on Mount Lovcen, which, among other things, is famous for the mausoleum dedicated to the greatest Montenegrin poet, Njegos. Traditionally, the first lecture is also held on the top of Mount Lovcen. Lovcen is the symbol of freedom and Njegos had been accused of being a liberal in the early 19th century. Therefore all of this is immensely symbolic!

If the ISSP and the postgraduate studies' program in entrepreneurial economics have been created in order to develop free market ideas and economic liberalism aimed at bringing state independence to Montenegro, then the cornerstone of the UDG is to integrate Montenegro into the global markets. The essence of this idea is to understand how people from Montenegro can use opportunities from the global marketplace in order to achieve a better quality of life.

Entering the private sector was personally challenging for me as well: my whole life I have been fighting for private property, while also earning my salary from the government as a professor at the State University! Now I can say that no matter how hard I fought for free markets, private property and entrepreneurship in the past, I've realized that earning 100 per cent of my salary through the market alone is much more difficult than I expected. Now I have a better understanding of why people fear the market, especially if they have the option of earning their income from the state budget. At the same time, I don't have a strong belief in people who fight for liberalism from expensive offices and who are not engaged in the market!

The idea of the UDG is being implemented. I hope that the young generation will accept it and continue to develop it in the decades to follow.

I still have two big unrealized ideas, born under the influence of the UDG. I plan to achieve them since I hope to live longer than my grandmother who died after she turned 107. Although the belief in spontaneous free market forces is the philosophy of my life, as time passes I have started to believe in genetic determinism as well!

26

Promoting Free Markets in Africa

Franklin Cudjoe
IMANI: The Center for
Policy and Education
(Ghana)

The quest to be an intellectual entrepreneur within a climate consumed by poverty, patronage and dependency, can be a very tough one. The tools to fight these ills are non-existent in our institutions of higher learning. Discarded theories of economic development or half-baked measures mired in statism were the norm for many students of economics. Such was the cross that I had to bear when I decided to tread the path of enlightened inquiry into understanding why, despite being blessed with physical and human resources, my country and continent were poor. What were elected governments to do, I asked? Didn't we install governments to guarantee our freedom from poverty, disease and ignorance?

Even though I erroneously argued for strong government intervention in building the assets of the poor, I realized much later, that to enhance freedom from poverty, governments must ensure a reduction in risk for private investors. They should do this through stable monetary and fiscal policy, stable investment regimes and a clear and transparent business environment backed by the rule of law and decentralized decision-making processes.

My mother's ordeal in getting a loan of US$150 as start-up capital from a moneylender seventeen years ago illustrates how a heavily regulated financial sector was a barrier to progress. My mother's business could only thrive after a decade of progressive financial liberalization when Ghana's economic books began reflecting a favorable balance of payments with a wider access to quasi venture funds.

My curiosity for unraveling other myths surrounding the government's invincibility at solving problems continued to grow. Reading recommendations from my good friend Nick Slepko, a Rotary Ambassadorial Scholar whom I met at a student symposium in Switzerland, as well as Jo Kwong of the Atlas Economic Research Foundation, and Linda Whetstone and Julian Morris of the International Policy Network, helped a lot. Thomas Sowell's *Knowledge and Decisions*, and Hayek's *Use of Knowledge in Society* and *The Road to Serfdom* were significant eye-openers for me.

Thomas Sowell taught me that all human institutions needed an authentication of the knowledge process since ideas are everywhere, but true knowledge is rare. Hayek's *Use of Knowledge* taught me that the knowledge we must utilize is not the exclusive domain of any one or group, but rather 'the dispersed bits of incomplete and frequently contradictory knowledge which all the separate individuals possess.' To which the transmission of this information occurs spontaneously, enticing the individual while seeking his or her own interest and doing what is in the general interest.

My understanding of Hayek, is that economics is a dynamic discipline because the concept of scarcity, its central problem, is weakened through the use of knowledge in freely allocating resources, rather than the statist view of resource coordination by 'all-knowing' central planners to address the question of resource allocation. And by extension, I realised how fatuous an argument it was that corporations put profits before people. Apart from asking where the money should come from, I was well aware of how dysfunctional and moribund Ghana's state-owned enterprises had become, even the few of them that were recuperating after heavy doses of private capital. These topics became the platform for all my media and speaking appearances.

However, I realized how comforting and costly it could be for one to rest on defeating a few vacuous philosophies. I was emboldened by the admonition that the only way to keep liberty's foes at bay was by giving meaning to John Blundell's summary of Hayek's advice in *Waging the War of Ideas.* That is, that one should 'Keep liberal thought relevant and vibrant; recognize the importance of history; be principled and steadfast; avoid special interests; eschew politics and instead search for leverage; recognize the critical role of the intellectual; and be Utopian and believe in the power of ideas'.

This was the signal that launched the birth of my think tank, IMANI: The Center for Policy & Education. IMANI was born out of the desire to create a springboard for generating and spreading workable ideas for a free and prosperous society with a mission to stimulate public discussion. This is what transformed IMANI into one of the most influential think tanks in Africa. IMANI has undergone remarkable growth since its inception barely five years ago, and has today achieved a stature that, in many ways, is truly astounding.

IMANI's competitors in Ghana are, on average, more than four times older, with extensive networks across governmental and corporate circles, which give them a pedigree born of the privilege that such access endows. It is therefore fascinating that IMANI is frequently cited in the same leagues as the most prestigious of these institutions. A weekly media citation index housed within IMANI shows that since May 2008, IMANI has been ranked number one among Ghanaian institutions for 'Web-presence' and number two when it comes to citations in the print press. Its profile in the broadcast media has also improved dramatically in recent times. Considering the resources available to these older institutions, IMANI's higher public profile constitutes a remarkable feat.

Over the course of the past four years here in Ghana, IMANI has consistently raised the level and quality of debate and discourse in the popular and specialist press. It has done this by highlighting neglected issues which touch on the four broad thematic pillars that IMANI views as the underpinnings in the development of free, stable, and prosperous societies. These themes include: 'Rule of Law,' 'Market Growth and Development,' 'Individual Rights, Human Security, and Human Dignity,' and 'Institutional Development.' Through careful and sustained marketing, these have been mainstreamed into the national discourse through IMANI's advocacy and public outreach efforts. Consequently, as indicated above, the organization has become the most consulted think tank in Ghana by such major media houses such as the BBC, the IPS (Inter Press Service), and more recently, the CBC. It is perhaps worthy to add that the inclusion of IMANI's work in international periodicals such as *The Wall Street Journal* outstrips that of any other similar organization in West Africa.

With only six staff and eight unremunerated fellows, IMANI nevertheless maintains commitments across the above-mentioned four thematic areas at a level that very few of its larger, older competitors have shown a willingness to match. The evidence for these claims is manifest in the breadth of subject matter covered by IMANI publications, press submissions and other commentaries.

The influence and scope of the organization's views have led to the modification of anti-market tax policies, the reversal of highly restrictive food and beverage safety regulations in Ghana and beyond, and to the wide-ranging redrafting of national primary healthcare policy.

IMANI's work has been cited by ministers of state when explaining policy changes, and has been referenced during sessions in the House of Lords in the United Kingdom and the High Court in South Africa. In addition, our publications have been mentioned by the Jamestown Foundation and the Association of South East Asian Nations. It is thought that its leadership has reframed the dominant trends in scholarship on China-Africa relations, as well as reshaping the debate about the interplay of energy geopolitics and the US-Africa strategic security relationship, as evidenced by follow-on publications in the *Asia Times* and elsewhere.

Yet, IMANI's focus has not departed from its core objective of training a new corps of future visionaries and leaders who will carry the torch of liberty and blaze the trail of prosperity in the coming dawn of African renaissance. IMANI's continental seminars have catered to dozens of youth from a dozen countries in Africa, and brought needy and academically underserved students in contact with Africa's leading thinkers and doers. In our most recent residential programs, 60 speakers, comprising Army generals, CEOs, senior technocrats, and academic deans and dons, have enkindled in the bright young minds of these 40 students a strong desire to become champions of liberty, proponents of the prosperity created by strong markets and human rights, and principled advocates for the rule of law and institutional growth here in Ghana and farther afield.

One beneficiary of one of these programs wrote: 'You have fertilized my mind; all my life I will bear fresh seeds of liberty.' Yet another beneficiary wrote, 'Even though the seminar did not change my left-leaning values, I have learnt that many of the entrepreneurs, the key drivers of the economy, are merely normal people who wish to do things for themselves. The seminar was a master piece of logistic efficiency; a testimony of the outstanding quality of a dedicated, even if rather small, staff.'

Another beneficiary of our seminar wrote, 'Events such as this are useful in raising public awareness of how knowledge properly applied could provide the tool for our societies to rise up to the challenge of eliminating poverty and for building prosperous societies for future generations of Africans.'

This aspect of our work has resonated so well with independent observers that, thus far, IMANI is the only think tank in Africa to have won an Atlas Economic Research Foundation Templeton Freedom Prize twice (beating 180 other think tanks across the globe). IMANI has since crowned this achievement by being awarded an Antony and Dorian Fisher Award from the Atlas Economic Research Foundation. Such recognition is clearly consistent with the notion expressed above that IMANI embodies a unique formula for success. That formula was recently noticed by the prestigious *Foreign Policy Magazine*, which ranked IMANI as the sixth most influential think tank in Africa, listed behind four think tanks based in South Africa and one in Senegal.

One Atlas Economic Research Foundation Templeton Freedom Prize judge remarked: 'I give them [IMANI] the highest points for being most specific and rigorous in applying free market solutions to an array of complex social problems. Their submission shows the importance of using rigorously derived, quantifiable research outputs to gain credibility in shaping the policy debate. Crisp, clear, compelling data is the most useful tool to provide to any media outlet, and it's easy for the media to use, without interpretation.'

It is without doubt always a testament to the viability of an organization if its members show excellence both within and outside. IMANI's principals have received awards ranging from the YAN Global Fellowship through Marie Curie Scholarships to St. Gallen Accreditation, as well as invitations to share panels with international leaders such as Bill Gates Senior, Mark Goldring, Anwar Ibrahim, Martin Wolf, and Maat Laar (the former President of Estonia).

And yet how much more, and how much better, could we have done? What greater developmental impact might we have made and what greater heights in scholarship would we have reached, had the support been more forthcoming? While we revel in our achievements, we are also well aware of our challenges.

In the context of the above-mentioned four thematic areas, we have initiated three major projects that constitute the strategic bedrock of our medium-term vision. Over the next five years, we aim to become the foremost authority in the world on the unfolding Sino-African relationship, through our Sino-African Virtual Institute (sinoafrica.org), and the leading developer of research methodology and practice guidelines for corporate social responsibility in West Africa through our upcoming ISBIX project. We are also aiming to be one of the three most prolific research houses in Africa working in the area of human security as a function of market institutionalization, through our upcoming "Big Debates" project.

Across these frameworks, public outreach will be consolidated through AfricanLiberty.org, the publication/syndication project run jointly with the Cato Institute, and the launch of Ghana's first Research Journalist Corps. Each element in this vision, upon critical analysis, reveal cracks in the current IMANI structure. Lack of adequate remuneration for adjunct and research fellows is increasingly limiting the organization's ability to carry out original research. The adjunct fellowship model has proved immensely useful in the past, and two of our current full-time staff began their relationship with us in this way. This model brings into the fold talented individuals who prefer the freedom of multiple affiliations in order to nurture interdisciplinary excellence, and helps to foster useful and potentially synergistic links between our institution and others.

Likewise, corporate governance would also most likely improve if IMANI were able to provide sitting allowances for board members. The present situation of strict pro bono conditions of service clearly limits the ability of management to draw on the vast experience of some board members.

IMANI would also prefer to be able to encourage a certain degree of specialization, in correspondence with the aforementioned themes and projects, amongst staff using customized training and core-competence augmentation. However, the unavailability of long-term core budget support has interfered with these longstanding plans.

IMANI enjoys healthy partnerships with a number of organizations in Africa and beyond, including the Cato Institute (United States), the International Policy Network (United Kingdom), the Initiative for Public Policy Analysis (Nigeria) and the Liberty Institute (India). The next level in organizational planning would be to enter into specialized partnerships with other institutions around strictly specified objectives. These kinds of relationship-based initiatives will clearly provide IMANI with an enhanced ability to define and monitor strategically shared goals and visions.

Five years from now, IMANI should be the most influential think tank in Africa. We know that this goal is achievable and we are happy to welcome donors and partners who identify with the vehicles for this strategic vision. However, interim funding will prove crucial to the sound development of these projects.

An Israeli Think Tank – Its Challenges and Discontents

Daniel Doron
Israel Center for Social
and Economic Progress
(Israel)

Israel is threatened with extinction and has suffered incessantly from war and terrorism since its founding in 1948. Therefore, it is not surprising that Israelis are almost completely consumed by concerns about security and its political ramifications, to the point of exclusion of many other serious challenges facing them, not least of which are economic ones.

It was in the wake of the 1973 Yom Kippur War, when Israel first suffered defeat, that Israelis finally lost faith in their governing institutions ruled by the Labor Socialist camp. They started asking why their economic system, which boasted some of the most talented people in the world, was lame. For the first time since the country was founded an opportunity to change Israel's economic system materialized.

After the 1973 war, my friends and I – who made up the first generation of graduates from after Israel's independence – developed a deep conviction that we could no longer ignore the countless failures of our entrenched political system and its sprawling bureaucracies. Up until 1973, we tolerated gross inequities and inefficiencies as long as our government assured our survival. It had become clear, however, that the rot in our political system was undermining even our defense establishment. It was posing a threat to our existence and, in the long run, was almost as deadly as the threats from a hostile Arab world.

A handful of us were disgusted by politics and we naively assumed we could bring change from outside of politics. We organized a group called 'The Movement for Change'. We were convinced that the key to reform was to change Israel's strict proportional representation system. This system, we believed, was the chief cause of the political 'factions' which James Madison, a Founding Father of the United States, identified as the chief threats to popular democracy. Factions and the politics of distribution led to ever intensifying struggles over political spoils and generated waste and inefficiency which plagued government services from health care and education to justice.

While raising funds for our fledgling movement we were rejected by many industrialists and merchants who sympathized with our cause but said they could not alienate a government they depended on in so many ways (subsidies, special tax concessions, permits, land zoning, etc). This made us realize the intimate connection between political and economic freedom. I had the good fortune to meet notable thinkers, such as Professor Irving Kristol, Arthur Seldon and Milton Friedman, and they deepened my conviction that Israel's political, social and economic problems were rooted in its socialist-statist system.

In the late seventies, I launched the Israel Center for Social and Economic Progress (ICSEP). Its mission: to help Israel realize its enormous potential by freeing its economy from the shackles of a regressive socialist and statist system.

In Israel, economic growth and liberalization are the keys to survival: only growth will enable Israel to address its many social problems, encourage its young to stay at home and meet its defense needs while striving for peace. It is only through growth that Israel can integrate the massive waves of immigration it has absorbed since its founding.

Israel's dysfunctional political and economic system is perpetuated by an iron triangle of a dominant political system and its unaccountable bureaucracies, oligopolistic businesses and militant labor unions. It is supported by a strong leftist ethos and a belief in big government.

While Israel has a number of successful, globally competitive enterprises (predominantly in high-tech), many of the locally oriented industries are monopolies or cartels. These enterprises restrain competition by keeping politicians and government bureaucrats 'satisfied' and maintain peace among laborers by 'feather-bedding' and inflating salaries. As a result, for decades, Israel has suffered from inflated costs, high unemployment, low productivity (half that of American workers) and slow real growth.

Many Israeli workers earn about US$1,200 a month, but prices and taxes in Israel are generally higher than in the United States. About one million Israeli workers receive supplemental government assistance and hundreds of thousands of families cannot make ends meet. Almost half of Israel's US$70 billion budget and about one third of its GDP are devoted to welfare, yet poverty remains and may even be growing. The economy operates well below its potential.

A competitive business environment would generate lower prices and could reduce the cost of all consumer goods by about one third. This would increase considerably the purchasing power of millions of poor Israelis who are dependent on government supplementary income and enable them to make ends meet. This, in turn, would enable the government to cut welfare costs and taxes. Basic structural reforms will also enable market forces to unleash the tremendous productivity potential of the Israeli worker and entrepreneur (evident in the high-tech sector), thus propelling Israel into the ranks of the world's most prosperous countries. Therefore, economic reform must become a top national priority.

ICSEP has been providing the know-how needed to fashion, implement and support pro-market structural reforms, and the intellectual ammunition to overcome resistance to them. It has achieved notable successes in generating crucial reforms, including the reform in the financial markets which broke a bank duopoly that was as damaging to the Israeli economy as Japanese banking was to Japan's economy. This was all done despite a culture dominated by out-of-date ideas that resisted and retarded reforms and strong political forces which were determined to perpetuate a monopoly-dominated system.

In addition, ICSEP is at the forefront of the struggle to overcome the pro-Marxist education that dominates most of our universities by inspiring Israeli students through pro-market thinking.

In our policy work, we identify crucial areas in which reform is most urgently needed, including land use, housing, small business regulation, de-monopolization, government structure and function, financial markets, the tax system, labor markets, education and health care. We conduct research in these areas and hold seminars and conferences to discuss our findings. We then design concrete reform plans and try to mobilize decision-makers and public-opinion-shapers in order to encourage coalitions in support of necessary reform.

In the mid-eighties, ICSEP laid the groundwork for successful anti-inflationary policies and for the 'privatized' immigrant absorption policies that facilitated the successful integration of the great mass of immigrants from the former Soviet Union. A subsequent ICSEP reform plan, 'Essential Conditions for the Renewal of Growth', detailed a number of concrete steps that could have huge effects if implemented. It was presented to the Israeli government under incoming prime minister Binyamin Netanyahu in September 1999 and to the Knesset (Israel's legislature). A follow-up plan, which updated the earlier plans and provided a detailed analysis of the causes of growing budget deficits and how to cut them, was prepared for Prime Minister Ehud Barak. A third plan suggested steps to enhance productivity by correcting grave distortions in the labor market.

We have also initiated several research projects on major issues, some in cooperation with other bodies, such as the International Center of Economic Growth (on political business cycles, published in Public Choice, 1992), and the Koret Foundation (on small businesses in Israel).

We have disseminated our research by organizing seminars and conferences for decision-makers which have attracted hundreds of policy people and have been widely reported in the media. They have had remarkable effects on public discourse and have resulted in some significant changes.

Since the early 1990s, we have held workshops and courses for over 9,000 young immigrants from the former Soviet Union, helping them integrate into a Western-style economy. In the mid-1990s, at the request of the Ministry of Education, we also held courses for high-school economics teachers.

Since 1998, we have been holding classes in economics in several Israeli high schools and have taught over 5,000 student participants. To attract students, we produced a series of short films depicting episodes from the students' lives to illustrate economic principles. The courses teach students basic economic concepts and theories and how they affect their daily lives and career prospects, as well as public-speaking skills. The classes are in high demand by students and schools, and we will expand as funding permits.

Since 2000, we have conducted university seminars on 'The Free Market and its Critics' in four Israeli universities. These seminars are primers in the theory and practice of market economics and are based on Milton and Rose Friedman's *Free to Choose* and Thomas Sowell's *Basic Economics*. Students participating in these seminars consist mostly of third-year students and occasional doctoral candidates who are on the dean's list from a variety of faculties.

Usually, the only Israeli students who receive instruction in market economics are those majoring in economics, but they tend to study mostly economic techniques, not philosophy. Other university students – especially in law, the social sciences and humanities – are largely ignorant of economics, which impairs their career decisions as well as their ability to analyze government policies and their cost-effectiveness. Even worse, students are brainwashed by the neo-Marxist and postmodernist ideas that dominate the social sciences and therefore they cannot act as enlightened citizens or decision-makers.

Our university seminars are based on a continuous dialogue between lecturers, students, Israeli entrepreneurs and business leaders and public figures such as former finance minister Binyamin Netanyahu, president emeritus of Dixons, Lord Kalms, and Sam Zell of Zell Enterprises. Close to 2,000 students have graduated from our university seminars and many more are on waiting lists. These graduates have changed the atmosphere on the university campuses from one of outright hostility to market thinking to one that is curious about and increasingly accepting of classic liberal thought.

Our alumni also participate in promoting free markets ideas in the public arena outside campus. Some have founded a not-for-profit organization called Citizens for True Social Justice and have undertaken numerous activities to promote economic reforms.

We are now designing an additional course and alumni club to deepen the students' understanding of market economics and provide them with skills for their public promotion.

In 2005, ICSEP launched a website of ideas, Kivunim, which features translations from *Commentary*, *The Wall Street Journal*, the *Weekly Stan-*

dard, the *City Journal*, the *Hoover Review*, the *National Review*, etc, to expose Israeli readers to a wider range of thinkers and ideas than is available in the mostly one-sided Israeli media. Kivunim also publishes original works by Israeli writers and its audience includes leading public and intellectual figures. In a short period of time it has gained over 10,000 steady visits a month.

Previously, we published a Hebrew-language periodical, *Lihiyot Hofshi* (To Be Free), which featured economic commentary, analysis and information on the Israeli economy. We have also published numerous papers in Hebrew, covering topics such as Britain's pioneering privatization experience, deregulation, the benefits of privatization for the environment, and the proceedings from our various conferences. There are over twenty titles in circulation. ICSEP has also translated into Hebrew seminal works such as Milton and Rose Friedman's *Free to Choose* and James D. Gwartney and Richard L. Stroup's *What Everyone Should Know about Economics and Prosperity*; adapting the latter to Israeli circumstances.

At the time of writing, we are preparing a book about the recent historic financial market reforms initiated by finance minister Binyamin Netanyahu in cooperation with ICSEP and other public bodies. This was the first time that a reform was launched in Israel with collaboration between government and voluntary bodies – providing a valuable lesson for Israelis who doubted that change could be made under existing political circumstances.

ICSEP has been bringing leading personalities to Israel to share their knowledge and experiences. Our distinguished guests have included: Nobel laureate Professor Milton Friedman, Professor Irving Kristol, Ambassador Stuart Eizenstat, US Supreme Court Justice Antonin Scalia, Judge Richard Posner, George Melloan of *The Wall Street Journal*, former UK Commissioner for the Common Market Sir Leon Brittan, and prominent businessmen such as Samuel Zell, Lord (David) Young and Lord (Stanley) Kalms. We are also regularly consulted about the Israeli economy by foreign study missions, such as the US–Israel Joint Economic Development Group and the US Congressional and White House study missions, as well as by foreign journalists and television networks and economic think tanks from Europe and the United States. ICSEP has also acted as a source of economic expertise for many other institutions, including the Israel Chambers of Commerce, universities, the Israel Supreme Court's Institute for Judicial Studies, the Israel Management Institute and others.

ICSEP has enjoyed extensive media coverage of its activities. Thanks to ICSEP's sponsorship, Israeli television has twice broadcast Milton Friedman's *Free to Choose* with Hebrew subtitles, a special on the difficulties of free markets in Israel and a film on immigrant entrepreneurship. Ironically, ICSEP's director, Daniel Doron, was a member of the Government Central Planning Board, on which he preached against central planning, and he also served on Prime Minister Netanyahu's Economic Advisory Group. He has appeared on international television and has been quoted on the topic of Israel's economy by *Business Week*, the *New York Times* and *Forbes* magazine. He regularly writes for *The Wall Street Journal*, the *Weekly Standard*, *The Sun*, and occasionally for the *Financial Times* and the *National Review*. Doron is also regularly interviewed on Israeli TV and radio and has published extensively in the Hebrew press. In addition, ICSEP's board members regularly publish articles, make media appearances and participate in public commissions on topics such as tax reform, housing and monopolies. These activities help to give ICSEP's ideas increased exposure.

ICSEP has focused its work on educating and engaging with the policymaking community. It has reached legislators, senior government officials, jurists, the media and academics, as well as leading figures in industry, labor and commerce. ICSEP has supplied them with the information necessary to pursue growth-oriented reforms.

ICSEP has transformed the terms of the economic policy debate in Israel. When it began its work, the concept of 'market economics' was unknown, ignored or derided. Today, public opinion has changed dramatically. Israeli policymakers do not wrestle with the question of whether Israel should reduce government interference in the economy; they consider exactly how, where and at what speed it should be reduced and how to overcome resistance to change. Each of ICSEP's conferences and seminars has attracted extensive media coverage along with participants from the highest echelons of the Israeli policy community: presidents, Supreme Court justices, government ministers, Knesset members and other leaders from a variety of fields. ICSEP was also the winner of two Atlas-sponsored Templeton prizes – one in 2005 for Institutional Excellence and the other in 2006 for Student Outreach. ICSEP's work has served as a significant catalyst for initiating reforms in various sectors of the Israeli economy.

It is precisely because Israel had such a statist economy that it presented great reform opportunities. We have learned a lot from experiences in other countries, but when it comes down to it, all reform proposals had to be modified to suit the specific nature of Israeli institutional structures. We also learned to take advantage of political opportunities, although much work remains to be done.

As for our integration in international efforts, it is a pity that despite the good work done by Atlas to create a network of pro-market think tanks, the achievements of these organizations do not come close to those of market adversaries, statists and collectivists. We must all strive to do more to devise new strategies and achieve better results.

28

Bringing the Market Back to Italy

Alberto Mingardi
Bruno Leoni Institute
(Italy)

CHAPTER

Italy is not best known for its free market economists, but it would be ungenerous to say that the country lacks a tradition of classical liberalism. During the 19th and 20th centuries, Italy was home to quite an active group of *liberisti*; that is, intellectuals who had a proper understanding of the virtues of the free market and who added considerably to the global capital of scholars versed in the ideas of liberty. Two figures that come to mind are Vilfredo Pareto and Gaetano Mosca. But it should not be forgotten that the school of *scienza delle finanze* exercised a decisive influence on James M. Buchanan and on the development of public choice theory. The extensive network of friends and admirers of Luigi Einaudi (president of Italy, 1948–55) shows the prestige that this important scholar garnered within the economic profession and beyond.

Nevertheless, despite their authoritative scholarship, these intellectuals have exercised a limited influence in the shaping of Italy's economic policies over the last century. The mastermind behind Italy's unification, Camillo Cavour, was by and large a free trader, and Marco Minghetti, a banker and one of Italy's first prime ministers, had a deep grasp of classical liberalism. The whole of Italy's political class from the beginning served the special interests of a few, however, and backed a policy agenda imbued with protectionism, industrial policy, compulsory welfarism and, eventually, war, which blossomed with the rise of fascism.

In the aftermath of World War II, the transition from monarchical to republican rule and from authoritarianism to universal franchise democracy left Italy's economic policy largely unchanged. While Mont Pelerin Society member, and friend of Ludwig von Mises, Luigi Einaudi was the governor of the Bank of Italy and the head of state, his popularity and ability to secure appointments was based on his fame and honesty, not on his classical liberal ideas.

As in many other countries, during the 1960s and 1970s the intellectual debate in Italy was completely monopolized by the academic left. Keynesianism was widely accepted as the only sensible approach to economic matters, and we were so good at producing socialist economists that we ended up exporting them, a prime example being Piero Sraffa. Only a small number of individuals had the courage to speak of the importance of private property rights, the free market and limited government. Bruno Leoni was the foremost Italian classical liberal scholar of the second half of the 20th century, but he died tragically in 1967 at the young age of 54. In the years after Leoni's death, Sergio Ricossa was the only prominent Italian economist to preach consistently the gospel of classical liberalism. Alas, he was almost entirely alone; on the left as well as the right.

I do not intend to bother the reader with a pedestrian sketch of contemporary Italian history, but we are today a product of our past. Ideas, both good and bad, have consequences. The dominance of statism in Italy can help explain why general government revenues were 24.8 per cent of GDP in 1960, 36.9 per cent in 1980, 42.4 per cent in 1990 and 47.9 per cent in 1997. It also explains why the number of Italy's government employees increased from 7.7 per cent of total employment in 1960 to reach 16.2 per cent in 1992, and why general government expenditure has risen dramatically since the late 19th century, from 13.7 per cent of GDP to around 30 per cent before World War II, 30.1 per cent in 1960, 42.1 per cent in 1980 and 53.4 per cent in 1990. What we see here are ideas at work. Ideas provided the impetus for an unprecedented growth of the state; a growth that faced very little opposition.

Italy was not lacking intellectual ammunition against statism, but the absence of intermediaries cultivating new 'second-hand dealers' in classical liberal ideas was certainly evident. The only attempt to create a classical liberal think tank in Italy dates back to the mid-1980s, when Antonio Martino, who had an extensive network of acquaintances both in academia and in the think tanks of the Anglo-Saxon world, founded the Centro Ricerche Economiche Applicate (CREA) in Rome. Martino, who headed the think tank, became the president of the Mont Pelerin Society and later the minister of foreign affairs in 1994 and the minister of defense in 2001–06. Virgilio Floriani, a successful entrepreneur with a firm belief in philanthropy who backed Martino's think tank, admired the success of the Institute of Economic Affairs and the willingness of his friend Antony Fisher to export that model all over the world.

CREA published the works of James M. Buchanan, Milton Friedman, Henri Lepage, Alvin Rabushka, Gordon Tullock and Roland Vaubel, along with those of well-known Italians such as CREA's Antonio Martino, Sergio Ricossa, Franco Romani and a giant of political science, Gianfranco Miglio. Under Martino's leadership, CREA was responsible for introducing concepts such as the flat tax and school vouchers into the Italian debate.

Unfortunately, CREA did not last long. Floriani, despite his business connections, was unable to raise enough money to sustain his brainchild. Italy does not have a tradition of philanthropy and an independent think tank is inconceivable in a country where the state is almost the only donor. Moreover, at that time the political parties dominated the entire political scene. Little was discussed outside of them and they engaged only minimally with others within civil society.

Something was about to change, however. At the end of the eighties, the scale of corruption – knowledge of which had been confined to a few political circles – became apparent to the general public. The vast expansion of the state, particularly in the south, was the method by which the political class relentlessly bought votes for itself. While it was not a revolution yet, crisis was in the air and the judiciary targeted part of the political system and jailed its main actors. The former Communist Party was a major beneficiary. Nonetheless, owing to overwhelming dissatisfaction with the old politics, the left was not able to secure power during the 1994 elections and the Italians voted in a complex coalition that included newcomers such as Umberto Bossi's Northern League and Silvio Berlusconi's Forza Italia.

While both of these parties ended up being disappointments to free market advocates in Italy, they did succeed in using free market rhetoric when fishing for votes. For example, Forza Italia's 1994 platform advocated a transition towards a flat tax. In the 1980s this idea was unheard of and now it was entering the political debate through the front door.

Alas, right-wingers have been poor allies of good policies. In 1994, they stayed in office for too short a time to be judged, and when they were in office during the second Berlusconi government from 2001 to 2006, little was accomplished. Although Berlusconi's government was successful in achieving a partial relaxation of hiring and firing regulations (though not on the firing side), on the whole its libertarian-leaning rhetoric went no farther than the paper it was written on.

At the same time, during the 1990s, the Italian state was rolled back. The main drivers in this process were not the 'freedom fighters' who joined the political right, but the technocrats who, for the most part, stayed with the left. In particular, the director general of the Italian treasury (now the governor of the central bank), Mario Draghi, was a key player in the privatization process. With left-of-center governments, Italy had an impressive array of privatizations, including highways, telecommunications and electricity. It can be argued that the process reflected the need to reduce public debt rather than an ideological affection for private enterprise. Regardless, Italians saw the light with privatization.

This is just one sign of how the world changed profoundly in only a decade. The end of the Soviet empire and the subsequent emergence of globalization rearranged the vocabulary of politics and the communist left had to start shopping for new ideas. Free markets, long considered a problem, now looked increasingly like the solution. The consensus in the economics profession began to change, and even though economists were by no means predominantly libertarians, they were no longer Sraffians either.

Thus it comes as no surprise that classical liberal ideas were reinvigorated in Italy. The 1990s brought a re-emergence of a free market movement that had not been seen since the early 1900s. Much of the credit for this reawakening is given to three small publishers: Aldo Canovari (Liberilibri), Leonardo Facco (Leonardo Facco Editore) and Florindo Rubbettino

(Rubbettino Editore). These publishers empowered a new wave of enthusiastic free marketeers who wanted to translate into their native language the classics of liberty ranging from F. A. Hayek to Murray Rothbard. The printing presses rolled and Italian readers had access to Murray Rothbard's *The Ethics of Liberty*, David Friedman's *The Machinery of Freedom*, Frederic Bastiat's *The Law*, and many others. Thanks to the enthusiasm of Professor Raimondo Cubeddu, Bruno Leoni's masterpiece, *Freedom and the Law*, was translated into Italian for the first time 35 years after its publication in the United States. The number of advocates of classical liberalism in academia and in journalism multiplied as well. The Internet proved to be the perfect mechanism to connect the few libertarians in different cities who thought that they were alone in their thinking.

Italy didn't have a free market think tank until late 2003, when the Istituto Bruno Leoni (IBL) was founded. Istituto Bruno Leoni was developed, in part, as a result of disillusionment with the Berlusconi government, which, instead of walking the road towards a free market, embraced the flag of protectionism. IBL also intended to foster a greater 'institutionalization' of the free market activities that had taken place in previous years. IBL was founded by three young scholars, Carlo Lottieri, Carlo Stagnaro and myself, with the support of three businessmen. The idea of starting such a venture was stimulated by a variety of factors. Personally, I had spent a few weeks in 1999 as a summer intern at The Heritage Foundation, Washington DC, and was fascinated by the extent to which think tanks are intellectual powerhouses in the United States. Moreover, I had the great fortune of being under the benevolent wing of Lord (Ralph) Harris of High Cross, and I was increasingly fascinated by his intellect as well as his charm, ethics and fierce commitment. I began to see his career and life as a model to follow; despite the fact that it would be impossible to be as good as him. My colleague, Carlo Lottieri, was convinced that there needed to be an umbrella institution to help younger scholars to pursue classical liberal research within Italy's academia, which was an inhospitable environment dominated by socialists of various kinds. Seeing the Centre for New Europe established in Brussels and other think tanks starting up in Europe gave us the courage to found IBL.

But unintended consequences are always more important than planned ones. I have found that thus far IBL has been responding to three basic outcomes which none of us could have conceived of accomplishing, but which exceeded our expectations.

The first is the extent to which the base of our movement is not defined by numbers, but rather by human types. Fundraising forces us to present our ideas in a bourgeois, 'presentable' fashion. It is not just a matter of attracting the money that interested individuals may want to spend on research, and the people interested in undertaking such research, it is about getting an intellectual movement more actively integrated into the real world. We can even say that part of our job is to educate our donors; not just about the research projects IBL is trying to develop, but also, at least initially, about the kinds of philanthropic efforts that lie behind a think tank.

The second outcome is that we started engaging in public policy. This was, and still is, a novelty in Italy. There is something to be said for the fact that there is almost no accurate translation of the word 'policy' in Italian. Right from the beginning IBL started publishing policy papers. By doing so it was competing with other actors that traditionally have proposed legislation – the labor unions and business associations. They, of course, have far more gunpowder than a small free market think tank. Nevertheless, it is important that we have succeeded in bringing our ideas into the marketplace as well, potentially providing the political class with the inspiration necessary to bring about change. This has not been an easy task. We have had to persevere and find a proper balance between the radicalism of our ideas and the practical policy recommendations derived from them. We wanted to keep open windows of opportunity, even for small, incremental reforms, without watering down our fundamental principles.

We have published a Briefing Paper every single month since our inception; which at the time of writing added up to 55. These papers are distributed to over 15,000 people, including all the Italian members of parliament. Over the course of three years, we have published 53 Occasional Papers (papers with a more theoretical and general touch), over 100 Focuses (shorter papers tailored to Internet readers) and over 30 books. Our website now has more than 9,000 pages and over 1,000 visitors a day, which is not bad for a website written exclusively in Italian. Far more important, the authors of our papers range from very established figures, such as Nobel Prize winner Ed Phelps, world-famous novelists like Mario Vargas Llosa and prestigious social scientists like Anthony de Jasay, Israel Kirzner and Vito Tanzi, to a number of committed young scholars, most of whom were not around when IBL was founded or were 'converted' to our ideas later on. While it is not easy, we do our best to find an appropriate balance between works with long-term objectives (in which IBL promotes fully fledged libertarian ideas) and policy-oriented publications, whose tone has to be different because their 'consumers' are directly involved in politics.

The third beneficial consequence of founding a think tank was that we reached a level of public visibility that was unthinkable without one. Being well organized is still the key to becoming known, and IBL's consistency in its work has given it the reputation of being the flagship of the type of policies that it pursues. The increase in the quantity and quality of our output has helped us to gain a reputation with the press. Moreover, our ideological consistency has resulted in us being viewed as extremists on some issues, but also as intellectually honest and therefore trustworthy. We tend to have dialogue with our enemies more often than fights. Italy is the country of Machiavelli and people can sense when you are selling out. Honesty has therefore been the best policy for us.

These three outcomes epitomize the 'intellectual entrepreneurship' behind the daily work of our think tank. Working in an organization whose survival is dependent upon its capacity to raise money to grow, and whose capacity to raise money depends (at least in part) on its output, we are forced to think differently and dynamically. A fair proportion of our time is devoted to developing ways to improve our communication and of taking advantage of all the possibilities that come with an Internet-based society. In addition, a fair amount of time is devoted to increasing our customer base by reaching out to politicians, journalists and other groups that can be convinced of the benefits of free competition.

A think tank can be seen as a vaccine against the tendency towards self-marginalization that is often typical of fringe intellectual movements. We are already beginning to see the fruits of our labor blossom.

To say that IBL has had a significant impact on policymaking would be self-indulgent. While we are making inroads, a major, truly revolutionary reform has not yet been accomplished. Nevertheless, we see the Italian public discussion evolving, day after day, in a better, more informed, more market-oriented direction, and our role in that process is not negligible. It is not the end, and it is not even the beginning of the end, but rather, merely the beginning.

29

Brazil: A Contrast of Ideas

Margaret Tse
Instituto Liberdade
(Brazil)

CHAPTER

INTRODUCTION

The history of Brazil suggests that dominant ideas have always had a profound influence on social and political issues. This chapter explains why the adoption and promotion of free market ideas could be especially powerful at moments of particularly rapid change and acute confusion, shaping human experience over time and underpinning the intellectual capital of the country. The Instituto Liberdade is playing a crucial role in influencing the climate of ideas in the contemporary scene.

HISTORICAL ROOTS FROM PORTUGUESE COLONIZATION

Many elements of the Portuguese colonization are deeply rooted in the fabric of Brazilian society. To properly explore these roots, it may be useful to go back in history. History professor José Murilo de Carvalho (2000: 8) theorises that the legacy of slavery has infected contemporary Brazilian society such that many people often consider themselves above the law. Slavery was introduced shortly after the conquest of the land by the Portuguese in 1500 and lasted for more than 300 years until it was abolished in 1888 after Brazil became an independent country. Research shows that around 4 million slaves, about 34 per cent of the total African slaves transported to the Americas, were brought to Brazil over the course of three centuries. Slavery was rooted in Brazil's social practices and value system. Clearly, at this time, individual freedom was not seen as a relevant social value.

The widespread emphasis on exploitation within Brazilian society was visible through the dominance of the large landed estates. The unequal and irregular distribution and occupation of land started in the 16th century, when the Portuguese crown conceded vast 'captaincies' to early colonists as a reward for services and, later on, for joining forces with the local oligarchies to maintain power. According to Carvalho, unlike the situation in the colonies of North America, there was no family farming in Brazil and landowners were slave-owners (ibid.). Even with the introduction of a land law which allowed the importation of free workers from Europe, the social and political impact of the latifundia (landed estates) was deep rooted. Landlords exploited their tenants' labor and, after democracy arrived, harvested their votes.

Patrimonialism, a type of rule in which the ruler does not distinguish between personal and public authority and treats matters and resources of state as his personal affair, was another major component of the Portuguese state and society during the country's conquest of Brazil. Portugal lacked the manpower to rule and explore the immense empire it had conquered, so it appointed the ruling class to the administration of the colony and this became a defining characteristic of the colonial government. Carvalho suggests that a lack of strong civil society and the large number of Brazilians incorporated into the colony's bureaucracy, compounded by clientelism and nepotism, contributed to the survival of patrimonial traits in present day Brazil (ibid.). After fifteen years of democratic rule, the widespread prevalence and tolerance of corruption – a consequence of patrimonial and clientelistic practices – is expressed through a high degree of impunity.

The combination of the indigenous Brazilians' lack of need for a plan, the Portuguese desire for quick enrichment, and the slaves' inability to own or invest in anything, formed the culture of today.

Moreover, Carvalho (2005) states that corruption is deeply rooted in the contemporary leftist Workers' Party in the country, not as a vulgar way of personal money-making, but as a technical instrument to erode the moral basis of capitalistic society and to fund the socialist revolutionary strategy. These two objectives are closely intertwined. Funded by corruption, the growth of leftist parties strengthens the credibility of the attacks they make against society. Capitalism would not appear so immoral without their deliberate efforts to degrade moral standards.

THE INFLUENCE OF POSITIVISM AND ITS FALLACIES

The concept of positivism, conceived by French philosopher Auguste Comte (1798–1857), influenced large parts of Latin America during the 19th century and was adopted by the military, technocratic and political elites in Brazil. In 1889, the republicans coined the phrase 'Order and Progress', which is still emblazoned on the Brazilian flag today. The goal of progress in this case was a 'socially responsible authoritarianism' which could provide 'scientific solutions' for society's problems.

According to Zimmermann (2007), 'Positivists argued that only such a "scientific" government could generate high levels of development, thereby supporting the "moral" superiority of dictatorship over constitutional democracy. In Brazil, the disciples of Comte were involved, decisively, in the overthrow of the monarchy in the hope that this would be succeeded by a dictatorial republic.'

Comte postulated an empirical science-based view of sociology and believed that an appreciation of the past, and the ability to build upon it towards the future, was crucial in transitioning from the theological and metaphysical phases.

AUSTRIAN ECONOMIST LUDWIG VON MISES (1985) EXPLAINS:

The sciences of human action start from the fact that man purposefully aims at ends he has chosen. It is precisely this that all brands of positivism, behaviorism, and panphysicalism want either to deny altogether or to pass over in silence . . . All that 'Unified Science' brought forward was to recommend the proscription of the methods applied by the sciences of human action and their replacement by the methods of the experimental natural sciences. It is not remarkable for that which it contributed, but only for that which it wants to see prohibited. Its protagonists are the champions of intolerance and of a narrow-minded dogmatism.

MUELLER (2002) DESCRIBES THE EFFECTS IN BRAZIL:

Comte's ideas have shown their greatest impact in economic policy. Given the facts that members of the military have played a central role in Brazil's political life and that positivism had become the leading philosophical paradigm at the military schools, economic policy in Brazil has been marked by an interventionist frenzy that affects all aspects of public life. The spirit of planning for modernity has turned Brazil into a hotbed of economic interventionism, with each new government promising the great leap forward.

GRAMSCI'S HEGEMONY THEORY

The Italian communist leader Antonio Gramsci (1891–1937) was a highly unique Marxist who was concerned about what strategies should be adopted by revolutionary parties operating in liberal democratic states. This led him to analyze the relationship between the economic base and the political superstructure and to introduce the concept of hegemony. Power, which is so deeply desired, must exist in a twofold nature: one formal and objective, essentially structural like the state, and the other more imprecise and abstract, with a conjectural basis relative to civil society. Coutinho (2002) states that in order to grasp power, as described in Gramsci's concepts, it is imperative to grasp hegemony first and make social institutions mere mechanisms of party propaganda, thereby destroying society from the inside in a slow but mortal attack to all forms of resistance.

COSTA (2004) ADDS,

Gramsci's concern with revolutionary violence is not moral, but instrumental. His complementary strategy of war of position – trench warfare – uses a lot of violent resources previously used by orthodox revolutionaries, such as misinformation, ideological manipulation of the masses, enlarging state (in an advanced stage of the revolution) and, at last, rupture, which would not refuse, if necessary, traditional violence as the last fatal and efficient strike.

Brazil is possibly the only country in the world where Gramsci's strategy is in an advanced position. Staying above the competition among political representatives was the left's strategy for maintaining its hegemonic position. Today, Brazil does not have any political opposition to facilitate any plurality of ideas.

According to Carvalho (2005), a well-planned and highly successful scheme aiming at establishing a communist regime has been under way in Brazil since 1964. In all sectors of the government, as well as in the Congress and Houses of Representatives of all 26 states and in about 5,000 municipalities of the country, most politicians came from former leftist movements, many of them ex-terrorists, including high-ranking officials. The 'São Paulo Forum' (SPF), founded in 1990 by Fidel Castro and the then president Lula, is the strategic headquarters of the Latin American revolutionary left. Their ultimate goal is to establish a dictatorship of one party, with absolute power in their hands and complete restriction of any demonstration of individualism, with the intent to resort to violence in order to reach their goals of socializing the country. Carvalho stresses that this revolutionary mentality is totalitarian and violent in itself because the imposition of ever more suffocating restrictions to human liberty has been combined with the dissemination of the revolutionary mentality among ever growing segments of the population.

COSTA (2004) CONTINUES,

What denounces the Gramscian revolution even more is that in Brazil, individual conscience is slowly being substituted by the concept of the political correctness and moral relativism. Examples of this abound: armed members of MST [Landless People's Movement] who invade farms are victims and farmers who defend themselves are criminals; drug-dealers who are provoking a civil war in Rio de Janeiro are victims of the system, and if they are found guilty, we, law-enforcing citizens, must share that guilt a bit (as the media informs us every day); priests who speak up against abortion and homosexuality are children-devouring monsters, but friars who embraced liberation theology and say that Cuba is paradise on Earth – no matter the 17,000 murdered – are portrayed as the highest models of Christianity.

RULE OF LAW VERSUS RULES OF SOCIETY

Brazilian social institutions are subject to two types of pressure. One is the universal pressure that comes from the bureaucratic norms and laws that define the existence of public service. The other is determined based on the webs of personal relations to which all are subjected and by the social resources that these networks mobilize and distribute. Brazil has a deep relationship-based society.

In Latin American countries such as Brazil, 'Constitutions typically contain a substantial number of aspirational or utopian provisions that are either impossible or extremely difficult to enforce. Some of these provisions contain social rights that seem far more appropriate in a political platform or a sermon than in a constitution' (Rosenn, 1990).

Brazil is a typical example of a country where the 'laws' of the society can easily overrule the laws of the state. DaMatta (1999) has argued that Brazilian society is pervaded by a 'double ethic', because methods for circumventing state laws can be obtained through a range of factors related to conditions of wealth, social status, family ties and friendship. Legalism in Brazil is the result of the problematic legacy of a convoluted legal system introduced by the Portuguese colonizers. Brazilians have acquired a certain tendency to soften laws by not applying them properly. As a result, we observe a chaotic and insecure environment for entrepreneurs.

Many of Brazil's national afflictions, such as crippling taxes, red tape, land invasions, endemic corruption throughout all levels of government and in all three branches of the country, lack of infrastructure and an unreliable judicial system, all contribute to the crowding out of enterprise or cause it to be driven underground. Everyone talks about wanting honest politicians, but few Brazilians complain about the size of the government, in spite of the creation of a tax meter by the São Paulo Chamber of Commerce, which tots up the government's tax rate in real time. Instituto Liberdade uses this meter to create awareness when celebrating Tax Freedom Day (the first day of the year in which a nation as a whole has theoretically earned enough income to fund its annual tax burden) in Brazil.

As Schor (2006) explains, 'constitutions are not entrenched in Latin America because political leaders do not fear citizen mobilization when fundamental rules of the game are violated'. In general, Congress ignores the problems of the people that it represents and legislators are rarely held accountable to voters or their party and are granted widespread immunity from prosecution. We also have a judiciary that administers the laws according to the power and the influence of the lawyers and the personal relationships between the interested parties. If the proposed reforms of Brazil's political, fiscal, judicial, social security and labor systems are achieved, it would solve the problems that we have with violence, property rights violations, poor public education, chaos within the healthcare system, the environment, government inefficiency and corruption.

The problem is that there is an absence of authentic classical liberal political parties. Classical liberalism, that is limited governments, free trade and private institutions apart from the state, is not present in politics today – not even in the form of a campaign promise. Classical liberalism has very few academic spokesmen in the country and the ones that do exist lack the political support to be able to offer attractive platform proposals that appeal to the intellectual and emotional sides of Brazilians.

Classical liberalism in Brazil was pioneered by Donald Stewart Jr. A businessman and civil engineer, he translated *Human Action* by Mises into Portuguese and wrote articles and books about liberal thought. In order to persuade Brazilian society of the advantages of a liberal order he founded the Instituto Liberal in 1983, in Rio de Janeiro. Although he passed away in 1999, his efforts and dedication to the cause changed the minds of future generations of intellectual entrepreneurs, who continued the work of promoting the ideas and expanding the debates.

Currently, there are few free market think tanks in Brazil and the most active ones are located in the southern regions of the country. The freedom fighters from the state of Rio Grande do Sul are typically descended from working-class European settlers and are characterized by their strong tradition of classical liberal values. In 1835, the overtaxation of beef jerky, the state's main source of revenue at that time, by the Portuguese Crown, angered local farmers and cattle raisers tied to the Freemasons, sparking an uprising called the Farroupilha Revolution. This was very similar to the Boston Tea Party in the USA, which sparked the American Revolution. The war lasted for ten years and ended with the defeat of the rebels. The revolution did not result in the state of Rio Grande do Sul becoming an independent country, but the traditional classical liberal spirit continues to live on.

This essay focuses on how ideas have impacted on Brazil, and also how the work of Instituto Liberdade, a small and independent free market think tank located in the southern region, is gradually affecting civil society by reaching out to intellectuals, teachers and entrepreneurs. Its continuous efforts over the course of 21 years in researching and analyzing public policy issues, publishing free market literature and organizing colloquiums and seminars show the dedication of Brazilian intellectual entrepreneurs to bringing their insights to the attention of policymakers, opinion leaders and the media. In order to promote a better political, economic and cultural environment in such a big and diverse country, the Institute is returning to its roots and engaging with the country's challenges directly, in the belief that the population is resourceful and capable of spontaneous creativity based on free market ideas.

One of the objectives of the Institute is to continue producing academic studies, but no longer limited to the field of economics. By putting a greater focus on Aristotle's ideas of natural order and the political science based on the ideas of philosophers from the Age of Enlightenment – that is, where the law exists to serve justice and the state is not the only source of answers – we could develop a more positive approach towards liberal democracy, and more specifically a more truly democratic government that follows the rule of law, emphasizing the protection of rights and freedoms of individuals from government power.

We hope that in the near future the country will reflect the predictions of John Blundell, Director General, and Ralph Harris, Fellow, at the Institute of Economic Affairs:

Massively rising expectations, greater knowledge, growing life expectancy, failing public enterprises, continuous improvement in the private sector, falling voter turnout, failing parties, growing pressure groups: these are all powerful trends, but together they add up to a monumental sea-change. The politicians who embrace these changes and work with them will be the ones my great grandchildren will read about in modern history, say 50 years from now. (Blundell, 2007: 132–3)

REFERENCES

Blundell, J. (2007), *Waging the War of Ideas*, 3rd edition, London: Institute of Economic Affairs.

Carvalho, J. M. de (2000), *The Struggle for Democracy in Brazil: Possible Lessons for Nigeria*, Amsterdam/Port Harcourt: SEPHIS and the University of Port Harcourt.

Carvalho, O. de (2005), 'Brazilian left: from victory to defeat to victory again', Presentation delivered at the Atlas Economic Research Foundation Seminar, 18 September.

Costa, J. (2004), 'Gramsci's violence in Brazil', Mídia Sem Máscara, 25 May.
Coutinho, S. A. de A. (2002), *A revolução Gramscista no ocidente* (The Gramscist Revolution in the West), Rio de Janeiro: Estandarte Editora.

DaMatta, R. A. (1987), 'The quest for citizenship in a relational universe', in *State and Society in Brazil: Continuity and Change*, Boulder, Colorado: Westview Press, pp. 318–19.

DaMatta, R. A. (1991), *Carnivals, Rogues, and Heroes: An Interpretation of the Brazilian Dilemma*, Notre Dame, Indiana: University of Notre Dame Press, pp. 187–8.

DaMatta, R. A. (1999), 'Is Brazil hopelessly corrupt?', in *The Brazil Reader: History, Culture, Politics*, Durham, North Carolina: Duke University Press, p. 295.

Fausto, B. (1977), 'O Brasil republicano', in *História geral da civilização brasileira*, São Paulo: Difel, vol. 3, p. 138.

Hardy, H. (2006), *Isaiah Berlin's Political Ideas in the Romantic Age*, Princeton, New Jersey: Princeton University Press.

Mises, L. v. (1978), *The Ultimate Foundation of Economic Science: An Essay on Method*, Kansas City, Kansas: Sheed Andrews and McMeel, p. 122.

Mises, L. v. (1985), *Theory and History*, Washington DC: Ludwig von Mises Institute, pp. 3–226.

Mueller, A. P. (2002), *The Ghost that Haunts Brazil*, Auburn, Virginia: Ludwig von Mises Institute.

Rosenn, K. S. (1990), 'The success of constitutionalism in the United States and its failure in Latin America: an explanation', University of Miami Inter-American Law Review, vol. 22.

Rosenn, K. S. (1998), 'O jeito na cultura jurídica brasileira', Rio de Janeiro: *Renovar*, p. 528.

Schor, M. (2006), 'Constitutionalism through the looking glass of Latin America', *Texas International Law Journal*, 1: 20.

Tse, M. (2007), H'ostile Environment in Brazil for Entrepreneurs', Porto Alegre: Instituto Liberdade.

Véliz, C. (1980), *The Centralist Tradition of Latin America*, Princeton, New Jersey: Princeton University Press, p. 195.

Zea, L. (1980), *Pensamiento positivista latinoamericano*, Caracas: Biblioteca Ayacucho.

Zimmermann, A. (2006), 'The left-wing threat to Brazil's democracy', *National Observer* (Council for the National Interest), 68: 48–54.

Zimmermann, A. (2007), 'Legal and extra-legal obstacles for the realization of the Rule of Law in Brazil', *Murdoch University Electronic Journal of Law (E-Law)*, 14(1).

30

Victories for Freedom in the Republic of Georgia

**Paata Sheshelidze
and Gia Jandieri**
New Economic School
(Republic of Georgia)

WHAT IS NESG?

The New Economic School – Georgia (NESG) is a non-governmental organization (NGO) that studies economics, law, philosophy and public policy; disseminates ideas of liberty and principles of free market cooperation; promotes free, voluntary and market-exchange-based cooperation among individuals, as well as non-coercive policy solutions inside Georgia and the whole region of the Black and Caspian Seas, especially in the neighboring countries of Armenia and Azerbaijan.

NESG's strategy is the facilitation of peaceful social change toward economic freedom and, consequently, emancipation from the mental slavery of social-welfarism, warfarism and aggressive nationalism via the education of young and socially active people.

The target group of NESG activities consists of young individuals from different universities and colleges, political parties and socially active NGOs, open-minded teachers, businessmen, farmers, political activists, members of parliament, government employees, journalists and professional commentators.

The doors of NESG are open to anyone who is inquisitive and eager to learn.

ORIGINS

Despite the many changes that took place after the collapse of the Soviet Union, support for the ideas of liberty, free markets, and limited government came much more slowly than expected. More importantly, support was slower than was necessary to put the country, as well as the whole Southern Caucasus region, on the right track, in the direction of increasing economic freedom. Many people became disillusioned with what they interpreted as the quasi failure of capitalism and the propaganda for leftist and populist policies spread by Western institutional 'advisors' such as the European Union, the International Monetary Fund and the World Bank, which did not help the cause for freedom.

It was the danger of missing an unique opportunity to nurture freedom that motivated the founders of the New Economic School in 2001 to oppose this trend by establishing a non-profit-making organization and taking an active position within society. This effort was driven by Mr. Paata Sheshelidze and Mr. Gia Jandieri and some of their like-minded friends. In order to promote free markets and leverage some initiatives taken at the end of Soviet times, in April 1989, they established the Association of Young Economists as the first legal NGO in Soviet Georgia. This organization completely rejected the Marxist studies coming out of the economic faculty of Tbilisi State University, and created its own educational program based on Western market-friendly ideas and experiences.

ACCOMPLISHMENTS

From the point of its inception until August 2010, NESG had organized more than 350 local and international seminars and training sessions, with more than 14,500 participants of different ages, occupations and educational levels. It has published dozens of books, including seven volumes of a series of articles under the general titles of *Library of Liberty* and *Guide to Economics for Journalists*. It has also produced several dozen articles on property rights and state interventionism, entrepreneurship and contractual society, market-based education and sound money, protectionism and taxation, monopolies and regulations. Through active media coverage and social networking, hundreds of people from Georgia and the Southern Caucasus have been involved in the dissemination of the ideas of freedom.

NESG has created the best private library in the region, which combines more than 1,000 donated and purchased books, videos and audio materials. The library is open to the public. In addition, NESG also offers research facilities for those who like to study and who seek to improve their knowledge and become more competitive in the market.

Parallel to this activity, NESG has been spearheading many public policy reforms, working directly with politicians and government officials. Their strategy consists of inviting world-famous reformers to support reforms in Georgia, and then training high-level public officials. This strategy has turned out to be a success and, in many cases, has resulted in changes including deregulation and the liberalizing of the country's economy, as well as expanding the number of pro-market people within political circles.

Through the involvement in international activities by its top managers, NESG has not only been able to develop better skills, but also meet and build friendships with a large network of organizations. NESG is also using networking to promote intensive discussions on economic freedom in neighboring Azerbaijan and Armenia.

RESULTS

One of most important outcomes of NESG activities has been the growth in the groups of talented young economists who have been invited by the minister of state in charge of coordinating reforms to join his staff and be in charge of policy making. Through the activities of its students and the intellectual pressure via its educational efforts and media activities, NESG has played a role in the following decisions made by the Georgian government since 2005:

- The Program of Institutional Deregulation of the Economy 2005-10;

- A new law on free trade and competition policy was adopted by the Georgian parliament in the summer of 2005. This revolutionary law, which has almost no analogues worldwide, prevents government officials at various levels from creating monopolies and giving special positions on specific governmental bodies, agencies and private companies;

- License and permit system reform was adopted in the autumn 2005. The number of licenses and permits required was reduced from 1,000 to 150. Now, government licenses are primarily required for activities related to people's health and livelihood;

- 'One Stop Shop', 'Silence is Consent' and 'One Umbrella' principles were introduced for business registration and licenses in autumn 2005;

- The law on agricultural land privatization was adopted in autumn 2005 and allows privatization of all agricultural lands in favor of the citizens of Georgia and resident companies;

- Reforms since 2006 on natural resources which allow individuals and companies to lease mines, forests, lakes, and rivers for a long period (25-plus years);

- The energy sector reform plan, where the basic elements include the complete privatization of supply and distribution and the partial deregulation of tariffs, which was partially adopted by the Georgian government in autumn 2005;

- The regulatory authority reform project of 2006 which reduces the power of regulatory authorities through a gradual elimination of its functions;

- The 2006 delegation of power from state agencies to private ones;

- The deregulation of banking activities in Georgia which redefines commercial banking activities, the criteria for licensing, bank management, prudential standards, etc. The banking sector was opened to non-resident owners and investors;

- The certification, standardization, accreditation and metrology system reform was adopted by the Georgian government in the beginning of 2006. The system was simplified and partly privatized. All standards were voluntary, and only some technical regulations remained mandatory;

- The institutional reform of state inspections was adopted in the beginning of 2006. It simplified and defined the issues related to human life and health, and laid out clear obligations and responsibilities of state authorities;

- New standards for food and safety regulations were adopted in the beginning of 2006, and self-regulatory practices were introduced;

- A new Labor Code was adopted by the Georgian parliament in the summer of 2006. This revolutionary law gives priority to mutually agreed contracts based on the relationship between an employer and an employee, and removes state interventions;

- Mass privatizations of state-owned hospitals began in Georgia in 2008, with the aim of converting all state hospitals to private ones;

- Since 2008, financial reforms have been advanced, with the aim of simplifying accounting and other tax-related procedures. There have also been plans to reduce taxes in the future.

Thanks to NESG's advocacy efforts, the most visible and direct results in policy include:

- NESG supporter Mr. Mart Laar (a member of the Estonian parliament and the 2006 prime minister of Estonia) remains an advisor to the president of Georgia and heavily influences many economic decisions;

- Another great supporter of NESG, Dr. Andrei Illarionov, became the leading advocate of Georgian reforms and democratic transformation, especially against the Russian invasion in 2008;

- The analysis of the potential privatization of Georgian railways with the assistance of foreign experts – Mr. Iraj Hashi, Mr. Karl Ziebarth and Mr Ronald Utt;

- Through the facilitation of NESG, Dr. Pierre Garello, director of IES-Europe (Institute for Economic Studies) was invited by the UNDP (United Nations Development Program) in Georgia to research the possibility of a free trade agreement with the European Union.

UNIQUE ECONOMIC IMPACT

Three generations of NESG students have received unique opportunities to participate in economic reforms and to be key figures in their design and implementation.

There is no other similar example of such an extensive participation of students from a free market think tank in economic reforms, nor of the direct and indirect impact that one free market think tank can have on economic reforms and freedoms in the very short period of just four to five years.

HOW TO MEASURE NESG'S IMPACT

NESG activities facilitated an interest in free market solutions to economic and social problems within the country. Elimination of poverty, and guarantees of growth, were debated among Georgian parliament members, the government, the media, the business community, academic circles, youth organizations, influential political parties and individuals, and various social networks.

Two interrelated aspects can be measured: the quality of NESG's activities and the qualifications of former students.

The quality of NESG's activities can be measured by the following: the reach of its Student Outreach program (full-time education activities since January 2002), the number of its events (more then 350) and the number of participants they attracted (14,500).

To measure the qualifications of NESG students, one can do an evaluation of those who have participated in the design of government deregulation reforms, and the recognition of those reforms. Accordingly, within well-known, global studies such as the *Doing Business* report from the World Bank, the *Economic Freedom of the World* report by the Fraser Institute, and *Index of Economic Freedom* by The Heritage Foundation, Georgian reforms have been well received and systematically praised during the last four to six years. Employers such as banks, insurance companies, developers and state agencies think very highly of NESG recommendations.

MEDIA PERFORMANCE

After years of public activities, the leadership and experts at NESG are now very popular in the media (newspapers, Web, TV and radio). There are regular media appearances by NESG representatives, in the form of interviews andarticles, In some cases, especially during important events such as the announcement of reforms or international agreements, these media appearances occur on a daily basis.

Interest in NESG from media sources has allowed them to organize special international training seminars and the book *Guide for Journalists* in cooperation with CIPE (Center for International Private Enterprise) and twelve seminars and twelve workshops on economic reforms for media representatives with international development consulting firm Chemonics.

Georgia Public Broadcasting, the national public TV broadcasting company, translated and broadcast the film, *Free to Choose*, which NESG secured thanks to the help of the Atlas Economic Research Foundation.

PARTNERS AND VISITORS

Since 2003, NESG's most important donor has been the Friedrich Naumann Foundation (FNF), Germany. The FNF was a major contributor towards NESG's educational programs, and the representative of the FNF in the Southern Caucasus, Dr. Wolfgang John, helped to extend NESG's work in Azerbaijan and Armenia. Other supporters of NESG include the Atlas Economic Research Foundation in the United States, and the Knowledge Fund in Georgia. NESG's closest partners include IES-Europe, Cato institute (USA), FEE (USA), ISIL (USA), Liberty Fund (USA), Istituto Bruno Leoni (Italy), the Hayek Foundation (Slovakia), the Hayek Institute (Austria), and many others, including private individuals.

An initiative of the NESG is to bring successful and well-known market-oriented reformers and thinkers to Georgia in order to study their experience and to analyze their recommendations. During the period from 15 October 2005 to 1 August 2010, NESG organized visits for the following:

1. Honorable Ruth Richardson, Minister of Finance of New Zealand (2–9 October 2005)
2. Mr. Mart Laar, Member of Parliament and former Prime Minister of Estonia (several times since January 2006)
3. Dr. Marc Miles, Heritage Foundation (16–18 February 2006)
4. Dr. Krassen Stanchev, Institute for Market Economics (several times since 2004)
5. Dr. Andrei Illarionov, Senior Fellow of Cato Institute, Advisor to the President of Russia 1999–2005 (several times since October 2006)
6. Dr. Lajos Bokros, Member of the European Parliament, former Minister of Finance of Hungary (29 October to 2 November 2006)
7. Dr. Vernon Smith, Nobel Prize winner (29 October to 2 November 2006)
8. Dr. Warren Coats (29 October to 2 November 2006)
9. Dr. Tom Palmer, Senior Fellow of the Cato Institute (29 October to 2 November 2006)
10. Becky Dunlop, Vice-President of The Heritage Foundation (June 2007)
11. Dr. Steve Hanke, Professor of Applied Economics at The Johns Hopkins University (October 2007)
12. Dr. Pierre Garello, Director of IES Europe (several times from December 2007 to July 2010)
13. Jaroslav Romanchuk, Director of Mises Center (February 2008)
14. Johnny Munkhammar, Timbro (June 2008 and May 2010)
15. Martin Chren, Hayek Foundation and Slovakian Member of Parliament (January 2010).
16. Professor Pascal Salin, Université Paris-Dauphine, France (April 2010).

INTERNATIONAL RECOGNITION

Since 2005 the achievements of NESG have been acknowledged on several occasions with awards and prizes in different categories, and most notably through award nominations from the Atlas Economic Research Foundation.

If you are coming to the Southern Caucasus and are looking for professional assistance or analysis, or if you need to know more about economic theories, economic conditions and business opportunities in the region, contact NESG. It is an organization that works 24 hours a day, seven days a week, and in any place where a laptop can be plugged in. NESG is changing and improving the world around it by changing the views of many people. NESG was created to disseminate not only economic knowledge, but hope as well.

EPILOGUE

THE CHALLENGES AND OPPORTUNITIES AHEAD
by Brad Lips, CEO
Atlas Economic Research Foundation

To borrow some words from the proverbial "Chinese Curse," we are certainly living through "interesting times." Government has grown unsustainably, almost guaranteeing a reckoning of one sort or another.

I'm optimistic that the think tanks profiled in this book – and those in the broader Atlas network that touches more than 80 countries – will play important roles in the years to come. Crises will emerge, and we will need effective, principled Freedom Champions to move opinion toward sound policy solutions.

Atlas's mission is to find such people, and help them establish effective think tanks and carry the message of freedom to all who will listen.

To succeed in our mission, we need to learn from the successes and also from the failures of our think tank movement. We need to be attentive to new challenges and new opportunities in our market.

I like to remind my Atlas colleagues that we are able to spend our days working for the most moral calling that I know of: assisting the spread of human liberty. But if we are careless, we will be doing something *immoral* instead – that is, squandering the resources entrusted to us by generous individuals who share our noble goals. We must always remain vigilant to find ways to better leverage our resources to fulfill our mission.

In that spirit, I thought I'd share some of our team's best thoughts about how the war of ideas is changing.

THE CONTINUING TECHNOLOGICAL REVOLUTION

The manner in which ideas are spread continues to evolve rapidly. Think tank veterans remember when the fax machine (now headed toward extinction) was an absolutely revolutionary technology. Today's think tanks wrestle with the question of whether to focus on traditional research (books, white papers), shift to a world of viral videos and 140-character tweets, or somehow bridge the two.

CITIZEN ACTIVISTS AS AN EMERGING
CUSTOMER OF THINK TANK PRODUCTS

The Internet has opened new opportunities for think tanks to concentrate on providing more than pure research. Think tanks are providing tools that equip citizens with information and empower them to become active in local policy battles. Transparency initiatives are making it easy to decipher government information and hold public officials accountable. Watchdog Web sites encourage citizen participation, and other online forums encourage the "crowd-sourcing" of new ideas and strategies.

OPPORTUNITIES TO FILL THE VOID IN JOURNALISM

The revenue model used by most print media institutions has been hard-hit by the online revolution. Some think tanks are taking advantage of the change by employing investigative journalists (no longer employed in great numbers by struggling daily newspapers) and directing attention to the costs of bad public policy and corrupt governing officials. The evolution of journalism is sure to continue, and it seems likely that nonprofit educational and policy institutes will figure significantly in the profession's future.

THE COMING TRANSFORMATION OF ACADEMIA

The coming decade may be as unkind to universities as the last one was to the newspapers. We're only at the cusp of a boom in online educational options, and think tanks need to stay attentive to new opportunities in this arena. It's fair to say that the think tank industry grew up, in large part, because academia had turned so inhospitable to those with free-market views. Scholars that might have stayed at universities under other circumstances opted instead for work in the policy world. One of the happy consequences of this has been that their work has been more responsive to a market, whereas the incentives at universities often encourage publishing on narrow topics, mainly of interest to only specialists in the field. Today, we see some colleges addressing this, along with the related problem of a strong leftward political bias on campus, by allowing faculty members and motivated alumni to establish academic centers on campus that are friendly to free-market concepts, and natural allies of the existing think tank network.

THE NEED FOR "CULTURAL ENTREPRENEURS"

Increasingly, friends of the free-market movement are recognizing that winning policy arguments only goes so far; ideological affiliations are more often born from emotion and a sense of what's fashionable. There has long been a lively argument about whether the case for liberty should be made on utilitarian grounds ("it works best") or moral grounds ("it is what is right"). Think tanks have tended to stress the former, but we know that the novels of Ayn Rand – with their passionate sense of life, and harsh condemnation of the statist mindset – have attracted more advocates of liberty than any cost-benefit analysis. We need efforts to build an artistic movement that can complement our intellectual movement and broaden the appeal of the principles of a free society.

THE RISE OF ONLINE SOCIAL NETWORKS

We need to improve how we interact with the rising generations that have grown up with the Internet, and who presently live on Facebook (I offer no prediction about where they'll spend most of their time in five years). Their online social networks revolve around shared interests. As with so many of our partners, Atlas is experimenting with different strategies for getting more young people engaged with the thoughtful, idealistic Freedom Champions that are connected to the Atlas Network.

OUR INTERCONNECTED WORLD

There is an increasing awareness that many of the future's gravest challenges do not respect national boundaries. Whether it's financial contagion or radical ideologies at war with modernity, it's clear that we all have an interest in moving societies worldwide toward greater individual liberty and responsibility.

It's this global perspective that is perhaps the most unique and innovative aspect of our work at Atlas. The reach of the Atlas network has grown from about a dozen institutes at its founding, to 400+ in nearly ninety countries, just three decades later.

The credit for the results achieved by these organizations belongs entirely to those who have led them and invested in them through the years. Atlas's role is to act as a catalyst and connector, providing resources and advice that accelerate their progress. We have made significant investments in recent years to improve our training programs and advisory services.

We also are reaching out to discover advocates of liberty in parts of the world that have been isolated from classical liberal ideas. Tom Palmer joined Atlas in 2009, bringing innovative international outreach programs in Arabic, Chinese, French, Hindi, Persian, Portuguese, Russian, BehasaMalayu, and four other languages. Through those platforms millions of people are being reached who previously had no access to the ideas of liberty, and from those platforms new think tanks and ventures are emerging.

Atlas also uses its unique position within the larger freedom movement to put a spotlight on its successes. Thanks to the John Templeton Foundation, we run the largest prize program devoted to honoring excellent work by think tanks to advance the ideas of freedom: the Templeton Freedom Awards. During the seven years that we have run this prestigious program, Atlas has been able to honor 145 different organizations from 46 countries, boosting their profile and credibility in their own local environments.

Those various aspects of our mission are perfectly complementary. We discover, train, and honor Intellectual Entrepreneurs who are changing their societies for the better by championing the ideas of freedom. We help establish new organizations. We spread the message of liberty to every corner of the globe. It is a highly leveraged and multilayered strategy for promoting liberty.

At Atlas we have our heroes, whose bravery inspires us every day. Let me share with you the sentiment, which is prominently displayed on our walls at Atlas, of Joaquim Nabuco, a nineteenth century Brazilian writer, diplomat and abolitionist:

> "Educate your children, educate yourselves in the love for the freedom of others, for only in this way will your own freedom not be a gratuitous gift from fate. You will be aware of its worth and have the courage to defend it."

I hope you are motivated to join with Atlas and the Freedom Champions in this book to face the challenges of our times.

ABOUT ATLAS

For three decades, the Atlas Economic Research Foundation has been a leader in the worldwide movement for individual liberty, free enterprise, and limited government under the rule of law. Its mission is "to discover, develop and support Intellectual Entrepreneurs worldwide who advance the Atlas vision of a society of free and responsible individuals."

Atlas relies entirely upon voluntary contributions from individuals, foundations, and corporations, to finance its own programs and operations, as well as the seed support it offers to promising free-market think tanks. Atlas accepts no government funding to carry out its programs, which include:

- Training programs that increase the effectiveness of think tanks, so they are using "sound business practices" to promote sound policy solutions.

- Educational platforms in Arabic, Hindi, Russian, Chinese, and ten other languages to jumpstart classical liberal movements in parts of the world with little experience with freedom.

- Policy programs, on topics like Sound Money, that mobilize and foster collaboration among the think tanks and scholars connected to the Atlas Network.

- Prize programs, such as the Templeton Freedom Awards, that recognize the best contributions to liberty and put financial resources where they will have the greatest impact.

Visit **AtlasNetwork.org** to learn more about Atlas and the Freedom Champions in this book who are connected through the Atlas Network. At the Atlas Web site, you will find a map-based directory of more than 400 think tanks dedicated to the principles of a free society.

Please contact Atlas today at 202.449.8449 or info@atlasnetwork.org to learn how you can support this important work to foster a future of freedom.